Entextualizing Domestic Violence

OXFORD STUDIES IN LANGUAGE AND LAW

Oxford Studies in Language and Law includes scholarly analyses and descriptions of language evidence in civil and criminal law cases as well as language issues arising in the area of statutes, statutory interpretation, courtroom discourse, jury instructions, and historical changes in legal language.

The Legal Language of Scottish Burghs: Standardization and Lexical Bundles (1380–1560)
Joanna Kopaczyk

"I'm Sorry for What I've Done": The Language of Courtroom Apologies
M. Catherine Gruber

Dueling Discourses: The Construction of Reality in Closing Arguments
Laura Felton Rosulek

Entextualizing Domestic Violence: Language Ideology and Violence Against Women in the Anglo-American Hearsay Principle
Jennifer Andrus

Entextualizing Domestic Violence

LANGUAGE IDEOLOGY AND VIOLENCE AGAINST WOMEN IN THE ANGLO-AMERICAN HEARSAY PRINCIPLE

Jennifer Andrus

OXFORD
UNIVERSITY PRESS

OXFORD
UNIVERSITY PRESS

Oxford University Press is a department of the University of Oxford.
It furthers the University's objective of excellence in research, scholarship,
and education by publishing worldwide.

Oxford New York
Auckland Cape Town Dar es Salaam Hong Kong Karachi
Kuala Lumpur Madrid Melbourne Mexico City Nairobi
New Delhi Shanghai Taipei Toronto

With offices in
Argentina Austria Brazil Chile Czech Republic France Greece
Guatemala Hungary Italy Japan Poland Portugal Singapore
South Korea Switzerland Thailand Turkey Ukraine Vietnam

Oxford is a registered trade mark of Oxford University Press
in the UK and certain other countries.

Published in the United States of America by
Oxford University Press
198 Madison Avenue, New York, NY 10016

Cataloging-in-Publication Data is on file with the Library of Congress.

9780190225834

9 8 7 6 5 4 3 2 1

Printed in the United States of America on acid-free paper

For my teachers.

CONTENTS

ACKNOWLEDGMENTS

Many years ago, I was taking a class on gender and discourse with a colleague, Susanne Green, who had volunteered with 911 for a number of years in a city in west Texas. During a conversation about agency and language, she described a legal concept called "the excited utterance" that she had learned about while working at 911. She had learned about it in the context of domestic violence calls and utterances blurted by hysterical women to the police. She further explained that these utterances are treated as true because they lack the hallmarks of self-concerned, planned speech. Sue wondered if spontaneous exclamations could be considered arhetorical in this way, if for example, the speaker didn't speak English well or wasn't in the country legally. Wouldn't even spontaneous exclamations under such contexts be shaped by the speaker's relationship to law enforcement and their daily lived experience? The idea of a spontaneous utterance divorced from speaker intention got me thinking. Even if the speaker was faultless, is there any way that this or any utterance could be fully divorced from the expectations and prior experiences of the interlocutors, power dynamics, and the features of interaction? Though I didn't realize it at the time, the conversation formed a kernel that would develop into a research program. Some years later, while working on a different project about violence against women, I recalled that conversation and began my own research on hearsay, the excited utterance exception to hearsay, and its relationship to domestic violence. I owe a deep debt of gratitude to Sue Green for introducing me to the concept and pointing out the assumptions about the speaker and agency that have driven my research for nearly a decade and for her friendship through the process.

Many other colleagues and friends have given me invaluable support as I've worked on this project. I am so happy to have had the opportunity to work with my friend and mentor, Barbara Johnstone. Barbara not only helped me work through complex sociolinguistic theories and spent countless hours working with me on the analysis and arguments in this book, she has also included me in many intellectual projects and opportunities, encouraging my intellectual development in many ways. Barbara models the kind of careful, ethical scholarship I hope to do and a perspective on balancing work and life that has guided me. I'm also grateful to Andreea Ritivoi, Michael Witmore, David Kaufer, and Paul Hopper who have read and given important and ongoing feedback on this research. I sincerely appreciate the time, feedback, and intellectual support of Susan Ehrlich, who models a thoughtful and careful analysis of law and violence against women that dissects the linguistic details of power and mysogeny. I also appreciate the support and feedback of Roger Shuy, Diana Eades, and Gregory Matoesian. I owe a special thanks to Ann Sinsheimer, who took time to discuss my research and the law of evidence and hearsay, and who taught me to read opinions, briefs, and other legal documents. Over the years, I have received invaluable feedback on papers presented at rhetoric, sociolinguistic, and legal humanities conferences. I owe special thanks to Elizabeth Britt, who heard my first conference paper on domestic violence and the excited utterance and has since given consistently valuable feedback and opportunities to develop my work. The excellent feedback from anonymous reviewers of the proposal and manuscript is also greatly appreciated.

I am grateful for the engaged responses and discussion of the students in my Forensic Discourse Analysis class at the University of Utah in the spring of 2012, who helped me work through some of the arguments in part I. I am grateful to the University of Utah Writing Program and College of Humanities for research funds, leave time, and course releases that have allowed me the time to complete the research and to write. I could not hope for better colleagues than Tom Huckin, Jay Jordan, Casey Boyle, and Maureen Matheson, whose friendship and mentorship have supported me as I've developed this project.

This project would have been impossible without the support of Nathan Atkinson, Thora Brylowe, Peter Cramer, Emily Klein, Erin Friess, Chris Weigel and Becca May, who have been willing to listen to me explain legal concepts and argue about theories of discourse, agency, violence, and bodies, and whose friendship and encouragement have energized me. Finally, I'll forever be in the debt of Valentine Santarromana, who has consistently supported me in all things since that first conversation about the excited utterance, many years ago.

PERMISSIONS

I developed some of the arguments in Chapter 2 in "The Development of an Artefactual Language Ideology: Historicizing the Metadiscourse of the Hearsay and the Excited Utterance Exception Rules in the Anglo-American Law of Evidence," which appeared in the October 2009 issue of *Language and Communication*. Some of the extracts and analysis in Chapter 4 were used in "Beyond Texts in Context: Recontextualization and the Co-Production of Texts and Contexts in the Legal Discourse, Excited Utterance Exception to Hearsay," published in *Discourse & Society* in March 2011. Portions of Chapter 5 appeared in "A Legal Discourse of Transparency: Discursive Agency and Domestic Violence in the Technical Discourse of the Excited Utterance Exception to Hearsay," *Technical Communication Quarterly*, January 2011, and "Victim Agency: Fractal Recursivity in the Language Ideology of the US Law of Evidence and Domestic Violence," *Language in Society*, December 2012.

NOTES ON ABBREVIATIONS AND LEGAL CITATION

I have used the following abbreviations and pseudonyms for the participants of the trial *US v. Hadley*, analyzed in Chapters 4 and 5 and mentioned throughout.

PH	Person to whom the excited utterance is attributed and wife of the defendant.
JH	Person accused and convicted of felony possession of a gun.
Officer 1	Male officer who was the first to arrive after two calls to 911 and who was the first witness during the trial.
Officer 2	Female officer who was the second to arrive at the home of PH and JH, and who was the second witness during the trial.
TSA Officer	TSA Officer who testified during the trial.
Prosecution 1	Lead attorney for the government. Of note, she questions Officer 2 (during the trial) and PH (during sentencing).
Prosecution 2	Attorney for the government. Of note, he questions Officer 1 (during the trial) and JH (during sentencing).
Defense	Attorney defending JH.
Judge	Federal District Judge who heard the case and issued the sentence.

When I cite trial transcript, I use this citation format:

Witness, Date: Transcript page number: (Officer 1, November 2002: 7)

When I cite the appellate opinion for *US v. Hadley* and other judicial opinions, I use this format:

Abbreviated case name, year: page number: (*Hadley*, 2005: 37)

Entextualizing Domestic Violence

Introduction

LEGAL LANGUAGE IDEOLOGY, REPORTED SPEECH, AND DOMESTIC VIOLENCE

> "Legal language flattens and confines in absolutes the complexity of meaning inherent in any given problem." Patricia Williams (1991, 6)

> "The postmodern position locating human experience as inescapably within language suggests that feminists should not overlook the constructive function of legal language as a critical frontier for feminist reforms. To put this 'principle' more bluntly, legal discourse should be recognized as a site of political struggle over sex differences." Mary Jo Frug (1992, 1045)

The modern legal system in the United States is made up of a series of statements—written rules, codes, statutes, precedents, oral examination and testimony, judicial decisions, briefs, and the list could go on. Thus Peter Tiersma (1999, 1) explains, "law—virtually by definition—comes into being through language." Nearly every legal process takes place in language, and, as Gregory Matoesian (2001, 3) argues, language itself is fundamental in the (re) production and circulation of law, "constitut[ing] and transform[ing] evidence, facts, and rules into relevant objects of legal knowledge." Law is deeply connected to language, or as Austin Sarat and Thomas Kearns (1996, 1) put it, "the law can never escape the intricacies and imprecisions, as well as the promise and power, of language itself." The relationship between law and language is fraught because language is powerful, complex, and durable, *and* it is slippery, subjective and indefinite. Indeed, at least part of language's power is derived from its semantic and rhetorical openness. A number of discursive mechanisms have developed to respond to the semantic and semiotic excesses of language, one of which is a referentialist language ideology, or the idea that language is primarily a way of referencing something in the world (cf Ehrlich, 2012). Such a view only sees language as a way of referencing a world that is external to language, eliding or even obscuring the pragmatic and interactional aspects of language. There exists in the law an "assert[ion] that what's real is not language or the use of language, but what language represents, what it refers to" (J. Frug 1988, 880). Conceiving of language's potential only in referential terms gives law a way of controlling its imprecision and managing its excesses. By perceiving "the real" as prior to and outside of language, the law is able to explicitly fix meaning, a process that creates an erasure under which the interactional flexibility of language is hidden from scrutiny. Not only does the law look outside of language for the real, but as Kim Lane Scheppele (1990, 44) argues, the law works hard to minimize the differences between events, occurrences in the world, and the linguistic recounting of those events in court and in legal documents. That is, the law treats linguistic accounts of events as essentially the same thing as the event itself, and at the same time, it locates the real in the world that language refers to. I discuss this so-called referentialist language ideology as an empiricist language ideology, switching the focus from the action of the language to the things it is thought to refer to. That is, an empirical language ideology highlights the material world to which words are thought to point. I shift attention this way because law focuses quite explicitly on what is visible and what happened, and because empiricism plays a fundamental role in the hearsay principle that is at the center of this book.

This book identifies some of the ways that language ideologies circulating in law and larger society fix the accounts of events and what they can mean. At the same time that an account of the event is given, the person said to have given the account is also accounted for. This is at least in part because law has the "capacity to impose and affirm culturally powerful definitions of social reality" (Ehrlich 2001, 18). At the same time that the law limits and fixes versions of events and subject positions, it also legitimizes its own function. "The law is a particularly potent source and badge of legitimacy, and site and cloak of force. The force underpins the legitimacy as the legitimacy conceals the force" (MacKinnon 1989, 237). Thus, as Elizabeth Mertz (1996, 149) argues, legal language is "socially transformative" because it "[renders] diverse realms of cultural experience in a common language." Legal language "constantly effects a translation of people in their roles (plaintiff, defendant) and actions into their legal categories (tort, breach of contract)" (Mertz 1996, 158). In other words, legal language creates a world that law can manage.

A central goal of scholars studying language and law is to understand these and other social ramifications of legal language. Perhaps the most common project has been analysis of in-court processes—for example, the form and function of direct- and cross-examination and attorneys' question-asking strategies (Atkinson and Drew 1979; Conley, et al. 1979; Conley and O'Barr 2005; Eades 2008; Ehrlich 2001; Matoesian 1993, 2001); the ways that some witnesses are able to resist the question-asking strategies of attorneys (Ehrlich & Sidnell 2006); and the effects of legal discourses and lawerly strategy in co-opting and altering victims' accounts of their own experiences (Ehrlich 2001; Trinch 2003). Others have been concerned with language associated with policing, identifying the ways police officers question victims and those accused of crimes (Shuy 1998; Berk-Seligson 2009; Tracy and Agne 2004), while others have analyzed the relationship between gender and policing (McElhinny 1995, 2003).

This book continues to probe the ways that the law conceives of its relationship to language, applying theories of language ideology (Silverstein 1979, [1981]2001; Irvine 1989; Woolard & Schieffelin 1994; Woolard 1998; Irvine & Gal 2000; Kroskrity 2000) to understand the relationship between ideology, constructions of fact and evidence, gender, and domestic violence. A language ideology consists of ideas about what language is, how it functions, and how it relates ideologically to the social groups. Kathryn Woolard (1998, 3) describes a language ideology this way:

> [I]deologies of language are not about language alone. Rather, they envision and enact ties of language to identity, to aesthetics, to morality, and to epistemology. Through such linkages, they underpin not only linguistic form and use but also the very notion of the person and the social group, as well as such fundamental social institutions as religious ritual, child socialization, gender relations, the nation-state, schooling, and law.

That is, language ideologies create links between aspects of language and ideas about speakers that draw on social expectations and norms. Or as Matoesian (2001, 40) puts it, language ideologies consist of "taken-for-granted cultural beliefs about the role of language structure as these relate to power in the constitution of reality." Law is thus not only made up of language, but ideas about what language is, how it functions, and how it relates to the world of experience. We can see social values and how they are naturalized in legal procedures in the language ideologies circulating in the law of evidence. Witnesses and their talk are products of and "filtered through cultural and institutional ideologies which themselves are manifest in 'talk'" (Ehrlich 2001, 4). That is, the speech of witnesses is brought into the legal text in interactions that perform cultural and institutional values as they make the witnesses' speech legally useful. For example, Eades (2008, 25) analyzes direct- and cross-examination strategies used against Aboriginal speakers in Australia, showing how ideas about language, dialect, and race "that underlie the linguistic mechanisms allowed by the rules of evidence" justify manipulative courtroom practices. Matoesian (2001, 38) has shown how "sexual rationality and linguistic hegemony" work together to make "the victim [of rape] complicit in her own subjugation." Cultural assumptions about women's bodies and experiences, for example, are used to make sense of rape complaints. "Law [is] not [. . .] a gender-neutral and free-floating institution but [. . .] a socially structured and gendered component of patriarchal domination" (Matoesian 1993, 15). Though law explicitly presumes neutral, objective positivity, Hirsch (1998, 19) shows how "understandings and enactments incorporate cultural notions about linguistic usage. In short, being a woman or a man means being (or being taken for, or being expected to be) a certain kind of speaker" (19). Deeply androcentric and patriarchal, law has developed to account for adult, white, male bodies (cf. Muhammad 2010). The structure of common law works as a filter that accounts for all bodies using a logic developed to account for enfranchised white male bodies ultimately leads to the systematic translation of the embodied and linguistic experiences of women, people of color, queer people, people with disabilities—anybody who doesn't neatly fit within the white male paradigm in which Anglo-American law has developed—into those already circulating in the law.

This project considers the intersection of legal language ideologies and legal gender bias in the context of domestic violence in the US law of evidence. Narratives and storytelling are particularly important in legal discussions of domestic violence and gender. As Shonna Trinch (2003, 3) puts it, "it is through this speech activity that testimony is borne as events come alive linguistically." Narratives told in legal settings are shaped by social and legal presuppositions about "*truth* and *authorship* serve in the construction of authority and credibility for the production of appropriate and meaningful representations of [domestic] abuse" (Trinch 2003, 1). That is, the law has an ideology of language that identifies and in many ways produces credible and authoritative texts and speakers, in the same discursive processes that naturalize authority and truth. Narratives about domestic violence are "about language and the reproduction of power and powerlessness" (Trinch 2010, 180). From initial interactions with police, meetings with advocates to get help filing for protective orders, interviews with prosecutors, and in-court testimony, victims of domestic violence are asked to say what happened (Trinch 2003). Speakers are put in a position to give an account of a situation underpinned by multiple dimensions of power—from the patriarchy of the home to that of institutions such as law and medicine. The question Trinch (2003, 16) raises is "what makes an account of domestic violence credible?" That is, what institutional markers must a story about domestic violence have for it to function as a piece of evidence rather than simply as a story about family and home? Trinch (2010, 188) describes the interaction this way:

> The interview will result in a written account of intimate-partner violence, formalized as public property. Once the story is inscribed in the legal document, these women continue to lose control over their stories, as they can no longer tell it their way, and they can no longer decide what can be done with it. The prosecution for example, can always use a sworn affidavit against an "uncooperative" victim who recants in a criminal investigation.

An account of violence at the hands of an intimate partner gains credibility in the process of becoming a part of public record, which simultaneously deauthorizes the speaker of the story about a violent act against her. The story itself is reconfigured to fit the preconditions of the law, and what the law recognizes as an offense worthy of a protective order (Trinch and Berk-Seligson 2002).

Like Trinch, here I am interested in better understanding the consequences of legal language ideologies to victims of domestic violence,[1] by locating and analyzing a site in which women and their talk are described, explained, and interpreted within a legal framework. I analyze the metadiscourses of the hearsay rule and the excited utterance exception of the Federal Rules of Evidence,[2] a site that is explicitly concerned with evaluating language, but where we also find significant discussion of those whose speech is under scrutiny. The hearsay rule bans a witness giving testimony from repeating out-of-court utterances, spoken by a third-party. The excited utterance exception admits repeated out-of-court utterances if the third-party speaker had excitedly and spontaneously blurted an utterance. As I'll discuss in some detail in Chapter 1, this exception to hearsay is quite commonly used to admit the utterances of domestic violence victims without their consent, and sometimes in opposition to their express wishes. When the excited utterance exception to hearsay is used in cases involving domestic violence, we find a legal language ideology in which women's explanations of their own experiences are measured against the "real," as the law defines it, overlooking the semantic and rhetorical goals of the speaker. As O'Barr and Conley (1996) have noted in their research, legal ideologies do not match the lay ideologies, linguistic or otherwise, that witnesses/victims bring with them to the courtroom (cf. Conley & O'Barr, 1990). Legal language ideology controls the relationship between a linguistic account and the materiality and experience it is said to represent. When the excited utterance exception is used in the context of domestic violence, the criteria used to evaluate a proposed *excited utterance* are co-articulated with assumptions about the trustworthiness of domestic violence victims in ways that devalue victim speech and subjectivity.

Before moving on, let me comment on my use of the term "victim." Many feminist scholars advocate for the use of the term "survivor" rather than "victim." Lamb (1999), for example, persuasively argues that the word "victim" carries with it expectations of how a good victim behaves that hold back social and legal changes that would reduce domestic violence. According to Lamb (1999, 108–109), victims are "required" in psychology approaches to domestic violence, to develop pathology and "being victimized has become equivalent to having a chronic mental illness." At the most basic level, I use the word "victim" because it is the legal term used when the law talks about those who have been abused by domestic partners. Using "victim" consistently rather than switching between "victim" (when quoting the law) and "survivor" (when critiquing the law) allows me to minimize terminological confusion. More importantly, because this book gives an account of legal conceptions of domestic violence, I use the term "victim" to emphasize the fact that the law sees women who have been abused by domestic partners as victims. If she were not a victim, no intervention would be suitable. As Sameera Mulla has put it, the "state has little interest in the victim-patient as a survivor" (2011, 291). Positioning women narrating events of domestic abuse as victims allows the law to appropriate those narratives when it sees fit.

Positioning women as "survivors" potentially reduces the visibility of the crime as well. As Carine Mardorossian (2002, 770–771) argues, the term "survivor" implies a relationship in which the survivor receives help and the (feminist) advocate gives help. "The dominant perception is that survivors need to be helped, taken care of, counseled, talked about, spoken for, studied, rather than assured the decision-making power and opportunities for self-making." In order to avoid the pitfalls of both "survivor" and "victim," I turn to Trinch's (2013, 289) argument that the victim/survivor binary needs to be problematized in order to refute myths of "real rape" or recognizable trauma that are sometimes used by legal and lay audiences to evaluate accounts of violence against women (cf. Lamb 1999 and Gavey 2005). Trinch "cautiously propose[s] that we maintain the category 'victim,'" but that we do so as a way of presenting women who have been the victims of intimate violence "as complicated, competent, rational, thoughtful, strategic, and smart members of their families, workplaces, and communities" (2013, 302). That is, we keep the category "victim" because it has sociolegal purchase, but we do so without pathologizing or essentializing women who have been victims of rape and/or domestic violence. In this book, I primarily use the term "victim" in order to comment on that process of appropriation of words and subjectivity and positioning of the speaker that we see in legal uses of the term. Indeed, as I argue throughout this book, the legal treatement of victims and the talk about women who have been victims of domestic violence produces a subject position that authorizes legal dismissal of the individual who suffers abuse in the very same gestures with which the law appropriates her speech and uses it as evidence. My use of the term is always in the mode of legal critique, wherein I'm evaluating and analyzing the effects of that usage—not aligning myself with the legal position, and not conceiving of abused women as essentially victims.

Hearsay, Reported Speech, and Domestic Violence

This book critiques the hearsay rule and its exceptions particularly as they are used in domestic violence cases. Thus, from one perspective, this book is about reported speech. I analyze ideas about language and trustworthiness that are embedded in ideas about secondhand speech, twice-told tales. In discussions of reported speech, gossip, and hearsay, we find an interesting and well-developed discussion about how and why some language is more easily trusted, more referentially true. That is, discussions of reported speech do significant work describing the weaknesses of language. For example, as John Locke (1690, Book 4, XVI:10) explained it in *The Essay Concerning Human Understanding*, "A credible man vouching his knowledge of ['the being and existence of the thing itself'] is a good proof; but if another equally credible do witness it from his report, the testimony is weaker: and a third that attests the hearsay of an hearsay is yet less considerable." Credible testimony in this formulation is related not to the credibleness of the speaker, but rather it is about the firsthand knowledge of the "original truth" of "the thing itself" (1690, Book 4, XVI:10). The quality of the testimony of the report is directly related to referential fidelity, which is ensured if it is made by somebody with firsthand knowledge.

Locke's empiricism focuses on firsthand knowledge, but this theory of language interrupts the relationship between language and knowledge with ideas, which complicate signification. Where empirical knowledge presumes an ideal speech situation in which there is a speaker able to produce an utterance that does not subjectively corrupt the sensory knowledge, ideas are a sort of middle point in people's minds that a word used in conversation calls up. That is, for an account based on knowledge of the thing itself to be correct, the speaker must produce an objective account of what they saw, unobstructed by speaker purpose. A subjective speaker—a speaker motivated by personal motives and purposes—by comparison can manipulate and distort the "original" truth of the material world. The trustworthiness of an utterance is linked to an object in the world, then, because that is thought to circumvent the subjectivity of the speaker. Subjective secondhand speech is exemplified by gossip, which hearsay is sometimes likened to. Gossip, historically attributed to women in Western cultures, is not to be trusted because it is riddled with the goals of the speaker above and beyond fidelity to the world of experience.[3] Or as Park (1987, 57) describes the dangers of hearsay "a tale twice told is a tale altered."

Hearsay is not trusted because it is a twice-told tale that is not linked to empirical knowledge of "the thing itself." Legally, hearsay is the in-court repetition of an out-of-court statement said by somebody else. Hearsay is "a statement that: (1) the declarant does not make while testifying at the current trial or hearing; and (2) a party offers in evidence to prove the truth of the matter asserted in the statement" (Rule 801).[4] In other words, hearsay is when a person giving testimony repeats the out-of-court utterance of another person, and the repeated utterance is presented as a fact central to the case for or against the person accused of the crime. Hearsay is barred in Anglo-American legal systems, because the person with the sensory knowledge of the event is not available for cross-examination in the courtroom in front of the judge, jury, and the person being accused. The hearsay rule is meant to guard against "misperception," "faulty memory," "ambiguity," or "faulty narration" (Mueller and Kirkpatrick 1996, 118).

Hearsay evidence is always reported speech. Let me give an example. It would be hearsay if Jenny gave testimony that Casey said, "I saw Alex steal that pack of gum." It is hearsay, because Jenny did not see Alex steal the gum;

she only reported what Casey had told her. Jenny would only be allowed to give testimony about the theft if she had seen it herself. In Anglo-American law, the knowledge of the person who saw the crime must be cross-examined, and that person is not in the courtroom. Instead, the person he spoke to, in this case Jenny, is giving testimony. Typically, when a "fact" is presented to the jury in direct-examination, it is then tested when opposing council cross-examines the witness. The person with the knowledge, Casey, is not on the stand and so they can't be cross-examined. Instead, hearsay evidence is evaluated by the judge, using a set of legal criteria to which the jury may not even be made privy. If the hearsay evidence is admitted using an exception to hearsay, it is thus presented to the jury as a fact, but it is never subjected to cross-examination, because the person, Jenny, who saw the event and thus has empirical knowledge is not on the stand (more on exceptions to hearsay in the next section).

Hearsay is inadmissible because the person with the firsthand knowledge—the person who witnessed the event—is not the person giving testimony. As Sir Geoffrey Gilbert[5] (1791, 889) put it, "Hearsay is not evidence. [...] the *Attestation* of the *Witness* must be to what he *knows*, and not to that only which he has *heard*; for *mere hearsay is no evidence*" (emphasis in original). Hearsay is untrusted because it is linked only to the testimony of another person rather than firsthand, sensory knowledge. This exclusion presumes that the "natural world" precedes language, and thus that every iteration of the empirical world is a decaying facsimile of "the real." Knowledge stems from firsthand, sensory-based experience—what Locke called "material truths" (1690, Book 4, XVI: 10)—not secondhand, essentially linguistic narrative. A witness, then, must tell the court what they have seen happen, not repeat the words of somebody else (i.e., hearsay). "Nothing can be more 'indeterminate' than loose and wandering '*Testimonies*' taken upon the uncertain Report of the Talk and Discourse of others" (Gilbert 1791, 890). Where "testimony" based only on "Report of Talk" is merely linguistic, "evidence" is either material or at least directly indexical.

Reported speech, not all of which is hearsay, is nevertheless admitted during trials, fairly regularly. As Matoesian (2001, 105) notes, "Reported speech—speech from historical settings—constitutes the evidential infrastructure of the adversarial system of justice." This is because, of course, evidence comes from events that happened prior to the trial or other legal contexts. It is notable, then, that this one kind of reported speech, hearsay, is systematically banned and that there are so many exceptions to hearsay that allow in some kinds of speech, uttered under certain constraining circumstances. Here I trace the contours of the inclusion and exclusion of hearsay in the context of domestic violence to identify and begin to parse the complicating factors of language ideology and social context that ultimately result in both the production of hearsay evidence and the subjectification of the speaker associated with that evidence.

I focus on hearsay because it is a place where we can see the law talking explicitly about language, but also because it is a legal site in which we find a discourse about domestic violence. At this intersection, we find accounts of intimate violence framed and constrained in a metadiscourse about what language is, how it functions, and ultimately who can speak true utterances. The special social and legal circumstances of domestic violence—that it wasn't illegal until very recently; that it was legally, socially, and religiously justified/justifiable; that it happens in domestic spaces; that it often has no other witnesses—have made it a legal space in which language ideology is performed alongside gender ideology. That is, in hearsay case law, the discussion about the relationship between truth and language is developed and explicated in part in the context of litigating domestic violence—acts of violence situated in intimate spaces where husbands abuse their wives. Domestic violence certainly is not in all of the hearsay case law or even the majority of it, but it has a long-term presence in it that is all the more compelling for a few reasons. Firstly, because domestic violence wasn't illegal for the first three hundred years of Anglo-American law, it is interesting that it has any presence in the case law at all. Indeed, it is primarily when the battery resulted in the death of the wife that we find domestic violence discussed in the hearsay case law. Secondly, the relationship between domestic violence and hearsay has been steadily growing in explicitness over the last thirty years, coming to a head in a number of recent US Supreme Court opinions.

When the US Supreme Court hears and rules on hearsay, they take up the question of constitutionality, whether or not the promises of the confrontation clause of the Sixth Amendment are granted to the accused. This leads to a discussion of hearsay that comments explicitly on what it means to be a witness and bear witness combined with a discussion of reported speech. As the Court reminds us in the recent opinion *Michigan v. Bryant* (2011, 1163), "Of course the Confrontation Clause is not the only bar to admissibility of hearsay statements at trial. State and federal rules of evidence prohibit the introduction of hearsay, subject to exceptions." The present study analyzes confrontation clause issues, but focuses primarily on the discussion of hearsay circulated in that conversation and evidence law, generally.

The relationship between hearsay and domestic violence is developed in the discussion of exceptions to hearsay, instances in which hearsay is deemed admissible. Historically the deathbed statement was used. Since the criminalization of domestic violence, there has been an upsurge in the use of the excited utterance exception. The excited utterance, historically referred to as a spontaneous declaration (cf. Greenleaf 1899; Wigmore 1940; *White v. Illinois* 1992), is a type of hearsay that has traditionally been admissible. The excited utterance is defined in the US Federal Rules of Evidence (2013 [1973], §803.2) simply as, "A statement relating to a startling event or condition, made while the declarant was under the stress of excitement that it caused." In other words, an excited utterance is made spontaneously, in response to a shocking event that the utterance also reports. The rationale and criteria for admitting an excited utterance are significantly fleshed out in Anglo-American case law. In the appellate opinion for *US v. Hadley* (2005), the case analyzed in here, the excited utterance is admitted by citing *Haggins v. Warden, Fort Pillow State Farm* (1983) and *Idaho v. Wright* (1990). *Haggins* uses the framework provided in Wigmore's evidentiary treatise: 1) there must be a "startling" event; 2) "the statement must be made before there is time to contrive"; and 3) the statement must be made while the speaker is still under the stress of the event." From *Wright* (1990), *Hadley* (2005) has taken the standard definition: statements must be made "under circumstances *that eliminate the possibility of fabrication, coaching, or confabulation,* and that therefore the circumstances surrounding the making of the statement provide sufficient assurance that the statement is trustworthy and that cross-examination would be superfluous." (emphasis in original; *Hadley* (2005) actually cites *US v. Schreane* (2003), a 6th Circuit opinion, that cites *Wright* (1990)). The definition from *Wright* (1990), unsurprisingly, is itself based on Wigmore (1940).

The foundational definition of the excited utterance, discussed in detail in Chapter 2, claims that this particular type of utterance is made spontaneously after the reflective faculties of the speaker have been stilled. These assumptions are highlighted in cases in which the speaker to whom the excited utterance is attributed refuses to testify and/or actively complicates the excited utterance, by offering new versions of the event. This complication often arises when the speaker to whom the excited utterance is attributed is the only witness and (typically) also the victim of the gendered violence of domestic assault. The excited utterance exception to hearsay allows the court to use the utterance even when the speaker to whom it is attributed no longer sees that utterance as a viable version of events. When an utterance is translated into the legally intelligible excited utterance, the discursive agency of the speaker is made to seem essentially nonexistent.

The effects on speaker agency that are implicit in the excited utterance were not particularly noticeable or problematic until domestic violence was made illegal in the 1980s and 1990s and prosecutors began using the excited utterance exception a way of including prior utterances, often those spoken directly after the incident to police officers. In the mid-1990s especially, there was a proliferation of law review articles discussing the prosecution of domestic assault using the excited utterance exception to hearsay. During the 1980s, 1990s, and 2000s, domestic violence was going through a process of criminalization in most states, and police policies regarding domestic violence were being overhauled; for example, mandatory arrest and no-drop policies[6] were put in place. Because victims of domestic violence aren't called or choose not to testify against their abusers, the criminal justice system needed ways to proceed with criminal charges, using prior utterances made by the victim (often the only witness) in cases when she refused to testify or missed court dates (Beloof and Shapiro

2002; Byrom 2005; Ferraro 1995; Han 2003). Before the 1980s, the excited utterance was rarely used to represent the speech of a person such as a wife who was available and competent to testify; the excited utterance was more commonly used in cases where the original speaker was an anonymous bystander, had died, was missing, or was a child.[7] In the last thirty years, as domestic violence litigation has made significant headway in holding abusive partners legally accountable, it has become more and more common to use the exceptions to hearsay in cases involving domestic violence.

Entextualizing Evidence

Three goals drive this project. My first goal is to detail the language ideology that is circulated in the hearsay rule, which I do by analyzing a range of legal treatises and precedents that range from 1690 to 2010. My second goal is to describe how this legal language ideology functions in trials and appellate opinions, by identifying and appropriating victims' accounts of domestic violence. I will show that this occurs in the process of "entextualizing" (Bauman and Briggs 1990; Silverstein and Urban 1996) discursive evidence during a trial when legal history, rules, and precedents are indexed. This process makes accounts of events available for legal uses. My third goal is to understand how the language ideology impacts the victim whose speech is appropriated and reproduced, ultimately supporting rather than undermining the structural subjugation of women, of which domestic violence is a part. In short, the use of the excited utterance exception does not help domestic violence victims, but rather it draws on and reproduces problematic stereotypes about domestic violence victims, instrumentalizing the speaker-victim, making them function as instruments for legal processes, and infantilizing them, making decisions for them 'for their own good.'

The typical way of evaluating evidence in Anglo-American law is cross-examination: a fact is presented in direct examination, and then it is tested via cross-examination. It is up to the jury to decide if they find the direct- or cross-examination more persuasive. According to legal idealism, the jury determines the facts of the case. When the hearsay evidence is elicited in direct-examination, there is no cross-examination, which changes the situation in important ways. Notably, the reliability of the evidence is initially evaluated by the judge using a legal rubric that is not explained to the jury, or if it is, that they may not fully understand. Thus when hearsay evidence is determined admissible, it is presented to the jury with a judicial stamp of approval. The admissibility of hearsay evidence is determined using a language ideology that determines which utterances are so reliable that the speaker does not need to be cross-examined. The consequences of the language ideology become the most obvious and relevant when the hearsay rule and the excited utterance exception to hearsay are invoked in cases involving domestic violence. Moreover, the use of this pair of rules in current legal situations reveals deeply held beliefs that domestic violence victims are untrustworthy speakers.

The hearsay rule and the excited utterance exception explicitly measure and evaluate utterances against a legal standard that is thought to determine when the utterance is reliable beyond and against the credibility of the speaker. As such, this pair of rules circulates and (re)produces a language ideology. In Chapter 1, I will describe these two rules in detail. For now suffice it to say that the hearsay rule bans the in-court repetition of out-of-court utterances made by a person other than the one giving testimony. The hearsay rule has a number of exceptions, one of which is the excited utterance, commonly used in cases involving domestic violence. The excited utterance exception admits the in-court repetition of a hearsay utterance if the utterance was said by an excited speaker speaking excitedly about and in response to exciting circumstances.

By looking at the relationship between intimate violence, hearsay, and the excited utterance exception to hearsay, we get a sense of how legal language is productive and powerful—it creates the thing it names—but also that its productive power stems from its conception of language, or language ideologies. A language ideology is made up of ideas about what language is, how it functions, and how it relates to the world it purportedly represents. This book examines the metadiscursive language ideology circulated in rules that determine when a secondhand utterance (hearsay) is credible, and how the language ideology used to deem (or not deem) an utterance credible impacts the person who purportedly spoke it. Further, it interrogates the ways that social discourses about women who have been the victims of intimate violence impact legal decisions. In particular, my approach considers multiple layers of legal text and discourse, from trial to US Supreme Court precedent to legal history. Not only would it be difficult and arbitrary to disentangle rules of evidence from the trials they are used in, from appellate opinions that cite rules and trials, and from the precedents cited in those opinions, but it would also bypass the rich intertextuality of the legal language ideology that impacts the individual who finds herself risked in/by the law.

Discursive Agency

The question of discursive agency—the worry that language is out of our control—is at the apex of questions of admissible hearsay for a number of reasons. Discursive agency (Butler 1997; Medina 2006) is the potential for an utterance to be meaningful, regardless of or beyond the intentions of the speaker, and it is complicated by processes of contextualization (2006) and entextualization (Andrus 2012). Legal discursive agency is further complicated by the role that intention plays in so many legal principles. The process of making the utterance meaningful also provides the discursive resources with which the speaker is "recognizable" (Butler 1997). Discussions of credible utterances hinge on the ways the speaker's intentions are identified via the discursive mechanisms of rule and case law. The pair of rules that this analysis is interested in, the hearsay rule and the excited utterance exception, are explicitly looking for and measuring the goals (or lack thereof) of the speaker, and in so doing, discursive agency is assigned to either the speaker (falseness and lack of credibility) or the utterance (trustworthy and fully credible). This double bind is a function of the language ideology with which an utterance is entextualized as an excited utterance, and, as I show, social presumptions about victims of intimate violence impact and are articulated within this legal framework.

From a poststructuralist perspective, agency is historically saturated and situated, culturally bound and capable of producing effect (both strategically and accidentally). Alessandro Duranti (2004, 451) explains, "any act of speaking involves some kind of agency, often regardless of the speaker's intentions and the hearer's interest or collaboration," and thus we should "resist a definition of intentionality that implies conscious planning" (454). That is, people may speak with purposes, but the audience, context, and language itself alter, add to, and exceed the intentions of the speaker or the listener alone. Thus, people act with language, but the effects aren't under the singular control of the speaker. Take for example, speech act theory (Austin [1962] 2003; Grice 1957; Searle 1970). This theory looks specifically at the ways in which action is effected through language. Butler (1997, 7) thus argues that there is a view that "language is thought of 'mostly as agency—as act with consequences,' an extended doing, a performance with effects." That is, the common view is that language is a type of agency, an act that people can do. Upsetting the dependence on speaker intention, she suggests alternatively, "Language is a name for [...] both [...] the act and its consequences" (Butler 1997, 8). That is, language is both the performance and the performed. This disrupts the simple agency of language as an instrument for human action by considering language instead as the result.

The simple agency of intentionality forgets that speakers can have internally inconsistent goals and interact at cross-purposes with their interlocutor. And perhaps most importantly, it forgets that language in context is semantically excessive (Butler 1997). As Foucault (1972, 209) argues,

> To speak is to do something—something other than to express what one thinks; to translate what one knows, and something other than to play with the structures of language (*langue*); to show that to add a statement to a preexisting series of statements is to perform a complicated and costly gesture, which involves conditions (and not only a situation, a context, and motives), and rules (not the logical and linguistic rules of construction).

Foucault is arguing that speaking is an activity, but not one that is under the sovereign control of the individual who speaks. The action is constrained by the series of statements that constrain and enable any individual event of speech, and thus the speech is a practice made dense, complex, and risky by the discursive conditions and rules circulating in and about language—a lesson that the speaker of an excited utterance learns all too well. Likewise, rather than focusing on the speaker and audience and how they do or do not function as sovereign subjects, Laura Ahearn (2001) suggests agency is established and constrained in ongoing discourse. Discourse is "co-constructed by participants, emergent from particular social interactions" (Ahearn 2001, 111). Thus agency to use discourse is co-constructed by interlocutors in context. It is contingent on the contexts, prior texts, and sites of actual interaction. There is room for purposeful discursive interaction, but we must also acknowledge that agency is 1) constrained at the point of interaction by the prior discourses of the situation, and 2) that an utterance will always mean more than the speaker intended it to.

From a feminist perspective, the poststructuralist model of agency is problematic: "Any theory that denies women 'agency' retards the changes in patriarchal social structures for which feminism strives, because it denies the existence of an entity to attack those structures" (Gardiner 1995, 9). That is, in order for a theory to be useful for feminist projects, it must allow the scholar to advocate for change, a stance that requires space for people to have agency to enact change. This position is problematic because it does not take into account the discourses that constrain and enable agency. Such constraining and enabling discourses don't merely authorize or forbid a particular speaker to speak or do things, but rather they establish a normative framework within which language and behaviors are intelligible. A more nuanced view of agency is necessary to understand the relationship between a speaker and her utterance within the institutional structures of Anglo-American common law.

Discursive agency (Butler 1997; Medina 2006) provides an alternative to linguistic or rhetorical agency, because discursive agency doesn't locate agency (only) in individuals. Discursive agency circulates in the shifting discourses, effects, and speaker capacities and intentions at work in the institutional setting of "the law." Discursive agency acknowledges the capacity of language to act, but without reducing it to speaker agency or the capacities of a sovereign individual. Discursive agency is dependent on and regulated by the prior discourses and contexts in which the utterance is produced and those used by the audience or interlocutors who actively make sense out of interaction and the speech produced in it. Discursive agency is constantly in flux, as the prior discourses and contexts being cited in any act of discourse are themselves unstable and accompanied by issues of authority and power. Jose Medina (2006) explains that "discursive agency involves a process of constant recontextualization [. . .], in which our discursive acts are constantly being oriented by histories of use and at the same time they are constantly reorienting these histories as well" (Medina 2006, xiv). In other words, discursive agency is not centralized in the individual, because it is affected by contexts of interaction, participant histories, histories of usage, and the bodies who interact. Discursive agency is produced and functions between interlocutors who shift in and out of participant roles as a part of their interaction. Thus discursive agency is diffuse—distributed across people, things, spaces, and events. It occurs in "chains of performances through which linguistic practices are maintained and reproduced" (Medina 2006, xiii). Butler argues that "the one who acts (who is not the same as the sovereign subject) acts precisely to the extent that he or she is constituted as an actor" (1997, 16). That is, in as much as any individual is an agent, that subjectivity is produced by discourses that constrain and enable bodies *and* the discourses that make them recognizable within a particular context.

The discourse of the law constrains the agency that emerges from events by entextualizing an essentially trustworthy account (the excited utterance) and prohibiting alternative accounts. Importantly, alternative accounts most often arise when the excited utterance exception is used in cases involving domestic violence, when the speaker of the purported utterance is not a stranger or passerby but a domestic partner. In such cases, the process of entextualizing an excited utterance makes the agency of the person producing an utterance about the event invisible. In fact, the use of the excited utterance exception to hearsay hinges on presumptions about the agency of the speaker in the moment it "originally" was spoken. This reaching into the past takes place long after the fact, in the courtroom, rendering the agency of the speaker nonexistent at the moment the original utterance was made. The "original" event, of course, can never be fully in the grasp of the Court without this rule and its backward effects. I argue that the backward effects of the excited utterance work to construct the "original" utterance, along with the excited utterance, and the agency of that speaker. That is, in constructing the excited utterance, the court disattributes (takes away agency that may have been attributed previously) the agency that the speaker may have had when she made her original utterance. As the law determines whether the utterance is admissible, and indeed as the utterance is moved back and forth across the line between admissible and inadmissible in the appellate process, the discursive agency of the speaker of the statement is altered with little regard for her actual agency in her world.

(Critical) Discourse Analysis

This project uses discourse analysis and archival research methods to analyze contemporary and historical documents together. Discourse analysis focuses on "language in use," but that phrase elides the rhetorical and interaction features that give discourse its richness. According to Barbara Johnstone (2008, 3), discourse analysis focuses on the ways that "people draw on the knowledge they have about language, knowledge based on their memories of things they have seen, heard, seen, or written before, to do things in the world: exchange information, express feelings, make things happen, create beauty, entertain themselves and others, and so on." That is, any use of discourse is both based on prior ideas about language that are formed from interactions with it as both a speaker/ writer and a listener/reader; at the same time, any use of discourse causes effects, some purposeful and some accidental, that make and keep the discursive form in circulation. Discourse analysis pays close attention to the details of text and talk that do social, interactional, and institutional work. Following Johnstone (1996, 23), I use discourse analysis to "study relatively small amounts of data in relatively great detail." I use discourse analysis to analyze trial and judicial opinions, which are situated in and made legible via historical treatises and precedents. Judicial opinions and trials are intricately intertextual, using legal reasoning to weave together opinions and concepts across more than three hundred years and, in the cases studied here, two continents. In interaction, participants will use and anticipate future uses of intertextual chains, which expand outward as discursive networks. Matoesian (2000, 879) argues that trials operate on an economy of "intertextuality, decontextualizing speech from one speech event and recontextualizing it in a new one." In a trial and even more so in an appeal, speech is recontextualized so that it echoes past legal texts and also in response to the speaker's perceived social identity. In addition, inconsistencies between the prior text and the new text are obscured by foregrounding some aspects of the context of earlier speech events and backgrounding others (Matoesian 2000). Importantly, as Susan Ehrlich (2007) argues, institutional processes of recontextualization do not only affect the resultant text but also the identities of participants.

In this study, I also use discourse analysis to understand how the structure and function of ideas about language that are used to entextualize the legal object "excited utterance" also impact the contexts at which the utterance points and construct the identity and discursive agency of the person to whom the utterance is attributed. Paying close attention to the details of text and talk, this analysis considers the ways in which legal presupposition—embedded in the black-letter law of legal rules, statutes, and precedents—circulates ideology that affects on-the-ground legal interactions such as trials. That is, combining historical research with discourse analysis of trials and judicial opinions allows me insight into the ways that legal discourses circulate in trials and the ways in which such discourses are consequential. Thus my use of discourse analysis satisfies critical goals, looking for the ways in which "institution[s] simultaneously facilitat[e] and constrain the social action (here specifically verbal interaction) of its members" (Fairclough 2010, 41). In addition, discourse analysis allows me to identify places where social actors resist the constraints of institutions, however fleetingly.

TRACING INTERTEXTUALITY

Guided by the principle of intertextuality, I have collected data that allows me to describe how "the now-said reaches back to and somehow incorporates or resonates with the already-said and reaches ahead to, anticipates, and somehow incorporates the to-be-said" (Bauman 2005, 145). This research analyzes judicial opinions (US Court of Appeals and US Supreme Court), statutes (US Rules of Evidence), English common law treatises on evidence, US legal treatises, and trial transcripts. My data consists of US Supreme Court opinions, Appellate Circuit opinions, State Supreme Court opinions, trial interactions, statutes, and historical treatises. I trace out a network of precedent cases established in the Supreme Court in order to understand how that intertextual network is applied and shaped in the everyday processes and discourses of trials. The Supreme Court only deals with questions of constitutionality, and thus in these cases the issue is hearsay in general (with the excited utterance exception as an example in a number of opinions), and how to balance hearsay exceptions with the requirements of confrontation, prescribed by the Sixth Amendment to the US Constitution. The Court of Appeals circuits operationalize the opinions of the Supreme Court in a context not explicitly or not only dealing with constitutional law.

US Supreme Court

Between 1970 and 2010, the US Supreme Court has ruled on the admissibility of hearsay eleven times. Figure 1 shows the intertextual nature of precedential citation. *Ohio v. Roberts* (1980) and *Crawford v. Washington* (2004) are the two main precedents, with *Crawford* overturning *Roberts* in 2004. Both opinions

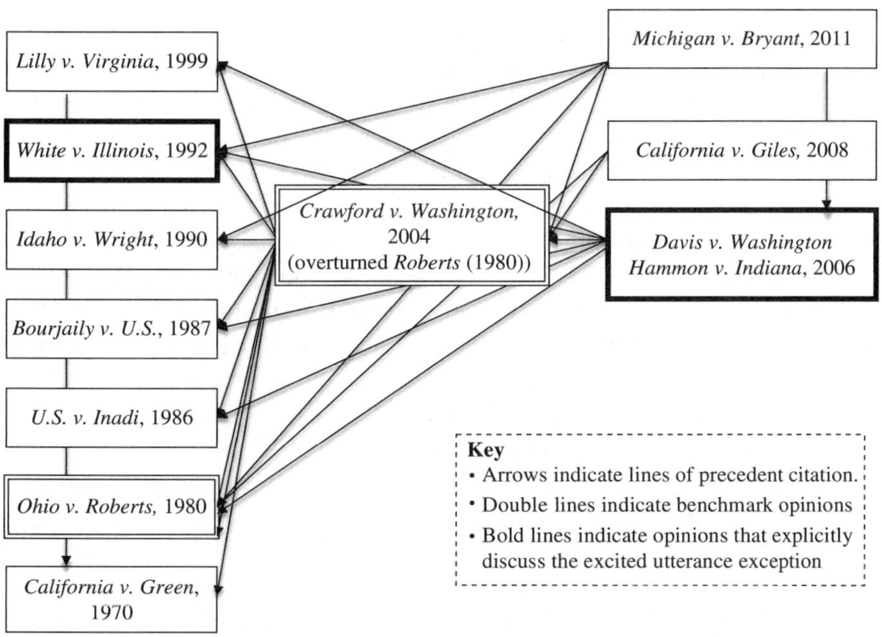

FIGURE 1 Hearsay Citation in the US Supreme Court.

are cited by every subsequent opinion. *White v. Illinois* (1992), which developed *Roberts* (1980), is also cited multiple times, even after *Crawford*, and the 2006 opinion for two cases, *Davis v. Washington* and *Hammon v. Indiana (Davis/Hammon)*, which developed *Crawford* is also important and well cited.

The opinions in Figure 1 are about many different kinds of admissible hearsay. *Lilly v. Virginia* (1999) and *United States v. Inadi* (1984), for example, are about co-conspirator statements. The cases marked with bold lines comment on the excited utterance specifically. Benchmark opinions about hearsay, *Ohio v. Roberts* (1980) and *Crawford v. Washington* (2004), are not about the excited utterance exception, but they are cited in nearly every hearsay opinion that followed. Benchmark opinions establish the parameters of hearsay and discuss what makes hearsay admissible. *Davis v. Washington/Hammon v. Indiana* (2006) and *Giles v. California* (2008) are opinions involving intimate partner violence. Because domestic violence is only recently illegal, these are some of the first US Supreme Court opinions to comment on domestic violence. Chapters 2 and 3 are devoted to analyzing these opinions.

US Court of Appeals and Trial Courts

I also reviewed all of the appellate opinions about hearsay from the US Court of Appeals from 2005–2007 to get a sense of a) how many cases were concerned with domestic violence and b) how exceptions to hearsay are applied, with the ultimate goal of selecting a case for which I could obtain the trial transcripts and use as a case study. Out of the available precedents, I have chosen *US v. Hadley*[8] (*Hadley*) (trial 2002–2003, appellate opinion 2005) as a case study, analyzing both the appellate opinion and trial transcript in Chapters 3 and 4. The *Hadley* trial was heard in the United States District Court for the Eastern District of Tennessee by a Chief District Judge. In that trial, the jury found JH guilty. The decision was appealed to the Sixth Circuit of the US Court of Appeals in 2004 on the basis of the admission of PH's excited utterances in the testimony of Officer 1 and Officer 2. *Hadley* is a case involving domestic violence, and a case in which the prosecution's (successful) argument hinges on the use of the excited utterance exception, which is used to admit this statement: "He has a gun. He's going to kill me" (Officer 1 Testimony, November 2002: 8). In this case, police were dispatched to a "domestic disorder with a gun," which was "Priority 1" or a call "that needs the fastest and quickest response to the call" (Officer 2, November 2002: 28). The police arrested JH "for the assault that occurred on PH" (Officer 1, November 2002: 23), and according to the police reports, PH pressed charges (Prosecution 1, March 2003: 12). The domestic assault charges were dismissed, however, and replaced with felony possession of a gun (*Hadley*, 2005: 3), a gesture that downplays the domestic quality of the crime, overlooking the physical impact that this particular crime has on the victim. Domestic violence is essentially stripped from a case that has domestic assault at its core, which works to make PH an instrument, an evidentiary index, for a crime having to do with a gun. Once translated, as the case is, to gun possession rather than domestic assault, PH is not called as a witness during the trial; instead, her utterances about a gun, made on the scene in an excited state, are admitted as evidence. In the process, she is circumvented and entextualized as essentially untrustworthy. PH attends the sentencing of her husband, JH, and insists that she be allowed to give testimony in defense of her husband then.

I analyze *Hadley*, both the trial (2002–2003) and appellate opinion (2005), in Chapters 4 and 5. I've selected *Hadley* as a case study because the *Hadley* appellate opinion was published just after the Supreme Court issued *Crawford v. Washington* (2004), which overturned part of an earlier precedent *Ohio v. Roberts* (1980). *Hadley* thus walks through the admissibility of the excited utterance in question according to both the reasoning of *Roberts* (1980) and *Crawford* (2004), commenting on the history of the hearsay ban and excited utterance exception and the most recent developments in the law. The trial is also rich for analysis, because PH, who is said to have spoken the excited utterance in that case, comes to court during sentencing and demands to be allowed to give testimony, in which she argued that she did not speak the excited utterance in question, and if she did, the court misunderstands what she meant by the statement. This case thus comes at an important moment in the history of legal developments regarding hearsay at the same time that its unique features call attention to the ways in which domestic violence victims are at risk in this body of law.

The excited utterance and its recent relationship to domestic violence case law provides a discursive and interactional site in which to interrogate and reassess the ways in which agency is performed and attributed in a context in which discursive agency is put at risk in a number of different ways: in the violence of the domestic situation; in the discourses of gender (used by women, their intimate partners, the police, and the members of the court); in the metadiscourse of the rule of law; and even in advocacy stances that have led to no-drop policies that disallow abused women from dropping charges against abusive domestic partners.

Outline of the Book

What follows is what Butler (1997, 53) has called "a rhetorical reading" of hearsay, or a reading "distinguished from a reading that follows established conventions of legal interpretation." That is, while I stay close to the legal concepts, this analysis does not argue for legally correct interpretations but instead, identifies the consequences of language ideologies embedded in the legal concepts. I make two complementary arguments. First, I argue that the language ideology circulated in the law of evidence is co-articulated with ideas about victims that work together to entextualize a legally intelligible utterance and also produce a legally intelligible subject position related to the utterance. Chapter 1 details developments in legal responses to domestic violence and feminist legal responses to violence against women, and explains how domestic violence and the excited utterance exception to hearsay fit together within the paternal structures of the law (cf. Matoesian 1993). I explain how gendered/sexist speech, paternalism at home, and paternalism in the law work together when the excited utterance exception is used in cases involving domestic violence. This discussion is continued in Chapter 2, where I describe recent developments in hearsay law in US Supreme Court opinions, some of which are about cases involving domestic violence. In the 1990s, the precedents about hearsay, many of which remain cited, are about the reliability of an utterance in the context of children's speech and children's testimony. When these opinions are applied in cases involving adult women's speech, the result is infantilization of the domestic violence victim. The arguments made in the 1990s are extended and complicated by refinements in hearsay law since 2004, in which a co-definition of "testimonial" and "witness" has developed. This chapter traces the developments of the last two decades to identify the legal discursive resources of the hearsay language ideology and the presumptions about credibility and reliability articulated in this language ideology that are applied in the lower courts.

My second argument is that discursive agency is a product of language ideological processes that entextualize and recontextualize utterances, thus positioning discursive agency apart from, or at least not essentially linked to, speaker intention. The process of giving an account of what happened, which often includes repeating previously spoken utterances, "entextualizes" evidence (cf. Bauman and Briggs 1990; Silverstein and Urban 1996) in an after-the-fact process that identifies a bit of ongoing discourse as a text. "Entextualization" occurs when a bit of discourse is extracted from ongoing discourse when it is appropriated by or made useful in a new context; such "recontextualization" renders the bit of discourse as a discrete "text-artifact" (Silverstein and Urban 1996). Forming the text outlines the boundaries of the event of which it gives an account. Thus, entextualization forms both the text and the event with which it is associated. When something is entextualized, the resultant text-artifact and its meaning are made to seem independent of the stretch of ongoing interaction in which it was produced. The now decontextualized text can be easily moved into new interactional settings and contexts with clearly demarcated boundaries. Entextualization decontextualizes a text thereby making it available for use in future contexts, future discursive events. In Chapter 3, I develop this argument by describing the language ideology that facilitates the entextualization of an utterance as an excited utterance—extracting an utterance from ongoing discourse in order to make it intelligible and useful in legal discourse. In Chapter 4, I describe the discursive agency shaped in the process of entextualizing an excited utterance, and the impact of the language ideology on the person to whom the excited utterance is attributed.

Taken together, these two arguments show the ways in which subjectivity/subject position is a product of the same processes of entextualization that produce a legally identifiable text. Legal discourses about language infantilize the domestic violence victim, making her what Judith Butler (1997) has termed "recognizable" as essentially untrustworthy. In the context of domestic violence, ideology, social practice, and expectations precede the interaction between police and domestic violence victims, giving shape to the interaction, the treatment of the victim, descriptions of her in police reports, and decisions to make an arrest or not, and ultimately making the speaker "recognizable" in institutionally salient ways. I conclude the book by considering the out-of-controlness of language that puts the victim at risk in these ways. The out-of-controlness of language works in concert with legal language ideology that treats language not only as controllable but typically in the intentional control of speakers. The ideology of language in the law treats language as though it is fully within the control of the individual, assuming intentionality and sovereign agency at every turn. The excited utterance exception to hearsay identifies a particular type of utterance that the law believes was never under the control of the speaker, working against the presupposition that typically speech is intentional. To put it another way, the excited utterance exception to hearsay is functional precisely because of an intentionality-related view of language—people mean to speak and they intend a particular meaning when they do (cf. Grice, 1957). The speaker of the excited utterance is caught between intentional and unintentional speech, and the social expectations of the domestic violence victim tighten this bind when the utterance is spoken by a victim and is reporting domestic violence. When the speaker is a domestic violence victim, the speaker mirrors the out-of-controllness of the utterance—she refuses to stay in her place, is out-of-control and recalcitrant, an affront to the law. This final chapter suggests that the excited utterance is the exception that proves the rule and that the victim of domestic violence fulfills much the same role. She is the out-of-control woman who reveals the continued paternal value of the rule of law.

1

The Legal Discourse of Domestic Violence: Language Ideology and Trustworthiness

The bulk of Anglo-American legal history has treated the husband's use of physical punishment to correct his wife as commonsensically right. According to *The Lawes Resolution of Women's Rights* ([1632]2005, 67), "The wife as long as she liveth is subject to the law of her husband." As the subject of her husband's law, wives were regularly subjected to physical punishment. As the person responsible for her behavior, it was the husband's responsibility to correct her as needed, including corporeally, much like a child (Foyster 2005). Tolerance for the types and severity of domestic violence in Anglo-American law has changed throughout the years. *Joyner v. Joyner* (1862, 325), which denies the complainant a divorce, argues that the husband is legally responsible for the wife and thus has the right to use violence to punish or correct her: "There may be circumstances which will mitigate, excuse and so far justify the husband in striking the wife 'with a horse-whip on one occasion and with a switch on another, leaving several bruises on the person.'" The mitigating factors discussed all rest on the presupposition that women are not autonomous civic agents, they have flights of temper, and they talk too much. Though not arguing that the practice was good, just or reasonable, the 1868 opinion for *State v. Rhodes* argued, "We will not inflict upon society the greater evil of raising the curtain upon domestic privacy, to punish the lesser evil of trifling violence" (*State v. Rhodes* qtd. in dissenting opinion in *Giles v. California* 2008, 2704). The suggestion is both that violence inflicted on a wife by a husband is "trifling" and that the domestic sphere should be protected from public scrutiny. Taken together, the suggestion is that the patriarchal structure of the home is more important than the safety of women. It only became explicitly illegal to batter one's wife in the twentieth century, and only criminal in the last few decades of that century. That is, domestic assault was not considered a police matter until the end of the twentieth century (cf. *Thurman v. City of Torrington, et al.* 1984).

Here I argue that shifting language and changes in the details of acceptable abuse all participate in the "legal facticity" of domestic violence, to borrow phrasing from Gregory Matoesian (1993, 2001). This research uses hearsay case law to show that the specifics of acceptable domestic violence prove to be malleable over and over, producing a body of law in which domestic violence is the legal and social norm—as long as it is done within limits that are determined after the fact. The discourse circulating in various bodies of civil and criminal law is consistently aimed at explaining, justifying, and describing the situations and contexts in which domestic violence is appropriate and the types of abuse that are reasonable, supported by a social dismissal of and underplaying of the evil of domestic violence. Relatedly, whether the treatment of the domestic partner crosses the line into domestic violence is established by cataloguing the marks left on her body, pathologizing the behavior of the victim (cf. Lamb 1999), and/or appropriating her story.

Because it was not illegal for a husband to physically punish his wife, case law that gives a legal account of domestic violence is not readily available in a single body of law. In Anglo-American legal history, the discussion of domestic violence is disturbingly scattered across civil and criminal cases, largely located in homicide cases, because domestic assault became illegal when punishment resulted in death. We also find accounts of domestic violence in divorce cases (see Foyster 2009). In the early nineteenth century Sir William Scott created a heuristic for determining what the correct punishment was for any given wifely crime. Judge Scott's benchmark ruling in *Holden v. Holden* (1810) pronounced, "For the reason which would justify the imputation of blame to the wife will not justify the ferocity of the husband" and granted Mrs. Holden's petition for divorce (*English Reports: Ecclesiastical, Admiralty, and Probate and Divorce* 161, 616). Such changes at the beginning of the nineteenth century didn't make wife-beating illegal, but it did create precedent that stated that some kinds of abuse justified divorce, quite a large leap forward for the time. Nevertheless, only in very rare cases was even severe domestic assault grounds for criminal prosecution, and then only typically if the wife had been killed by her husband (cf. *The Queen v. Brooks*, 1843). In addition to being the subject of her husband's law, married women were considered the property of their husbands and lacked civil autonomy: "the [husband's and wife's] [i]nterests are absolutely the same" (Buller 1785, 286). These are the very complaints listed one hundred years later in "The Declaration of Sentiments" written by Elizabeth Cady Stanton and presented to the US Congress in 1848. Though there were improvements in the legal status of women, such as getting the vote in 1923 and the federal disavowal of domestic violence in 1920, it was not until well into the twentieth century that a wife was no longer defined as both the property of the husband and a part of him, both of which made it virtually impossible to identify the violence of husbands against wives as criminal.

Though this trajectory seems to show positive developments for women who have been abused by their husbands, and indeed there have been significant improvements, the story is not quite so clean. Women are still abused by their intimate partners at startling rates. Additionally, women are consistently blamed for the violence that they sustain and/or are infantilized as children incapable of reasonable decisions, which allows for state intervention in their marriages. Spousal abuse was discussed in commonsensically paternal terms, creating a legal facticity of domestic violence.

This research identifies a central if implicit articulation between law and domestic violence in the metadiscourses of the hearsay principle of the Anglo-American law of evidence. This chapter maps the points where law, gender, violence against women, and ideas about language intersect to argue that ideas about language, or language ideologies, shape the social and legal intelligibility of domestic violence victims. Much of the feminist research on legal language and power has looked at the ways that gender intersects with the power and dominance inherent in legal interaction, which is largely linguistic. Carol Smart (1989, 94) argues that "law constitutes the bodies of women in discourse," drawing on and reproducing "notions about women's bodies (e.g., as diseased, hysterical, immoral) in the construction and practice of law." That is, notions about women's bodies that circulate in the law reflect and participate in the social constitution of that body. Aviva Orenstein (1997, 162) argues that one place to look for legal discourses' production of gendered bodies is in the law of evidence. "This area of law regulates and reflects the construction of courtroom 'truth.' It perpetuates the cultural values, legal rules, and social norms that our society uses to assess credibility." The law of evidence traffics in truth, truth that is identified in terms of referential correctness: this is what happened (cf. Trinch, 2003). This view of truth reproduces social norms and expectations of credibility at the same time that it refuses to acknowledge that metadiscursive legal rules determine what counts as truth and who has the credibility necessary to speak the truth.

The law of evidence, rules, and procedures, "are drawn from the culture's general understanding of how we 'know' things to be true" (Shapiro 1991, 2). M. J. Frug makes a similar argument, arguing that the law plays a significant role "in the production of the meaning of the female body." She goes on to argue:

> Legal rules—like other cultural mechanisms—encode the female body with meanings. Legal discourse then explains and rationalizes these meanings by an appeal to the "natural" differences between the sexes, differences that the rules themselves help to produce. The formal norm of legal neutrality conceals ways in which legal rules participate in the construction of those meanings. (M. J. Frug 1992, 1049).

For Frug legal rules are one of the "cultural mechanisms" that make women's bodies meaningful, hiding legal effectuality behind a veil of positivity and neutrality. Following Frug, I analyze the US Federal Rules of Evidence, arguing that this is a discursive site in which a woman who has been the victim of domestic violence is made meaningful in ways that fit the evidentiary structure of the law and social norms of intimate relationships.

In the rules of evidence, ideological presuppositions about and expectations of women are co-articulated with legal ideologies of truth, fact, and reliability, creating filters through which the speech of victims and witnesses are filtered (Ehrlich 2001, 4). "Male and female sexuality and violence against women are reproduced and recirculated in the 'talk' of . . institutional contexts," and further, such institutional discourses "shape and/or constrain the kinds of gendered identities that are produced" (Ibid.). Ehrlich is concerned with the ways in which presumptions about the sexual behavior of men and women are circulated in institutional settings, in a process of prohibition and enablement that also forms identities. Like Ehrlich, my approach also considers ways institutional contexts circulate ideas about violence against women, locating language ideologies that are used to make the woman who has been abused by an intimate partner "recognizable" as a legal subject. According to Judith Butler (1997, 5), being "recognizable" is a function of and performed through address, which "is not merely to be recognized for what one already is, but to have the very term conferred by which the recognition of existence becomes possible." That is, the discursive resources that facilitate the recognition of an individual circulate and are recirculated in address, which instantiates the subject (again). Expectations about how a woman will and should react to intimate violence, presuppositions about women's speech and behavior, and presuppositions about truth and credibility work together to legally address the victim of domestic violence, bring her into legal subjecthood. As M.J. Frug (1992, 1046) argues, "Because [gender is] semiotic—that is, constituted by a system of signs that we produce and interpret—each of us inescapably produces herself within the gender meaning system, although the meaning of gender is indeterminate or undecidable." In Frug's configuration, gender is both a sign system that constrains the interpretation of the body, and a self-productive process, an achievement. Recognizability doesn't only enable identity performances, but it also forecloses some. "Cultural norms [also] render other gendered identities inappropriate or unintelligible, and often subject to social and physical sanctions and penalties (e.g., ostracism, homophobia, gay bashing, the 'fixing' of intersexed infants)" (Ehrlich 2007: 453). That is, not all gender performances are acknowledged or authorized in the institutional context(s) of the law. Legally recognizable subject positions are produced and reproduced via linguistic legal practices that draw on social categories and expectations of gender, reifying them within the objective, binary structures at work in the Anglo-American law of evidence.

As I describe in what follows, the subject position, victim[1] of domestic violence, comes stocked with social and legal expectations about the victim—female, untrustworthy, willing to lie for her partner, abused woman's syndrome, not credible—that work in concert with legal rules about truth and trustworthiness to create a subjectivity that is presupposed as essentially untrustworthy and not credible. That said, when a victim or witness is allowed to speak, such static categories such as domestic violence victim are contested in interaction, in part at least because the victim does not think of herself the same way the law does (see Kitzinger 2000 on interaction and gendered identity). The witness/victim tends to represent her situation in more complexity. In interactions like those in courtrooms and district attorneys' offices, identity is "accomplished" again and again, every time the static preconceptions of the law are contested in interaction with the person whose experiences and utterances are evaluated (cf. West and Zimmerman 1987; Butler 1993). The excited utterance exception to hearsay, which I analyze here, is a legal structure that bypasses legal interaction (the victim is not called to the stand in the trial, but her words are imported via another's testimony) in a process that reimagines the interaction between police and the victim as unidirectional—she spoke to them, while they controlled the situation. And as I argue here, the shape of legally recognizable subject positions are not only implicated in practices that are explicitly about bodies, but also in discourses about language circulating within the law, determining which speech and, by extension, which speakers are trustworthy and which are not.

Gender, Language, and Law

Victims of intimate violence are caught within a matrix of androcentric structures, three of which are particularly important here: language, gender, and law. Language is integral to the relating of law and gender, in part via indexicality. Indexical forms do both social and semantic work by relating linguistic and social meaning. Social gender discourses are implicated in legal discourses via indexicality, or the strategies used to point to and establish "social alignments" (Johnstone 2008, 133). Indexical forms thus support gendered, sexist social norms, and when they are brought into the law, the indexical forms bring sexist presuppositions with them. According to Sally McConnell-Ginet (1998) language and sexism are circulated and articulated together, and thus sexism is built into semantics. "To understand the source of sexist semantics, the way sexism in society and culture interacts with the system of linguistic meanings" we need to look for the ways that meaning is dependent on prior interaction and prior discourses (McConnell-Ginet 1998,199). Similarly, Luce Irigaray (1993) argues that there are "cultural injustices of language" that are linked to "generalized sexism," which can be "found in grammar, in vocabulary, in the connotations of a word's gender." That is, sexism is built into the structure of language itself. Irigaray is working with French, which has explicit gender marking, but as Ann Bodine (1975) has shown, English has its own structural sexism in its pronominal system. Dale Spender (1980) calls language "man-made," having structures that value masculine experiences and desires and presenting them as natural standards against which feminine/female experiences and desires stand out as deviant (cf. Lakoff 1973; de Beauvoir 1949). Moreover, some experiences, for example domestic violence, that are unique to or more common in female experience, lack labels and are thus unidentifiable (Smart 1989). For centuries, violence against women was, in the words of Gloria Steinem (1983, 149) "just called life." Feminist linguistic research has thus made important inroads in calling attention to ways in which language is heavily weighted toward typically male values and experiences, excluding what McConnell-Ginet has called "a 'woman's eye view.'" Deborah Cameron (1998, 11) argues "to the extent that our lives are carried on in language [. . .], the sexism of language must constantly reenact and reinforce the commonsense 'normality' of sexist assumptions." That is, sexism is embedded and secreted in language in ways that make sexist constructions and conceptions seem ordinary. Woman's place at home taking care of children and household duties, for example, is made to seem commonsensical in scientific discourses creating an indexical link between the home and child birthing (cf. Lerner 1986).

Much of the scholarship that approaches gender, sex, and language has been critiqued, and rightly so, for essentializing femaleness distilled in language. Elinor Ochs' (1992) critique argues that very few linguistic phenomena are directly or simply linked to gender. Susan Gal (1995, 171) argues that "categories of women's speech, men's speech, and prestigious or powerful speech are not just indexically derived from the identities of speakers," but rather, they are dynamic and related to "other areas of cultural discourse." Eckert and McConnell-Ginet (1999, 189) argue that creating "gender identities is mainly accomplished as people engage directly with others in common ongoing projects—jointly developing shared ways of doing and thinking about things, shared ways of understanding." That is, gender is a feature and product of actions and ideas that are created and refined in interaction with others, who may or may not share all of the same practices and values. Gender identity is not singular and an internal and cohesive element of the individual, but rather it is situational and rhetorical, developed and deployed in different ways depending on what the interaction calls for. Thus McElhinny (2003, 35) argues, "Crucially, the assignment of situational meaning is interactionally governed." The idea that gender emerges in interaction is related to early work on gender as a performance by Candace West and Don Zimmerman (1987, 126): gender is "a routine, methodical, and recurring accomplishment [that] involves a complex of socially guided perceptual, interaction, and micropolitical activities." Gender is a performance of reproducible social practices that are recognizable within a matrix of gendered possibilities. That is, what is recognized/recognizably gendered about speech will change in relationship to shifts in social discourses, and ultimately, identity and gender are situational.

Sociolinguistic analysis of rape trials has made significant headway in identifying and interrogating the linguistic structures that circulate sexist ideas within the law. Such studies give us important insight into the discursive structures with which the law conceives of violence against women. For example, Conley and O'Barr (2005) argue that during rape trials, victims are revictimized via the cross-examination strategies commonly used to impeach testimony. Gregory Matoesian (1993, 22) develops this claim, arguing that "through artful linguistic maneuvers and elegant conversational devices, through the complex and emergent design of sequential-syntactic structures, the local (indexical) particulars about the rape incident are assembled and fashioned into powerful blame implicative inferences against the victim." According to Matoesian (1993) and others, rape is a "social fact" in which aggressive male sexuality is fitted into a spectrum of "natural" male behavior, and in which the victim is put in a syntactic position that blames her. In the rape trial analyzed by Ehrlich (2001, 57), the judge reasoned that "young women . . . must realize that when a young man becomes aroused during sexual activity beyond a moderate degree there is a danger that he will be drive by hormones rather than by conscience." This position, she continues (2001, 60) "license[s] a view of male sexuality and masculinity that portrays violent men as not being the 'agents' of their own actions." Additionally, trial interactions about rape often use miscommunication models to argue, often successfully, that the victim hadn't adequately shown that she did not want to have sex. Such arguments position the accused as an accidental rapist who merely misunderstood (cf. Tannen 1991) the victim's inadequate "signals." Such arguments put the bulk of responsibility and blame on the victim to be a better communicator (Ehrlich 2001; Kitzinger & Firth 1999). These arguments are embedded, for example in prevention training that focuses on teaching women how to say "no" more effectively (Corcoran 1992; Firth and Kitzinger 1997). Celia Kitzinger and Hannah Firth (294) argue that both women and men have a "sophisticated awareness of . . . culturally normative ways" of refusing sex that don't involve "just saying no." "Male claims not to have 'understood' refusals which conform to culturally normative patterns can only be heard as self-interested justifications of coercive behaviour" (295). That is, men know when they are being refused sex, they just don't respond to the request by stopping their sexual advances. Such research shows that legal processes co-opt and transform women's speech so that it works against her express interests, and it shows the depths to which victims are in an always already culturally untenable position.

In short, gender and law draw on the discursive practices of the other. Though there is nothing in language that is inherently gendered (Ehrlich 2001, 9), and, as Ochs (1992) notes, explicit links between language and gender are difficult to identify, there are indexical forms that draw on and point to the social performance of gender. Certain linguistic forms become associated with gendered performance, if only momentarily, so that their performance can come to index gender in some contexts. Such indexical forms function and circulate in legal arguments. The legal context coordinates with and complicates the indexical relationship between language and gender. On one level this is simply because law and gender are both discursive practices consumed, performed, and circulated in language. But on another level, it is because in the law ideas about (trustworthy) language are co-articulated with ideas about speakers in ways that are deeply indebted to presuppositions about social identity. That is, gender is a factor in, a product of, and affected by legal language ideologies located in the intertextual discourses of the law from the trial to the precedent.

Domestic Violence and Law

As Gregory Matoesian (1993) and others have noted, the law tends to support and reproduce patriarchal ideologies circulating in the broader culture. "Culturally mediated interpretive devices" and more generally "patriarchal ideologies provide the linguistic rationalizations and interpretive framework [. . .] for making sense of what happened" (13). Matoesian is talking in particular about sexual violence, but his thoughts can be expanded to consider domestic violence. Domestic violence has long been justified in the law by a script of domesticity and privacy; patriarchal discourses of one domain reinforce similar discourses in the other. The male dominance of the law and home are linked and reinforced via the language that moves between the two domains. The private violence of the home is reinforced in the public violence of the law, leading in many cases to moments of victim-blaming. As Trinch (2010, 197) notes, legal professionals, even those there to help the victim of abuse such as advocates and police officers, "inevitably ascribe some blame to victims." In order to get the protective order, make an arrest, or secure a conviction, "institutional definitions" are privileged, often sacrificing victims' goals and concerns in the process (Trinch 2010, 197). Victim-blaming is in part a result of what Smart (1989, 2) calls "a congruence between law and what might be called a 'masculine culture.'" Law is sexist because it is embedded in and reinforces the masculine culture of which it is a part. As a part of this "masculine culture," domestic violence has a troubling legal history, in which the wife was not only relegated to the domestic sphere but also the property of the husband and denied legal individuality (cf. Blackwell 1766; Olsen 1983). Only the male head of household could earn wages, and only he could inherit. He could also chastise his wife (and children) as he saw fit. The infamous *State of North Carolina v. Black* (1864) explains to the twenty-first century reader: "A husband is responsible for the acts of his wife, and he is required to govern his household, and for that purpose the law permits him to use towards his wife such a degree of force as is necessary to control an unruly temper and make her behave herself." The takeaway message is physically punish your wife as you see fit, just don't use unnecessary force that will necessitate legal involvement.

The criminalization of domestic violence is thus a relatively new development in the United States and other Anglo-American legal systems. Before 1920, the legal stance on domestic violence was that the private matters of the home were none of the business of the law; in fact, the husband was the head of the household authorized and expected to discipline the family, including the wife, as he saw fit. Sir William Blackstone's (1766, 366) famous commentaries on English law justify the violence of husbands against wives:

> The husband also (by old law) might give his wife moderate correction. For, as he is to answer for her misbehavior, the law thought it reasonable to entrust him with this power of restraining her, by domestic chastisement, in the same moderation that a man is allowed to correct his apprentices or children.

That is, because the husband is legally responsible for his wife's behavior, he should and does have the right to correct her behavior just as he would a child. Blackstonel[2] (366) goes on to say that in the "politer reign of Charles the Second" at least a husband can't "beat his wife severely with scourges and sticks." Blackstone creates a distinction between "old" (Roman) ways and English law that supports burgeoning English common law. He also positions both the father and the law as having the woman's best interests at heart when chastisement must be given. He writes, "even the disabilities, which the wife lies under are for the most part intended for her protection and benefit: so great a favourite is the female sex of the laws of England" (Ibid.). These ideas are imported in US law in the infamous *Bradley v. State of Mississippi* (1824). The Supreme Court of Mississippi affirmed the conviction of Mr. Bradley for beating his wife severely. Still the sentiment that husbands have the right to beat their wives in moderation persists:

> Family broils and dissentions cannot be investigated before the tribunals of the country, without casting a shade over the character of those who are unfortunately engaged in the controversy. To screen from public reproach those who may be thus unhappily situated, let the husband be permitted to exercise the right of moderate chastisement, in cases of great emergency, and use salutary restraints in every case of misbehaviour, without being subjected to vexatious prosecutions, resulting in the mutual discredit and shame of all parties concerned.

Not only does *Bradley* (1824) support "the [husband's] right of moderate chastisement," but it also states two times that wives shouldn't bring charges against their husbands because public knowledge of this particular private event brings shame and embarrassment to the wife as well as the husband. Such a trivial matter should be dealt with privately, not publicly. This ruling also uses the euphemism "family broils and dissention," which dresses the violence of husband against wife in language of family dysfunction, obscuring the violence and subjugation that is part and parcel of domestic assault.

The view expressed in *Bradley* (1824) values private rights and privacy at the expense of the wife. It also establishes a boundary between the law and the home that is reinforced in other case law. For example, *State of North Carolina v. Black* (1864) states:

> Unless some permanent injury be inflicted, or there be an excess of violence, or such a degree of cruelty as shows that it is inflicted to gratify his own bad passions, the law will not invade the domestic forum or go behind the curtain. It prefers to leave the parties to themselves, as the best mode of inducing them to make the matter up and live together as man and wife should.

The law's sovereign domain is the world outside of the home, because it is the duty of the husband to control the world within it, and like the law, he had the power to exercise sovereign control by punishing the bodies of his subjects. Reminding the husband that he is only an arm of the law's paternalism, he is warned not to inflict "permanent injury" or use "excessive violence."

Though legal reform has insinuated the law into the home, the division between the law and home remains active in nefarious and often invisible ways. Martha Minow (2000, 852) argues that "a conception of inviolable boundaries" that divide the public sphere from the private sphere put "violence in the home [. . .] beyond the reach of the law." The curtain that protects the home from public scrutiny continues to function. Even after it is illegal to abuse one's wife, legal discourses have difficulty recognizing abused bodies, looking for certain kinds of identifiable marks, while ignoring others; assuming that abused women won't leave their husbands due to damaged psyches; ignoring the pernicious romantic, cultural, and legal edicts that demand a wife support her husband as the head of the domestic sphere; and using legal reasoning, which relies on precedent and thus continues to circulate discourses that maintain paternal social and institutional structures. The boundary between the law and home also provides protection for institutional principles and norms. We see this, for example, in the 1789 case *King v. Woodcock* in which Silvia Woodcock was badly beaten by her husband, dying about forty-eight hours after she was found. In that time, she gave an account of what had happened to the Magistrate. In debating the admissibility of the account, the judge argued that "[g] reat as a crime of this nature must always appear to be, yet the inquiry into it must proceed upon the rules of evidence." We see this logic again in *Regina v. Bedingfield*[3] (1879). After having her throat slit, a Ms. Rudd ran into the courtyard of her home and said, "See what Harry has done!" to two women who worked for her (1879, 345). The prosecution attempted to admit the utterance via the *res gestae* rule or the dying declarations exception to hearsay but was denied. According to Justice Cockburn it is regrettable but undeniable "that according to the law of England, any statement made by the deceased should not be admissible." That is, legal rules simply cannot be circumvented, even to retrieve the accusations about the killer made by a woman who had been killed. In both cases, legal rules of evidence are given clear supremacy to the crimes against both Silvia Woodcock and Ms. Rudd. Also in both cases the judge says that there is enough physical evidence that the story of the victim is unnecessary. That is to say, in these cases, circumstantial evidence is viewed as superior to a carefully told narrative about abuse told by the victim.

I've spent time describing this history because it underpins and informs the treatment of domestic violence victims in the current US law of evidence. In cases such as these, judges are quick to refuse the admission of statements made by women who had died at the hands of their abusers. In fact, this reasoning was used to ban the accounts of murdered women from the court in a number of twentieth and twenty-first century cases, including a recent US Supreme Court case, *Giles v. California* (2008), which I'll discuss in detail in Chapter 2.

Recent Developments in Domestic Violence and Law

Law is both a sociocultural resource and a sociocultural product. That is, law works together with social, cultural, and linguistic mechanisms, values, and ideologies even as it is affected by changes within those mechanisms. According to Peter Goodrich (1987, 174), "legal language, like any other language usage, is a social practice and [thus] its texts will bear the imprint of such practice or organizational background, and further, that as a discourse or genre, legal discourse is inevitably answerable to or responsible for its place and role within the political and sexual commitments of its times." That is, law and the discourses in which it is circulated is deeply social and thus saturated with the values and agendas in which and with which it is used. The legal treatment of a social problem like domestic violence has been, not surprisingly, profoundly affected by the culture in which it participates even as it shapes that culture. Legal presuppositions about domestic violence are co-articulated with and mirrored by social discourses that participate in and produce victim-blaming. Institutional distrust of the domestic violence victim has led to an ever-increasing use the excited utterance exception to hearsay as a way of admitting the speech of a domestic violence victim who is not otherwise called to testify, either because she refuses or because she is not called to the stand.

The paternalism of this legal history described above is presented unapologetically as commonsense. Husbands were legally responsible for their wives, and thus they had the right, if not duty, to discipline them. Feminist legal reform in the 1970s and 1980s led to, among other things, the recognition of intimate violence as a serious crime, though it has been a struggle to get police, lawyers, judges, and juries to recognize the problem and appropriately respond to it. "Studies [in the 1970s and 80s] revealed that the police were reluctant to respond to battered women's calls and that battered women's experiences were sometimes trivialized as 'non-crimes' by prosecutors and judges" (Murphy 1993, 1263). As a non-crime, "criminal justice personnel, including police, view battering in gender-neutral terms as a problem of pathological family interaction" (Ferraro 1995, 265). That is, police often conceive of battering not as oppression against women but as a product of a dysfunctional family of which the victim is a full and equal participant. Presuppositions about the victim of abuse are inscribed in law, where they continue to recirculate in legal discourses.

Domestic violence may be considered wrong, a public harm, but social and legal conceptions also often inculpate the victim in the allegations of violence—pathologizing the victim, looking for her participation in the fight, distrusting her for staying in the relationship, and ignoring the social, cultural, and economic factors that preclude leaving. The legal treatment of domestic violence is mirrored and often co-articulated with social discourses about gender and intimate relationships, which necessarily find their way into the court via the very real human actors in the courtroom. The victim herself is treated as a roadblock to stopping the violence, due to the fact that victims of domestic violence sometimes return to their abusive partners, drop charges, miss court dates, and invoke the spousal immunity to avoid giving testimony. Take for example the response of the popular news media to Chris Brown's violent attack against Rihanna in 2009, in which Rihanna was caught between discourses that wondered whether she was telling the truth about Brown and those that pathologized her. Implying that the truth of the attack was questionable, MTV.com contributor Gil Kaufman suggested that the photo was leaked to provide proof of abuse, allowing the public to scrutinize "the evidence of Rihanna's injuries" in order to "settle" questions about the truth of her allegations (MTV.com, 02/23/09). The implication is that women lie about abuse, and that only visible injuries can substantiate such claims. Other coverage explicitly pathologized Rihanna. As one columnist for CNN.com wrote, "[Rihanna's] reported reunion with Brown enables his allegedly abusive behavior and is, in my opinion, a classic case of battered woman's syndrome" (Velez-Mitchell, CNN.com, 03/10/09). Note that Brown's abusive behavior is alleged, but Rihanna's battered woman's syndrome is not. Such discourses pathologize the victim as essentially broken by the abuse and unable to make "rational" decisions. In fact, she is put in the position of "enabling" Brown's position. She is the cause of her own abuse, while Brown's role as perpetrator is passive. In this way, Rihanna was also assigned an equally culpable role. Kimora Lee Simmons was reported in VH1 News as saying, "Sometimes I think young lovers go through things and I really don't know what happened, so I wish everybody the best" (Vena, MTV.com,

2/19/09). Here we see the violent attack in which Rihanna was choked, bitten, and had her head bashed into a car window chalked up to a squabble between "young lovers." News coverage also characterized the abuse as a misstep. For example, Chris Brown's father said this in the days following his son's attack on Rihanna: "This is unfortunate, this stumble, this situation. [. . .] We all have our shortcomings. We all trip" (MTV.com, 2/14/09). That is, this event of violence is little more than a bump, no worse than other people's weaknesses. In this coverage, Rihanna is fit into a set of assumptions about how domestic violence victims act. Her actions aren't characterized as unique but as typical. They amount to the following:

- Victims of domestic violence, like children, are not full civil agents and are prone to falseness;
- Victims of domestic violence are unwilling or unable to leave the abusive relationship of their own accord;
- Victims of domestic violence are often equally culpable participants in an unhealthy relationship (cf. Ferraro 1995); and/or
- Victims of domestic violence are recalcitrant witnesses and thus legally unhelpful.

As the Rihanna case exemplifies, many of the presuppositions circulating in legal and social discourses about domestic violence victims have to do with the credibility of the victim. "What if she's lying?" is the question hanging in the air in lay and legal domains. The research by Elizabeth (1981, 1982) showed that when prosecutors screen domestic violence complaints, they chose cases to prosecute by considering the credibility of the victim, in the process revealing a distrust of abused women and how they tell their stories. The perceived lack of credibility of victims of intimate violence is exacerbated by the legal doctrine of innocent until proven guilty. For all of its importance, assuming the innocence of the accused assumes the deceitfulness of victims. Because the burden of proof lies with the prosecution in criminal cases, in both the contexts of rape and domestic violence, there is significant pressure put on the victim to prove her story (cf. Ehrlich 2001, 35). The other side of credibility and the expectation that abused women lie about abuse is the expectation that women lie to protect their abuser. We see this in the joint opinion, *Davis v. Washington/Hammon v. Indiana* (2006), which states: "This case presents an all too familiar scenario: the police respond to a report of domestic violence, an apparent victim reports a battery, and the victim then does not testify at trial for reasons that are not conclusively documented in the record" (6). Here the Court is obscuring the fact that it is a very common practice that abused women are not called as witnesses (Stanko 1982; Lewis 1993) (e.g., in the case study in Chapters 4 and 5, *US v. Hadley* [trial, 2002; appellate opinion, 2005] PH, is not called to testify) by indirectly suggesting that Mrs. Hammon didn't show up in court but that she was supposed to. Domestic violence may be considered wrong, a public harm, but social and legal conceptions therefore often inculpate the victim in the allegations of violence—pathologizing the victim, looking for her participation in the fight, distrusting her for staying in the relationship, and ignoring the social, cultural, and economic factors that preclude leaving. Domestic violence victims are thus constructed in various ways as essentially untrustworthy speakers, a point that I will develop throughout this book.

Legal reforms have made strides in identifying and trying some abusers, but still, the best estimates show that 4.8 million women are subjected to assault by an intimate partner every year (Tjaden and Thoennes 2000, 7), and one in four women will be victims of severe intimate violence in their lifetime (National Intimate Partner and Sexual Violence Survey, CDC, 2010). This begs the question: if as a society we disdain domestic violence, why does it remain so pervasive? Donna Coker (1999, 39) suggests a compelling answer:

> [Intimate violence] may be experienced as a personal violation, but it is an act facilitated and made possible by societal gender inequalities. The batterer does not, indeed could not, act alone. Social supports for battering include widespread denial of its frequency or harm, economic structures that render women vulnerable, and sexist ideology that holds women accountable for male violence and for emotional lives of families, and that foster deference to male familial control.

As Coker persuasively explains it, domestic violence remains pervasive for the same reasons it is sometimes difficult for women to get out of abusive relationships. Domestic violence is built into the societal gender inequalities that structure everyday interaction and complicate her extrication from the situation. As Mindie Lazarus-Black (2007, 7) notes, victims of domestic violence are constrained by institutional structures and variables such as the legal process, including "statutory law, contingent forms and fees, the hours the court is open," the availability of police and the behaviors that legal professionals "regard as 'real' domestic disputes." Added to this are "wider structural constraints of economy, polity, kinship, and gender organization that shape whether an abused woman knows her rights, whether she can afford to bring the case, whether there is someone to watch her children, whether she can withstand the fury of her husband, and whether she is pressured to preserve family honor by remaining silent." Though Lazarus-Black is specifically analyzing domestic violence in Trinidad, the same constraints are in play in the United States and other legal systems. The point is that domestic violence is a social problem that is deeply intertwined with the domestic sphere and expectations that "family troubles are private" (8). Ideologies of privacy and domesticity naturalize ideals of married life and certain values and behaviors associated with the domestic space—love, familiality, support—which are further complicated by indexical forms that urge women "to stand by their men." The structure of socio-gender stereotypes is supposed to be easily shed when the relationship becomes violent, at which point the wife is expected to make a quick egress from the domestic space into a safer space. Both the expectation to stay in a relationship to make it work and the one to leave an abusive relationship simplify and forget the complicated social structures of modern life and the emotional and psychological concerns of love and commitment. For example, the victim has a social responsibility for the well-being of her children, and she is economically dependent on her abuser. Furthermore, suggesting that it is entirely the responsibility of the victim to leave, and in fact, explaining her reasons for staying with abused woman's syndrome or "cycle of abuse" arguments shifts the burden of responsibility from the abuser to the victim. Such problems are exacerbated by too few women's shelters, which are always full and carry waiting lists. In short, the social structure of gender and domesticity make leaving difficult in the best of cases and protect the intentions and actions of the abuser.

The thirty-plus years that domestic violence has been going through criminalization have thus failed to curb domestic violence. One aspect of this reform that has contributed to the victim-blaming of domestic violence reforms is the development of a number of laws and police policies that take the decision out of the hands of the victim, with problematic consequences. Of note are "no-drop" policies, which disallow women from dropping charges once they've been filed, and "mandatory arrest" policies, which mandate an arrest for every instance of reported violence. Under this policy, one or both partners may be arrested, which reduces the victim's willingness to call the police in the first place. Especially if there are children in the home, a domestic assault arrest could lead to the removal of the children from the home, which is not a risk that some women will take. Many of these laws have been developed not in response to abusers' behavior, but in response to a sense that abused women don't want to testify, withdraw their statements, and the like. Domestic violence victims are recalcitrant—they don't behave in the way they should—and because the complicating factors are overlooked, they are treated as essentially unable to make a good decision. This problematically puts the victim of domestic violence in the same position she was in at home: under control. It also ignores problematic, lingering spousal immunities, which sentimentalize the home and "domestic tranquility." Such policies also put the onus of the decision to take the stand on the victim, ignoring the fact that prosecutors often don't want to put victims on the stand because they aren't reliable witnesses (cf. Stanko 1982; Lewis 1993). Finally, such laws assume that the abused victim should leave without legal involvement and that she has the power to do so. As Schneider (2000, 77) puts it, such policies "reflect a tendency to want battered women to assume responsibility, to take control, to act as agents [and, they] put the women's conduct under scrutiny." The victim is blamed and/or pathologized if she stays, and the abuser is underscrutinized—he is merely acting like a man/husband. Additionally, the woman's role in the fight is scrutinized, and if she won't testify, her psychological state and motives are scrutinized.

Perhaps in response to common police attitudes toward domestic violence victims, and perhaps in response to the treatment of the new crime as insignificant, domestic violence legal reform is already being chipped away. In 2011, Topeka Kansas decriminalized domestic violence, which was only a misdemeanor anyway, as a way to save money. In 2012, a Wisconsin senator, Donald Pridemore went on the record stating that abused women shouldn't leave their abusive partners, but rather, "If they can re-find those reasons and get back to why they got married in the first place, it might help" (Celock huffingtonpost.com, 03/12/12). The message to stay in the relationship and make it work is not a new one. It is embedded in popular representations of "standing by your man" and even in traditional marriage vows. Legal reforms regarding domestic violence are thus working against deeply held patriarchal social and legal values, and not surprisingly, before such reforms have been fully realized, they are already being undone.

As domestic violence is increasingly recognized as a public (rather than private) crime, and as the home is increasingly recognized as political/politicized, the home is also increasingly recognized as an extension of the public sphere. The effects are not all good. Jeannie Suk (2006, 7) argues, "In this regime, the home is a space in which criminal law deliberately and coercively *reorders* and *controls* private rights and relationships in property and marriage—not as an incident of prosecution, but as its goal" (emphasis in original). One way that this has occurred is the state appropriation of the civil protective order. A protective order is sought by the victim as a protection against an abuser, and it is civil—between individuals. Governmental agencies have begun filing for protective orders for individuals that disallow the accused abuser from returning home, even if his partner wants him to. According to Suk (2006, 116), this practice creates "'state-imposed de facto divorce' wherein prosecutors use the routine enforcement of misdemeanor [domestic violence] to seek to end (in all but name) intimate domestic relationships." That is, prosecutors, not victims, decide the space a couple will share.

All of the legal tactics described allow the law to prosecute without the participation of the victim. Ferraro (1995, 268) claims that proceeding with charges and trial without the open participation of the victim "[fails] to recognize the diverse needs and experiences of battered women [. . .] [as well as] the feminist principle that women are the best experts in their own lives." Proceeding with charges without the help of the victim can even put the victim of abuse at more risk, ignoring the social factors that surround abuse and conflating legal fixes with social fixes. "The criminal justice approach to women-battering focuses on the control of specific incidents without attention to the complex social and economic problems of women. The isolation of battering from the larger context of women's lives produces absurd contradictions" (Ferraro 1995, 269). That is, the typical approaches to domestic violence decontextualize the violence, identifying only that which is a legal violation and separating it out of women's lives. This disregards the fact that domestic violence is saturated with histories that make the situation far more complicated. The legal response to domestic violence also overlooks the complexity and differences across violent relationships. Schneider (2000) argues against one-size-fits-all solutions, arguing instead for a legal response rooted in "particularity." This perspective grounds responses to domestic violence in women's experiences and avoids one-size-fits-all solutions that ignore the complications and contradictions of women's lived experience.

Domestic Violence and Hearsay Evidence

As I explained fully in the introduction, hearsay is the in-court repetition of an out-of-court statement, and it is repeated in court by the addressee of the out-of-court statement. Hearsay is essentially reported speech, and it is banned in the Anglo-American legal system, with a number of exceptions. There is quite a long history between hearsay and domestic violence, in part because of spousal immunities in Anglo-American law. When women couldn't testify against their husbands because of marital privilege, or when men killed their wives in violent episodes, an exception to the hearsay rule was used, sometimes successfully, to import her speech into the courtroom as hearsay. However, as this book argues, whether admitted or not, the talk about victims of domestic violence that accompanies the arguments about the admissibility of hearsay reproduces many long-held presumptions about the trustworthiness of victims of domestic violence.

The excited utterance exception to hearsay has become closely associated with domestic violence, though traditionally and more commonly used in accident and male-on-male assault cases (McCormick et al. 2006). In the last 30-plus years, the excited utterance has become increasingly used in domestic violence cases, in response to the criminalization[4] of domestic violence. The excited utterance exception is used/useful in cases involving domestic violence, because it allows for the evidentiary use of a firsthand statement, without the presence of the speaker of that statement. As discussed above, victims of domestic violence don't take the stand for a number of reasons ranging from fear of retribution to prosecution finding them not credible and thus not calling them as witnesses. According to San Diego City Attorney Casey Gwinn, the use of the excited utterance is one way in which "the criminal justice system can assist in stopping the violence, making victims safer, and holding abusers accountable [. . .] with or without victim participation" (qtd. in Byrom 2005, 412). The legal reasoning used to admit an excited utterance makes it available for use in prosecution, whether or not the person who purportedly spoke the utterance considers the statement to be true. Douglas Beloof and Joel Shapiro (2002) suggest that this is a good thing. Fronting the legal goal of "truth-finding," they argue, "Batterers pressure domestic violence victims to recant, which typically results in the failure of victims to appear or, alternatively, in testimony at trial that is less reliable than the victim's initial report of abuse" (1). The evidence given in the initial report of abuse should thus be admitted, hearsay or not. The focus that Beloof and Shapiro place on the coercive power of the abuser is problematic in its strict erasure of the victim's personhood and social, economic, and parental concerns. Abused women are presented as a homogeneous and self-evident group that can't be trusted because of a fundamentally truncated ability to tell the "truth." Orenstein (1997) complains about the homogenization of abused women assumed in the excited utterance exception. When it is applied in cases involving female speakers, "excitement" is translated into "hysterical," and it is assumed that all women will respond the same way to trauma: hysterically.

The practice of using an utterance without the participation of the speaker ignores the importance of consent, and it ignores the actual differences between victims of domestic violence and of the male-on-male crimes in which the excited utterance case law was developed. As Figure 2 shows, these differences are important and worth noting.

Perhaps the most important difference between the two situations noted above is the relationship between the attacker, the victim, and the speaker of the excited utterance. In the traditional excited utterance relationship, each interactional position is filled by a different person, but in domestic violence, the victim and speaker are the same person; in the traditional situation, the attacker and victim often don't know each other, but in domestic situations, they are intimates. Anglo-American law has developed with the male body and experiences in mind, not those of a crime that was not even on the record as such. The law is saturated by male standards (cf. Olsen 1983; Smart 1989; Schneider 2000; Frug 1992); from the reasonable man principle to laws about rape, the status quo experience is masculine. As Justice Scalia reminds the Court over and over, the standard for the hearsay exclusion is the unlawful trial and execution of Sir Walter Raleigh, not *Regina v. Bedingfield* (1879), which would be equally suitable from a positive law perspective.

Traditional (accident or male-on-male assault)	Domestic Violence
speaker of the excited utterance is a witness	speaker of the excited utterance is the victim
speaker is a bystander, doesn't know one or both parties involved	speaker knows and is intimately involved with the assailant
speaker is physically unavailable to testify	speaker is physically available but doesn't testify for some reason (hers or legal counsel's)
speaker is typically male	speaker is typically female

FIGURE 2 Differences Between Domestic Violence and Other Types of Assault.

Excited Utterances and Infantilization

The excited utterance exception to hearsay allows a person giving testimony to repeat the out-of-court utterance of a third-party as long as the repeated utterance was said in exciting circumstances, by an excited speaker, and is about the event in question. I argue that this use of the exception talks over the victim and negates her relationship to trustworthy narrative about her own experience. This appropriation of the speech of adult women is justified in a discourse about truthfulness and fabrication that is developed in precedents dealing with children's speech, the result of which is a kind of legal infantilization that leaves the adult woman open to state intervention. An excited utterance is entextualized during a trial when it is elicited in direct examination or cross-examination, justified with precedential and statutory arguments, and ruled on by the judge. This happens again during the appellate process when the law with which a bit of evidence is produced is evaluated, again producing evidence. The precedents used to justify an argument in trial—and especially in the precedent-producing discourse of appellate and Supreme Courts—are extremely important, in that they produce evidence. They take a bit of discourse and convert it into a text with legal weight. In the case of hearsay, this process also produces a speaker to whom the utterance and its veracity are linked.

A set of precedents in the late 1980s and early 1990s developed well-cited criteria for evaluating a purported excited utterance in cases that involved the speech of children that had been the victims of sexual abuse, notably within two US Supreme Court opinions, *Idaho v. Wright* (1990) and *White v. Illinois* (1992), and a US Appellate court, *Haggins v. Warden, Fort Pillow State Farm* (1983). The discourse developed in these cases establishes an approach for disambiguating utterances that have been fabricated from those that have not via a standard of spontaneous speech. The unquestioned application of these precedents in cases involving domestic violence and the speech of adult women elides important distinctions between women and children. The competency standard used to determine whether or not a child witness understands the difference between fact and imagination plays a key role in cases involving children's speech. In each of the precedents listed above (*White*, *Wright*, and *Haggins*), the excited utterance exception is used after a child has been deemed incompetent to give testimony. The competency standard and the excited utterance exception to hearsay intersect in the evaluation of truthfulness, which is then applied in cases involving the speech of adult women.

The central issue in cases involving child witnesses and in precedents dealing with the excited utterance exception is distinguishing truth from contrivance: who lies, under what circumstances, and what is the best way to identify and limit false statements. Limiting testimony to firsthand accounts allows testimony to be cross-examined in front of the judge and jury who can see the demeanor of the witness, and it protects the constitutional rights of the accused to confront those who bear witness against him/her. The excited utterance exception admits hearsay as long as the speaker was excited and thus lacked the reflective faculties required to fabricate. According to *Idaho v. Wright* (1990, 820):

> The basis for the "excited utterance" exception, for example, is that such statements are given under circumstances that eliminate the possibility of fabrication, coaching, or confabulation, and that therefore the circumstances surrounding the making of the statement provide sufficient assurance that the statement is trustworthy and that cross-examination would be superfluous.

This well-used definition, taken from a case evaluating the speech of a child, focuses on the potential for the speaker to be lying, to be constructing false accounts of events. In this case, the child is unable to give testimony, and so her previous statements to doctors and nurses are admitted as hearsay in their testimony using the excited utterance exception. The question is whether the prior utterance of a speaker who is incompetent to testify was produced while the speaker was under the influence of a powerful event. The thing that can control the potential for falsification does not come from the speaker, but rather it must come from something external to the speaker: the event. Throughout this case law, the exciting event from which the excited utterance erupts is syntactically placed in the subject position. The event acts on the speaker, controlling the reflective faculties that will potentially lead to fabrication. A spontaneous utterance can thus be repeated as hearsay because, according to *Haggins* (1983), it "contain[s] inherent guarantees of truthfulness," which, as *Illinois* (1992, 356) explains, make the excited utterance more trustworthy than a similar utterance made in the comparative "calm of the courtroom." In other words, the utterance made non-self-consciously is self-referentially true, as opposed to contextually true, and thus needs no cross-examination. No fact given in testimony in open court is so privilged.

These precedents in which the discussion of fabrication and truthfulness is developed and circulated all admit an excited utterance because a child speaker is deemed incompetent to give testimony. When children have been the victims of and witnesses to violent crimes and thus need to give testimony, the first step is to evaluate their ability to understand the concept of an oath or promise, to distinguish between fantasy and reality, and ultimately to tell the truth, all of which are prerequisites to taking the stand that most adults are presumed to meet. There is no preset age limit or standard to determine when a speaker is too young to give testimony, but rather competency to give testimony is often evaluated in a separate hearing that precedes the trial. Part of the competency test is to determine whether the child has been influenced by the more powerful rhetoric of adults. According to *Idaho v. Wright* (1990, 813), "Expert testimony and child psychology texts indicated that children are susceptible to suggestion and are therefore likely to be misled by leading questions." Because children are both easily manipulated and understood to be prone to fabrication, Anglo-American law has developed explicit processes that can be used to determine whether a child has the capacity to tell the truth. All three of these excited utterance precedents admit excited utterances because the child is determined to be incapable of swearing to tell the truth.

Adult women don't undergo the same explicit evaluation of their ability to tell the truth. An adult is typically determined to be telling the truth or not through the fact-finding process of direct examination and cross-examination. In cases involving domestic violence, however, the victim of the crime may not take the stand for a variety of reasons. They may not show up for court dates; they may not be called to testify because they have been diagnosed with abused woman's syndrome; or according to some studies, they are not called to give testimony out of fear the jury won't find them sympathetic. All of the reasons women don't give testimony, but especially the last two, operate according to a social picture of women who are the victims of domestic violence in which they are either so damaged that they no longer have the capacity to stand up for themselves, or in which they are unable to tell the truth because they are under the spell of their abusive husbands. The victim of domestic violence is thought to be psychologically pliable and prone to fabrication, much like the child witness. And indeed, such presuppositions facilitate the use of precedents discussing the truthfulness of children's speech in cases involving the speech of victims of domestic violence, which then work to reinforce such presuppositions.

Like *Wright* (1990), discussed above, in *Haggins* (1983, 1052), the competency of the child witness to testify against an uncle came down to truthfulness: "[T]he child continuously stated that she would not tell the truth and, after full consideration, the judge ruled that she was not competent to testify." In trying to locate and vet the potentially truthful utterances of an untruthful child, *Haggins* (1983, 1057, quoting *Weinstein's Evidence*) further develops an explanation for the admissibility of the excited utterance: "The assumption underlying [the excited utterance] exception is that a person under the sway of excitement precipitated by an external startling event will be bereft of the reflective capacity essential for fabrication and that, consequently, any utterance he makes will be spontaneous and trustworthy." Following this comes a three-part test that can be applied to determine whether a hearsay utterance was in fact an excited utterance:

> Three elements are necessary for the admission of an excited utterance. First, there must be an event startling enough to cause nervous excitement. Second, the statement must be made before there is time to contrive or misrepresent. And, third, the statement must be made while the person is under the stress of the excitement caused by the event. (*Haggins* 1983, 1057).

The logic in *Haggins* (1983) follows this way: children who have not yet developed the capacity to either tell the truth or distinguish true from false are incompetent to testify; they may have spontaneously, accidentally blurted a true statement when their reflective faculties had been stilled; such statements can be repeated as hearsay, because exciting circumstances still the reflective faculties required to falsify, decontextualizing the utterance and rendering it trustworthy—even for children who require special procedures to determine whether they even understand the concept of truth. When this logic is applied in cases involving adult speech, the issue of the child's capacity to swear an oath to tell the truth is not discussed because the witness is not a child. Nevertheless, the line of logic in *Haggins* (1983) proceeds from this presupposition. The process of justifying the admission of a spontaneous utterance begins with an explicit analysis of the child witness's ability to distinguish fact from fiction. Such questions about the ability of the witness to tell the truth are presupposed even when they are not explicitly stated.

Haggins's three-factor test is applied in *US v. Hadley* (2005), a case involving domestic assault in which JH held a gun to the head of PH during a fight at their home. The officers who answered a call to 911 testified that she ran out to them and blurted, "He has a gun and he's going to kill me." What makes *Hadley* particularly interesting is that PH took the stand during sentencing and offered an alternative account of the event. Because the excited utterance functions as an exact account of the event, a new account either changes what happened in the event or is false. For this reason, the *Hadley* trial court had to explicitly operationalize a discussion of fabrication and motivation to determine when she was telling the truth and when she was not. The *Hadley* (2005, 496) appellate opinion used *Haggins* (1983) to re-certify the excited utterance established during the trial:

> More generally, we ask whether the statements at issue were made "under circumstances that eliminate the possibility of fabrication, coaching, or confabulation, and that therefore the circumstances surrounding the making of the statement provide sufficient assurance that the statement is trustworthy and that cross-examination would be superfluous."

This description of the excited utterance intertwines *White* (1992) and *Haggins* (1983), albeit with citations omitted. Thus, two cases involving child speakers are woven together to create a general measurement of truthfulness that is applied to an adult woman speaker, and the fact that these definitions come from precedents involving children's speech is erased with the omission of the citation. The evaluation of truthfulness in *Hadley* (2005) determines that PH is an unreliable speaker who did not tell the truth when she took the stand during sentencing. Her only reliable utterance was the excited utterance. *Hadley* (2005) applies the standard developed in *Haggins* (1983), and as a result, PH is equated with a child, unable to tell the truth.

I am not suggesting that a different legal code should be developed for different categories of speakers. However, because different rules and standards have been developed to deal with children, due to their still-developing morality and their reduced civil agency, cases dealing with child declarants are not equivalent or easily applicable in all cases involving excited utterances. In fact, these cases involving children's speech discuss the 'child-ness' of the witness on multiple occasions. The equivalency between women and children is equally problematic for children, I should point out. The adult standards of trustworthiness assumed in the hearing to determine competency to testify and the excitedness criteria of the excited utterance don't easily apply in cases involving child speakers. For example, as Aviva Orenstein (1997) argues, sometimes shock makes a speaker quiet instead of hysterical.

The use of children's speech to evaluate the speech of adult women has consequences. Children are thought to be at least potentially unable to tell the truth in open court, or even to distinguish between fact and fiction, and they are open to manipulation by more powerful agents, such as their parents, legal professionals, and doctors. Without direct testing of competency, an adult woman's testimony may be circumvented with the use of the excited utterance exception to hearsay developed in part in precedents considering the speech of child declarants. The competency of adult women to tell the truth about domestic violence, then, is questioned explicitly and implicitly throughout the legal process, and ultimately their speech is equated with children's. This equivalency is not without function. In assuming that adult women are untrustworthy in the same way that children are, the court is permitted to use their utterances for their own good and without their consent.

Legal Language Ideology and Domestic Violence

Talk about talk in cases that involve admissible hearsay, like the case of infantilization described above, is the product of a language ideology that such talk also circulates. A language ideology "[emerges] at the meta-level, where language signals reflexively about its own signaling" (Mertz 1998, 151). That is to say, we find a language ideology at the point where a text or utterance recognizes and comments on its languageness. According to Michael Silverstein (1979, 193), a language ideology is a "[set] of beliefs about language articulated by users as a rationalization or justification of perceived language structure and use." In other words, a language ideology also does more than just metadiscursive work; it relates ideas about what language is and how it functions with the social world. Language ideologies are used to rationalize beliefs about people that are based on the use of a particular linguistic form or style. In identifying the form as appropriated for a particular group, the language ideology justifies the reaction to or perception of the group by indexing something linguistic, an accent for example, rather than something social, such as gender, social class, or race. Thus, talk about talk also has consequences for those who use the linguistic form or style.

Language ideologies are developed with and circulate indexical forms that link speakers with values and norms. Susan Gal (1995, 171) explains that "ideological work is required to create cultural notions that link forms of talk to social groups in such a way that speakers come to think the relationship is natural." That is, links between talk and the social identities of groups and individuals are "load[ed] with moral and political interests" (Irvine, 1989: 255). A language ideology impacts individuals because it creates metadiscursive links between language and the larger discursive structures at work culturally, and the link is underpinned by moral and ideological presupposition. Such presuppositions, according to Irvine and Gal (2001), make the link between the linguistic and the social appear to be natural and normal, and its link to larger ideological issues is made to appear unimportant, ineffectual, or absent altogether. The link between the group and the marked linguistic form becomes naturalized. "Much of the meaning and hence communicative value that linguistic forms have for their speakers lies in the 'indexical' connections between the linguistic signs and the contextual factors of their use" (Kroskrity 2000, 7). In other words, much of the ideological work done by language lies in its nonreferential valences—the values and ideology embedded in language that go beyond the (potential) real-world referent for the word. The nonreferential value of language is layered on and interplays with the use of language to represent the world of experience. As Irvine and Gal (2000, 37) argue, "As part of everyday behavior, the use of a linguistic form can become a pointer to (index of) the social identities and typical activities of speakers." Linguistic features come to index more than just things in the world; they also index social structure, and they become an indexical foundation on which other social relationships can be built. When speakers "notice, rationalize, and justify" this indexical linkage, they create and circulate language ideologies that can be used to (re)produce indexical forms.

In the hearsay rule, we see the noticing and justification of indexicality that Irvine and Gal describe. The hearsay rule is explicitly metadiscursive, commenting directly on language. The hearsay rule and its exceptions include criteria that determine when an out-of-court utterance is credible and thus admissible as hearsay, and when it is not credible and thus inadmissible. This language ideology is made up of heuristics that can be used to evaluate, sort, and organize utterances. These criteria also comment on the speaker, creating less explicit correlations between types of speakers and the admissibleness of the hearsay utterance. The hearsay rule and its exceptions operate as a language ideology that creates a complex correlation between true accounts of events and trustworthy speakers. This legal discourse articulates a set of assumptions about where the meaning of an utterance is located (material referent, linguistic subjectivity, the utterance, interaction, etc.); when the utterance can be considered credible; the types of situations associated with credible utterances; and who can make them. The complexity of the language ideology is highlighted when the out-of-court speaker of a possible hearsay utterance is the victim of intimate violence. The language ideology of the excited utterance exception to hearsay supports and reproduces legal gender bias when it is co-articulated with the social status of victims of intimate violence.

Conclusions

The language ideology embedded and circulated in the hearsay rule and the excited utterance exception participates in the institutional production of a discourse of the facticity of domestic violence that "is at once controlled, selected, organized and redistributed according to a certain number of procedures, whose role is to avert its powers and its dangers, to cope with chance events, to evade its ponderous, awesome materiality" (Foucault 1972, 216). In other words, the legal rules that constrain speech are working to control for the instability of language, especially the language that reproduces the material world, thereby bringing into line the unplanned utterance. For Foucault, the utterance is fundamentally out of the control of the speaker, yet this prohibitive discourse affects the speaker as well as the utterance. Once spoken, an utterance is available to be swept up in discursive practices, in which intentionality becomes unidentifiable, assuming it ever was. Structures of control often emanate from metadiscursive processes that "both represent and regulate other discourses" and they also affect "who is authorized to speak or write or to be listened to or read, and in what sorts of social and institutional spaces" (Bauman and Briggs 2000, 142).

The hearsay rule and the excited utterance exception to hearsay function as a metadiscourse that authorizes speakers, by aligning or disaligning speakers with the credibility necessary to be heard in legal settings. The institutional language ideology circulated in the hearsay rule matches social expectations of truthfulness, and together, they actively shape the production of legal artifacts, while creating the resources that give rise to and constrain the discursive agency of victims and witnesses. The discussion of admissible hearsay has long overlapped with legal discussions about domestic violence that often equate women to children, discussions which have always been infused with social discourses about a woman's role in society, marriage, and her relationship to the domestic sphere, and her ability to make objectively true (rather than subjective) utterances. Together they produce a set of intersecting discourses that produce and circulate a legal facticity of domestic violence.

PART ONE

Anglo-American Law and the In/Admissibility of Hearsay

Chapters 2 and 3 analyze the hearsay rule, tracing it from English common law to the US Law of Evidence and constitutional law in order to understand 1) the language ideology developed and circulated in legal treatises, case law, and statute; 2) the treatment of domestic violence in legal texts and principles; and 3) the indexical relationship between domestic violence and hearsay that is underpinned by the empirical language ideology developed in hearsay case law.

The hearsay principle excludes secondhand speech in in-court testimony. That is, witnesses can only give testimony about events that they have seen with their own eyes. The exclusion of hearsay has been lauded as the "linchpin of the common law criminal trial" (Doak and McGourlay 2012, 333). In modern US law, this prohibition is encoded in the Federal Rules of Evidence, Article 8, which states that hearsay is a statement that "the declarant does not make while testifying at the current trial or hearing" and is offered "to prove the truth of the matter asserted in the statement." Chapter 2 argues that the hearsay principle presupposes a relationship between speech (language) and the empirically experienced world, in which 1) facts and evidence are objects in the physical world, 2) true linguistic accounts of facts will transparently represent the objectivity of the physical world, and 3) language is subjective and always has the potential to skew and manipulate the truth of the physical world. This language ideology, developed over three hundred years of common law (discussed in Chapter 2), is presupposed in the process of evaluating hearsay during the trial and again in appellate opinions. When it is admitted, it is because the relationship between the utterance in question and the physical world is assumed to be stable in the utterance itself. When it is not admitted, it is because the utterance in question is assumed to be subjective, self-interested. In contemporary

US Supreme Court opinions, this language ideology endures through a consistent reliance on historical precedents and due to a heavy emphasis on "objective circumstances" in cases such as *Davis v. Washington/Hammon v. Indiana*, (2006) and *Michigan v. Bryant* (2011).

When the admissibility of hearsay reaches the US Supreme Court, the focus shifts from a discussion of hearsay law to a discussion of the confrontation clause in the US Constitution. The admission of hearsay potentially violates the right of the accused to confront their accuser, because the person with the physical knowledge of the event—the person who spoke the hearsay in question—is not in the courtroom to be cross-examined. In the bulk of Supreme Court opinions, the law of evidence and Constitutional law are said to work together. Citing the key precedents, *Ohio v. Roberts* (1980, 66) states,

> Certain hearsay exceptions rest upon such solid foundations that admission of virtually any evidence within them comports with the "substance of the constitutional protection." *Mattox v. United States*, 156 U. S., at 244. This reflects the truism that "hearsay rules and the Confrontation Clause are generally designed to protect similar values," *California v. Green*, 399 U. S., at 155, and "stem from the same roots," *Dutton v. Evans*, 400 U. S. 74, 86 (1970).

This sentiment is expressed across the case law, accompanied of course by the qualification that the two are not to be fully conflated. *Bryant* explicitly uses the excited utterance exception to hearsay in its argument to admit the hearsay statement in that case. Prohibited as it is, the Supreme Court typically finds hearsay inadmissible, with the exception of a few key cases, notably *Mattox v. United States* (1892), *Michigan v. Bryant* (2011) and a number of co-conspirator cases (cf. *Lilly v. Virginia*), all of which evaluate (and admit) the hearsay of male speakers about non-domestic crimes. Only in *Davis v. Washington/Hammon v. Indiana* (2006) is the speech of a domestic violence victim determined admissible by the US Supreme Court. Table 1 lists the key precedents, the outcome, and the uptake of the opinion via citation (see the Appendix for more information).

Throughout the cases analyzed in these two chapters, we find a discourse about domestic violence that is consistently dismissive of the crime and distrusts the subjectivity of victims of domestic violence. What I argue is that the empirical language ideology circulating in hearsay and constitutional law, the gendered discourses about the reliability of women who have been victims of domestic violence, and social discourses that divide public and private spheres create a subject position from which victims of domestic violence are unable to make purposeful and reliable utterances.

TABLE 1

Relationship between Hearsay Admissibility and Speaker Type, with Shepardized® Statistics

Case name	Hearsay issue	Speaker	Hearsay	Shepherdized® Statistics	
Mattox v. US (1895)	On remand, the prior testimony of two witnesses who had since died (murder)	Two Men	Admitted	1142 Citations:	
				Warning Analyses:	Overruled (1), Superseded (1)
				Questioned Analyses:	Questioned (2)
				Cautionary Analyses:	Distinguished (11), Limited (1)
				Positive Analyses:	Followed (40)
				Neutral Analyses:	Concurring Opinion (33), Dissenting Op. (54), Explained (3), Quest. Precedent (4)
				Other Sources:	Law Reviews (492), Secondary Sources (1), Statutes (6), Treatises (84), Annotations (2), Court Documents (256)
California v. Green (1970)	Prior testimony at a preliminary hearing (giving marijuana to a minor)	Man	Admitted	3006 Citations:	
				Cautionary Analyses:	Criticized (2), Distinguished (37), Not Followed (1)
				Positive Analyses:	Followed (156), Concurring Opinion (72)
				Neutral Analyses:	Conflict. Authority (1), Dissenting Op. (113), Explained (29), Harmonized (3), Interim Decision (2), Quest. Precedent (15)
				Other Sources:	Law Reviews (692), Statutes (17), Treatises (214), Annotations (4), Court Documents (427)
Ohio v. Roberts (1980)	Prior testimony about the same case at an earlier hearing admitted at trial (check fraud)	Woman	Admitted	5219 Citations:	
				Warning Analyses:	Abrogated as stated in (89), Overruled (326), Reversal noted in (1)
				Questioned Analyses:	Questioned (291)
				Cautionary Analyses:	Criticized (19), Distinguished (72), Not Followed (1)
				Positive Analyses:	Followed (676), Concurring Opinion (112)
				Neutral Analyses:	Conflict. Authority (1), Dissenting Op. (159), Explained (87), Harmonized (1), Interim Decision (1), Quest. Precedent (24)
				Other Sources:	Law Reviews (1147), Statutes (20), Treatises (498), Annotations (2), Court Documents (789)

continued

TABLE 1

(continued)

Case name	Hearsay issue	Speaker	Hearsay	Shepherdized® Statistics	
Wright v. Idaho (1990)	Statements made to a pediatrician (sexual assault against a child)	Child	Not admitted	1942 Citations:	
				Warning Analyses:	Abrogated as stated in (2), Overruled (1)
				Questioned Analyses:	Questioned (6)
				Cautionary Analyses:	Distinguished (46)
				Positive Analyses:	Followed (259), Concurring Opinion (53)
				Neutral Analyses:	Dissenting Op. (80), Explained (24), Harmonized (2), Quest. Precedent (8)
				Other Sources:	Law Reviews (534), Statutes (17), Treatises (268), Annotations (3), Court Documents (263)
White v. Illinois (1992)	Spontaneous declaration or excited utterance exception and medical examination exception (sexual assault against a child)	Child	Admitted	1143 Citations:	
				Warning Analyses:	Abrogated as stated in (1)
				Questioned Analyses:	Questioned (10)
				Cautionary Analyses:	Criticized (2), Distinguished (17)
				Positive Analyses:	Followed (92), Concurring Opinion (23)
				Neutral Analyses:	Dissenting Op. (46), Explained (20), Interim Decision (2), Quest. Precedent (9)
				Other Sources:	Law Reviews (543), Statutes (6), Treatises (235), Annotations (1), Court Documents (212)
Lilly v. Virginia (1999)	Co-conspirator's statements against interest (robbery, abduction, murder)	Man	Admitted	1277 Citations:	
				Questioned Analyses:	Questioned (6)
				Cautionary Analyses:	Criticized (4), Distinguished (94)
				Positive Analyses:	Followed (187), Concurring Opinion (19)
				Neutral Analyses:	Conflict. Authority (1), Dissenting Op. (43), Explained (26), Quest. Precedent (6)
				Other Sources:	Law Reviews (301), Statutes (11), Treatises (193), Annotations (1), Court Documents (276)
Crawford v. Washington (2004)	Statements made during police interrogation in the formal setting of the police station.	Woman	Not admitted	12796 Citations:	
				Questioned Analyses:	Questioned (2)
				Cautionary Analyses:	Criticized (9), Distinguished (1516)
				Positive Analyses:	Followed (2610), Concurring Opinion (177)

continued

TABLE 1

(continued)

Case name	Hearsay issue	Speaker	Hearsay	Shepherdized® Statistics	
				Neutral Analyses:	Conflict. Authority (1), Dissenting Op. (241), Explained (552), Harmonized (17), Quest. Precedent (41)
				Other Sources:	Law Reviews (1412), Statutes (146), Treatises (961), Other Citations (4), Court Documents (2074)
Davis v. Washington (2006)	Present-sense impression exception (domestic assault)	Woman	Admitted	2865 Citations:	
				Cautionary Analyses:	Criticized (4), Distinguished (144)
				Positive Analyses:	Followed (773), Concurring Opinion (58)
Hammon v. Indiana (2006)	Excited utterance exception (domestic assault)	Woman	Not admitted	Neutral Analyses:	Conflict. Authority (1), Dissenting Op. (84), Explained (117), Harmonized (7), Quest. Precedent (11)
				Other Sources:	Law Reviews (519), Statutes (8), Treatises (376), Court Documents (564)
Giles v. California (2008)	Forfeiture of rights exception by wrongdoing (murder of girlfriend)	Woman	Not admitted	386 Citations:	
				Cautionary Analyses:	Distinguished (26)
				Positive Analyses:	Followed (93), Concurring Opinion (7)
				Neutral Analyses:	Conflict. Authority (1), Dissenting Op. (15), Explained (29), Harmonized (1)
				Other Sources:	Law Reviews (242), Statutes (12), Treatises (149), Court Documents (85)
Michigan v. Bryant (2011)	Excited utterance	Man	Admitted	446 Citations:	
				Cautionary Analyses:	Distinguished (21)
				Positive Analyses:	Followed (94), Concurring Opinion (13)
				Neutral Analyses:	Criticized (1), Conflict. Authority (2), Dissenting Op. (22), Explained (21), Harmonized (2), Quest. Precedent (2)
				Other Sources:	Law Reviews (125), Statutes (3), Treatises (154), Other Citations (1), Court Documents (56)

2

Legal Empiricism in/and the Language Ideology of Hearsay

In their article, "Ideological Dissonance in the American Legal System," William O'Barr and John Conley (1996, 114–115) consider the meaning-making processes of the law, defining "legal ideology as a system of beliefs about the nature and purpose of the law. These beliefs guide those who hold them in constructing meaning in the legal environment" (1996, 115). The law itself has ideological mechanisms about the nature and role of the law itself, which facilitate the interpretation of events and what they will mean in the legal context. This ideology is more available to legal professionals than it is to the lay people—victims, witnesses, and those accused of crimes—who need to navigate legal contexts, putting the people caught up in the law at an ideological and semantic disadvantage. That is, the law is a point in which individual and institutional values and epistemologies meet, but because they are not equally powerful—legal ideology is explicitly powerful—when they are brought into a legal context, other epistemologies, narrative styles, and subjectivities are filtered through legal ideologies, which render them legally recognizable.

One such filter that is also difficult to identify and thus has broad effect is language ideology, or "ideas about language and discourse and about how these articulate with various social phenomena" (Kroskrity 2000, 5). As such, language ideologies are as much about the nonreferential function of language as they are about the referential or denotational function of language. As Kroskrity (2000, 7) has put it, the "communicative value that linguistic forms have for their speakers lies in the 'indexical' connections between the linguistic signs and the contextual factors of their use—their connection to speakers, settings, topics, institutions, and other aspects of their sociocultural worlds." That is, language ideologies are indexical structures that link word forms, syntax, narrative style, etc., and social meaning and use them to evaluate and assess individual speakers. Ideas about the relationship between word and social world ultimately are used to comment on speakers—those individuals who use language in the particular context in which the language ideology is effectual. Because language and language ideologies are deeply social, they are necessarily flexible, open to negotiation and renegotiation as social context(s) and relationships change (cf. Silverstein 1981, Kroskrity 2000).

Ideas about language are incredibly powerful in a legal context if only because of the textual, precedential nature of common law and the important role of speech in the adversarial practices of courtroom direct- and cross-examination. Indeed, the point where common law intersects with in-courtroom processes—when the precedent and statute are used in in-court legal arguments and when the trial testimony is cited, evaluated, and commented on in judicial opinions—is where we can see the shape and features of legal language ideology, its indexical relationship to prior and future legal texts, and its effects on the speech and ultimately subject positions of the people whose lives will be directly impacted by legal outcomes. The hearsay rule and its exceptions function at this intersection; it is a courtroom practice that is based in and justified by precedent and the historical developments of common law. Hearsay is especially relevant because it is also a metadiscourse—the hearsay rule is explicitly about language itself, about how language does and/or can relate referentially to the world, and as such, metadiscourses have a constitutive effect. According to Bauman and Briggs (2000, 142), "Metadiscursive practices shape, both positively and negatively, processes of producing and receiving texts, affecting who is authorized to speak or write or to be listened to or read, and in what sorts of social and institutional spaces." Metadiscourses create, or entextualize, the discourses that they are about, and that also tends to have real world consequences, managing the relationship between social practices, authority to speak, and individual bodies. As an especially powerful metadiscourse, the hearsay rule actively validates certain types of in-court speech, simultaneously commenting on out-of-court speech. The metadiscursive evaluation of present and past speech in the same courtroom process circulates a language ideology, in that the metadiscourses of the hearsay rule articulate a legal conception of the relationship between the utterance, the material world, and individuals. The discourse circulated in the hearsay rule and its exceptions articulates a metadiscursive argument about what makes an utterance true at the same time that it circulates social discourses. The result is a metadiscourse that is also productive of subject positions.

The metadiscursive language ideology of the hearsay rule is established, circulated, and regulated intertextually, reaching back to seventeenth and eighteenth century developments in English common law. Hearsay is banned, because the Anglo-American law of evidence, with its roots deep in the seventeenth century, prefers "information which the speaker acquired through a direct experience" (Philips 1992, 251). Due to the precedential structure of common law and the regular citation of texts from the eighteenth and nineteenth centuries, the language ideology has clear overlaps with Enlightenment language ideology, especially the ideas of John Locke. Bauman and Briggs (2000, 143–144) argue that, in Locke's view, "writing and reading, speaking and listening must emerge from connections between language and knowledge that are systematically stripped of all contextual and intertextual associations." The divorce of language from social and subjective meaning streamlines and clarifies the referential relationship between words and the objects in the world, which Locke believed would reduce abuses of language.

As I will show in what follows, the belief about the relationship between word and world that locates truth in the world, what I call an empirical language ideology, is reproduced in the language ideology of the hearsay rule relatively consistently through the developments of the Anglo-American law of evidence. That is, even as hearsay law changes, this language ideology remains the same. In the metadiscourses used to evaluate the admissibility of hearsay, there is a language ideology, which consists of three parts: 1) original sensory knowledge is superior to other forms of knowledge; 2) human language has the potential to distort that which is seen and/or heard, because it can be affected by both social meaning and the rhetorical goals and values of individual speakers; and 3) reiterated speech is problematic, because it indexes a prior text rather than the original event. Thus, the language ideology of hearsay is rooted in a distrust of language.

As an extension of the English legal system, the US legal system has historically relied and built on English rules and precedents. Though the two systems have developed separately for more than two hundred years, they continue to share the same basic structure, combining adversarial courtroom procedure and common law, or law that is developed in judicial precedent. US Supreme Court opinions still regularly cite historical English cases. The US Supreme Court only recognizes as satisfying the Constitutional mandate of the so called confrontation clause, or the right to confront one's accuser in open court, those exceptions to hearsay that are "firmly rooted" and recognized as exceptions to hearsay at the writing of the Constitution (cf. *Ohio v. Roberts*, 1980 and *Crawford v. Washington*, 2004).

To understand the ties between the historical legal ideology of hearsay and the language ideology that underpins it, I analyze the historical development of the exclusion of hearsay and the contexts in which it is admissible and then show the relationship between that historical development and the admissibility of hearsay in US law. Because hearsay is essentially metadiscursive, much of the work performed in these treatments of hearsay describes how language works and how it relates to speakers, making a legal language ideology quite explicit. The law has a preference for objective, material evidence that can be seen, what they called primary evidence in eighteenth and nineteenth century treatises, which is embedded in the language ideology at work in the metadiscourses used to measure and entextualize admissible and inadmissible hearsay. Like other mechanisms of law, this language ideology makes bodies and experiences seeable in particular ways. Here, I focus on historical developments in the law of evidence and the rule against hearsay and a shift in hearsay admissibility between two twentieth and twenty-first century precedents, *Ohio v. Roberts* (1980) and *Crawford v. Washington* (2004).

The prohibition against hearsay is rooted in presuppositions that firsthand sensory knowledge is superior to what John Pitt Taylor (1897, 468) quoting Buller (1785) called "a mere speaking." The idea that mere speaking is inferior to firsthand sensory knowledge is embedded in the metadiscourses about hearsay. *Chettle v. Chettle* (1821) puts it quite succinctly: "What is the evidence here? Mere hearsay. Nothing seen" (161 Eng. Rep., 1399). Legal discourses found in case law and evidentiary treatises alike create an empiricist metadiscourse, which I claim is at the root of the language ideology circulated in the hearsay rule and the spontaneous declaration/excited utterance exception. I will show that the hearsay language ideology, which values sensory-based, objective knowledge provides discourses that transform some utterances into objects. Thus, the rule and its exceptions work together within the production of what Jan Blommaert (2008) calls "artefactual language ideology" that treats special forms and types of utterances as artifacts and rendering them durable. Such metadiscourses continue to be circulated in recent US Supreme Court hearsay precedents, in particular in the constructions of "reliability," "trustworthiness," "nontestimonial," and "objective circumstances." Importantly and especially in the twentieth and twenty-first century context of domestic violence litigation, the excited utterance exception to hearsay plays an important part in the assertion and reassertion of a language ideology that hinges on the object and objectiveness, a language ideology that is used to distrust the speech of domestic violence victims.

Hearsay, History, and Utterance as an Object

As Thayer (1898, 267) explained, "[T]he law of evidence is the creature of experience rather than logic." That is, law of evidence has developed in a practical manner in the in-court experience of both judges and lawyers through and in which the various rules and procedures developed. Such rules are codified and passed down through judicial opinion and historical legal texts such as the abstracts, abridgements, and treatises that catalogued the legal practices and outcomes of the seventeenth, eighteenth, and nineteenth centuries. According to McCormick (1999, 2:124), "The rule against hearsay taking form at the end of the seventeenth century was neither a matter of immemorial usage nor an inheritance from Magna Carta but was a relatively late development of the common law." Even then, the rule against hearsay that many consider a key value of the modern law of evidence wasn't in a form very close to our current rule or commonly used until the mid-eighteenth century (cf. Wigmore [1904]

1940; Langbein 1996). In the U.S. Federal Rules of Evidence (2013), we find this definition:

"Hearsay" means a statement that:

(1) the declarant does not make while testifying at the current trial or hearing; and

(2) a party offers in evidence to prove the truth of the matter asserted in the statement.

There are two speakers involved with hearsay: 1) Speaker 1, who saw the event and reported it to Speaker 2 ("That car hit him!"), and 2) Speaker 2, who is in court, where, in response to attorney-led questions, s/he repeats the utterance s/he heard Speaker 1 say out of court (Q: How did you find out about the accident? A: He told me, "That car hit him."). Boiled down to its bare bones, hearsay is reported speech: the repetition of a person's speech by someone who heard that speech. Such secondhand reported speech is (typically) inadmissible. The development of Anglo-American evidentiary law supplements and qualifies this statutory definition with arguments about the infidelity of reported speech.

Hearsay is rarely defined without accompanying legal and ideological arguments explaining why hearsay evidence is inferior and inadmissible. Hearsay's legal inadmissibility rests on two pegs of Anglo-American law: the oath and cross-examination. Embedded in legal arguments about the inadmissibility of hearsay is a metadiscursive argument about language itself indicating a legal conception of the relationship between the speaker, language, and the material world. In short, the hearsay rule lays out a language ideology. Presumptions about evidence, what counts and what doesn't count, allow the law to see and not see in ways that tend to support and be supported by cultural and ideological structures. As a textual animal, the law of evidence provides the discursive resources with which evidence is entextualized as such.

The ideological exclusion of hearsay evidence began to take shape during the Enlightenment, with citations to legal opinions about hearsay dating to the late seventeenth century (e.g., *Thompson and Wife v. Trevanion,* 1694) and early legal treatises in the eighteenth century. The Enlightenment is marked, in part, by a change in the conception of the relationship between language, the world, and the individual speaker—a change in the ideology of language. Max Horkheimer and Theodor Adorno (1972, 3) characterize "the program of the Enlightenment" as "the disenchantment of the world; the dissolution of myths and the substitution of knowledge for fancy." This "disenchantment of the world" led to changes in science and history that have been well studied. Bruno Latour (1993, 29) has argued that during this time, "facts," though "mute entities," were thought to "speak for themselves." Witnesses to scientific experiments "take testimony from natural forces, and they testify to each other that they are not betraying but translating the silent behaviour of objects" (29). As Michel Foucault (1970, 282) explains in *The Order of Things*, the Enlightenment also saw changes in the relationship between the world and language that Foucault laments have received less attention. He argues that during the Enlightenment language was divided out of nature. In previous historical periods, language was part of nature, its transparency dependent on a natural resemblance between language and things. "In its raw, historical sixteenth-century being, language is not an arbitrary system; it has been set down in the world and forms a part of it" (Foucault 1970, 35). In other words, prior to the Enlightenment, language was intertwined with that which it represented. Hearsay was similarly intertwined with firsthand knowledge. Juries were made up of community members who used what they knew from community discussion as well as their firsthand knowledge to come to legal conclusions (cf. Landsman 1990; Langbein 1996).

During the Enlightenment, language is divided out of nature and made to reference it; language becomes a medium by which nature can be mimicked or represented. "From the seventeenth century, [. . .] the arrangement of signs was to become binary," the relationship between nature and language reduced to "the connection of a significant and a signified" (Foucault 1970, 43). At the end of Locke's (1690, Book IV:xxi.5) famous *Essay*, he divides discourse into three distinct entities: "things," "actions" and "signs," with "*things*, as they are in themselves knowable; *actions* as they depend on us, in order to happiness; and the right use of *signs* in order to knowledge." Here only "things" are "knowable"; "signs" merely convey knowledge. The legal scholar Sir Geoffrey Gilbert admired Locke (cf. Shapiro 1991), even writing his own abridgement of the *Essay* for his law students to use (1752, 264). In the abridgement, he represents Locke as arguing that truth is in the "being and existence of things" not in language; "language is nothing else, but the connection of sounds to ideas." In Enlightenment empiricism, like that found in Locke and Gilbert, knowledge is a quality of things, the material world. Language is already once removed from the material world. Language is not knowledge; it can merely index what is knowable. Hearsay, then, is nothing but language, but rather than at least indexing what Locke called the "being and existence of things," as most language does, it precariously rests on an unsteady foundation of language. "Demoted" out of nature, language was viewed as merely referential rather than as an inextricable part of nature itself. The prohibition against hearsay is entirely dependent on the idea that the "significant" precedes the representation—the physical world precedes discourse. Repetition, such as hearsay, is only inferior to the "original" when the material world is conceived of as distinct from and prior to language. In such a view of language, each iteration of an utterance is further from the original—a copy of a copy, with each iteration showing deterioration simply by being further from the original. Or as Locke put it (1690, Book 4:XVI:10), "any testimony, the further of it is from the original truth, the less force and proof it has.

The being and existence of the thing itself, is what I call the original truth. [. . .] [I]n traditional truths, each remove weakens the force of the proof." Testimony is only as good as the empirical knowledge on which it is based.

Locke doesn't go as far as Sir Francis Bacon, a notable (notorious) English jurist and philosopher, who called words the "idols of the market place," because they "lead men away into numberless empty controversies and idle fancies" (Aphorism XLIII). Still, he does recognize and thus attempt to control language's subjective and social dimensions. According to Bauman and Briggs, Locke created "tools for stripping language of direct connections to things or social forms, [which] would come to form some of the most important bases for constructing [rational] modern subjects," as a way of "saving language" from being dismissed for being fundamentally imprecise (Bauman and Briggs 2003, 31). By stripping language of its interconnection with the world and asserting instead that accurate language is that which most transparently indexes what it references, Locke proposes a theory of language in which the meaning of a word is more or less stable, as long as the speaker uses it consistently. By asserting that accurate language is neither the product of social interaction or intertextuality, "[Locke] rendered [the intertextual and social nature of meaning and language] less visible" (Bauman and Briggs 2000, 144). The rules that generally prohibit hearsay but admit some types of hearsay utterances, like the excited utterance, circulate an empiricist language ideology, which is similar to a referential language ideology. A referential language ideology locates meaning in the word, a denotational view of language (Ehrlich 2012). An empirical language ideology also understands language denotationally, but it understands correctness empirically, that is, a word or phrase is correct when it correctly points to something real in the world. The language ideology that we find in hearsay is deeply invested in the indexical relationship between word and world. An empirical language ideology distrusts subjectivity, and thus it ignores the ways that discourse is subjective, contextual, interactional, and interdiscursive. The dismissal of subjectivity, context, interaction, and prior texts that are present in empirical and referential veins of language ideology create an environment in which an utterance, like the excited utterance, can be seen as true in and of itself.

Given that the Anglo-American law of evidence developed at the same time that this empiricist language ideology was being articulated by Locke and others, it isn't surprising that the legal view of language is equally empiricist. This view of language is on the surface in the earliest explanations of why hearsay is inadmissible, found in Gilbert's *The Law of Evidence* (1791 edition[1], 889):

> The *Attestation* of the *Witness* must be to what he *knows*, and not to that only which he has *heard*; for a *mere hearsay is no Evidence*: for it is his *Knowledge* that must direct the Court and Jury in the Judgement of the Fact. [. . .] If the first speech was without Oath, an Oath that there was such a Speech makes it no more than a bare speaking. (*sic*)

Here we see a legal description of the relationship between speech and knowledge, specifically oriented to determining what kinds of speech constitute evidence. If an utterance is not rooted in "knowledge" and averred through "oath," it is "no more than a bare speaking." Legal discussions of Gilbert have tended to focus on the oath aspect of this discussion (cf. Landsman 1990; Langbein 1996; Macnair 1994), but from a metadiscursive perspective, the ways that "knowledge" mediates the relationship between speech and evidence is worth some discussion. Witnesses must speak about that which they know, not what they have heard. The distinction between the two is a distinction between knowledge, which is based in firsthand experience of the world, and language, which in the seventeenth and eighteenth centuries was largely thought of as a representational or secondary medium for communicating knowledge (cf. Foucault, 1970).

In Gilbert's legal treatise, we find unease with spoken language, in general. Gilbert's discussion of hearsay, reiterated by other eighteenth century legal experts, is situated in a larger theory of "best evidence," a legal theory that remains to this day; the Court should be presented with and consider the "best evidence" available. For Gilbert, best evidence is written evidence; the vast majority of his three-volume opus is about written documents, certifying copies, identifying signatures, and the like. Contrast this to current legal evidence law's focus on witnesses, direct- and cross-examination, and the presentation of verbal evidence in court. Hearsay is problematic because it is too far removed from the material world, and because it lacks the tangible, durable qualities of written documents. As Gilbert (1791, 890) puts it, "nothing can be more 'indeterminate' than loose and wandering (sic) '*Testimonies*' taken up on the uncertain Report of the Talk and Discourse of others." Here Gilbert not only qualifies hearsay as "uncertain," but testimony itself is "loose and wandering." Testimony based on hearsay is, as he puts it, "no evidence." Repetition of speech is always already potentially invalid because its referent is an utterance and *not* the original event. The material world is twice removed from the utterance. Each iteration puts more referential distance between the utterance and the event that it indexes.

With the emphasis on sensory experience and the event, then, the prohibition against hearsay is rationalized in this historical narrative in two ways, illustrated in Figure 3. First, hearsay is at least two steps removed from the original event. Second, because it is a step further away from the event, hearsay is essentially linguistic, essentially intertextual, because its referent is another statement. The law of evidence prefers representation of the world that can be experienced

	"original" utterance	hearsay
physical event	said by person A who witnessed/was the victim of the event *to* person B	repeated *by* person B in in-court testimony

FIGURE 3 Reiterative Relationship between Hearsay and Event.

with the senses. Hearsay is distrusted, then, because it is a citation of a prior utterance rather than a sensory experience.

NINETEENTH CENTURY DEVELOPMENTS IN HEARSAY JURISPRUDENCE

As Anglo-American common law developed, it did so underpinned by the idea that language was only accurate if it referenced the world that could be experienced with the senses, not other texts or social contexts. That is, the truth value of language is always empirical—in its relationship to the world of experience—not the non-referential information such as emotion, purpose, etc., that also figure into discursive interaction. Only sense-based knowledge could be cross-examined. Thus, in the late eighteenth century and early nineteenth century, we see a strengthening of empiricism as the law of evidence codified and the concern with swearing of an oath was combined with the necessity of the adversarial process through which empirical knowledge could be tested.[2] In-court testimony is considered the next best evidence, and thus it must be cross-examined. Although in the nineteenth century we see the legal arguments against hearsay shift from a focus on the oath, as the promiser of truth, to cross-examination, as the tester of truth, the view that the truth of language is found in its reference to the "real world" remains quite steady. In Starkie's *A Practical Treatise on Evidence and Digest of Proofs in Civil and Criminal Proceedings* ([1824] 2nd ed 1833), we find an empiricist language ideology articulated within a discussion of adversarial legal practice. Starkie's (1833, 36–37) discussion of in-court testimony (secondary evidence[3]) draws a distinction between "immediate" information, which is based on firsthand knowledge, and "mediate" information, which is reported through a third party: "Information derived mediately through another person is in its own nature inferior in point of certainty to that which is derived immediately from an eye or ear witness." Hearsay is mediate; it is not derived from firsthand experience. Starkie (37) places significant weight on empirical knowledge derived from sensory perception.

> Information which we derive, not immediately from one who has had actual knowledge of the fact by the perception of his senses, but from one who knows nothing more of the fact than that it has been asserted by some other person: this species of evidence, which is generally termed hearsay evidence, is evidently inferior, in point of certainty, to the former, even for the common purposes of daily intercourse in society.

Hearsay is evidently inferior because it is not grounded in the sensory knowledge of the speaker. "The highest degree of certainty [. . .] consists in a knowledge of the fact derived from the actual perception of the fact by the senses; and even this degree of evidence is obviously capable of being strengthened or weakened by particular circumstances" (Ibid.). That is, sensory knowledge is made all the more sound when it is supported by evidence from the event itself. By the end of the nineteenth century, this is called "Autoptic Proference," or seeing for oneself, in which "the object itself [is presented] for the personal observation of the tribunal" (Greenleaf, Wigmore's ed., 1899, 25). That which is seeable is "real evidence," and should always be presented to the court when available. As Greenleaf (25) puts it, "[the law] assumes the objectivity of external nature." That is, that which can be experienced with the senses is objectively real. Hearsay is excluded because it denies the right to cross-examine and it isn't accompanied by a sworn oath, but also because it isn't linked to empirically observable reality, which Taylor (1897, 471) following Greenleaf ([1846] 1899, § 99) calls "its intrinsic weakness." Hearsay is, after all, language, "merely speaking" all the way down.

EXCEPTIONS TO HEARSAY

As the hearsay rule was used more consistently, it went through different phases, becoming more nuanced. Eventually, treatise writers began drawing distinctions between types of reported speech that are hearsay and those that are not hearsay. Utterances that show the state of mind or knowledge of the speaker, for example, are not barred by the hearsay rule because they are not hearsay[4] (cf. Taylor 1897, 483; Greenleaf [1846] 1899: §§ 100–114). With such strongly worded and long-lived prohibitions against hearsay, it is perhaps a bit surprising that more than twenty-five exceptions to the rule have developed over the years, many accompanying the rule from the beginning. One reason is that it took a number of years before the jury trial, the adversarial process, and the law of evidence codified into anything like what we have today, and so even after explicit prohibitions against hearsay were written down in legal texts like Gilbert's, it was still regularly admitted (Wigmore 1940; Landsman 1990). The law of evidence also developed explicit exceptions to the hearsay rule to admit important evidence that was otherwise unavailable: utterances of people too young to give testimony or people no longer available, either because they had moved or because they had died. Excluding utterances such as these would, according to Taylor (1897, 471), "work considerable injustice."

The first explicit discussions of the types of hearsay that are admissible are found in early nineteenth century treatises. In the second edition of his treatise, Phillipps (1820, 178) includes a discussion, albeit a brief one, of "spontaneous declarations" in his discussion of exceptions to hearsay, which included statements about pedigree, birthplace and reputation; old leases and rectory documents; declarations against interest; dying declarations; and statements accompanying an act (*res gestae*). Starkie (1833) contains a similar list. As the law of evidence became more formalized, such lists became more organizationally refined and in depth, culminating in the work of Wigmore. Both his 1899 version of Greenleaf's *A Treatise on the Law of Evidence* (16th edition) and his own 6-volume opus, *Evidence in Trials at Common Law* ([1904]1940), give a detailed and copious list of hearsay exceptions that are still cited and indeed are recognizably like the list of hearsay exceptions in the US Federal Rules of Evidence ([1973]2013).

The lists of exceptions given in Greenleaf (1846), Taylor (1897), and Wigmore (1940) are substantially the same as those written in the first half of the nineteenth century, with the exception of the *res gestae* exception. This class of utterances is not part of the *res gestae* group of utterances to which the hearsay rule doesn't apply. *Res gestae* utterances are not hearsay "because the utterance is used, not as an assertion to prove the truth of the fact asserted, but independently of the truth of the utterance as an assertion" (Greenleaf 1899, 263). A spontaneous declaration is an utterance that accompanies an act, but in this case, "the assertion is used as testimonial evidence of the fact asserted" (263). That is, a spontaneous declaration asserts what happened, whereas a *res gestae* utterance simply explains or gives legal significance to an act: uttering "I claim this land as my homestead," while staking a claim. Greenleaf, Taylor, and Wigmore all make the argument that the *res gestae* class of reported speech is admissible, just not as exceptions to hearsay. They are admissible because they are not a repetition of what someone else knows but what someone else did. To put it another way, *res gestae* utterances are themselves actions rather than a report of action. In fact, in his famous lectures on speech acts,[5] J. L. Austin alludes to *res gestae* utterances. "[I]n the American law of evidence, a report of what someone else said is admitted as evidence if what is said is an utterance of our performative kind: because this is not so much of something *said*, as which it would be hearsay and not admissible evidence, but rather as something he *did*, an action of his." A *res gestae* utterance coincides with a physical act in such a way as to give the act legal significance, as in staking a claim (Wigmore 1940 §1732). Hearsay is not a performative, in Austin's sense, because hearsay is "something said." As such, *res gestae* utterances are not hearsay at all but rather what Greenleaf called "original" evidence, not "mere speaking."

Greenleaf and Wigmore in particular make a strong case for spontaneous declarations to be divided out of the general *res gestae* principle and treated separately as an exception to hearsay. Because "it is universally accepted that they are admissible under certain limitations, it seems proper to treat [spontaneous declarations] frankly as the subject of a real and separate exception to the Hearsay rule" (Greenleaf 1899, 263). In fact, by the end of the nineteenth century, there was general unrest, especially among American jurists regarding the use of *res gestae* as a catchall (cf. Taylor, 1897; Thayer, 1898; Wigmore, [1904]1940). One infamous example of the misuse of *res gestae* can be found in *Regina v. Bedingfield* (1879), which many believed erroneously excluded a spontaneous declaration because the standards of the *res gestae* principle had been applied (cf. Wigmore, 1940: §1756; Thayer, 1898).

Wigmore traces the admittance of a spontaneous declaration as an exception to hearsay to *Thompson and Wife v. Trevanian* (1694), in which Lord Holt "allowed, that what the wife said immediate upon the hurt received, and before that she had time to devise or contrive any thing for her own advantage, might be given as evidence" (King's Bench Reports, Skinner 402). This still cited passage avoids reference to *res gestae,* and it gets at the heart of the admissibility of spontaneous declarations such that they become more than "mere speaking" and thus admissible evidence. An utterance blurted out because of an injury is admissible because it isn't self-interested or rhetorically purposeful and therefore doesn't require testing via cross-examination. A blurted utterance encapsulates the first-person knowledge of the original speaker, and so it can be repeated by those who heard the original utterance. Such an utterance may still be hearsay, but it is said in such a way as to satisfy the requirements of the oath, cross-examination, and, in the United States, the constitutional right to confrontation. In his edition of Greenleaf, Wigmore (1899, 264) develops this root justification for admitting spontaneous speech, citing the instructions to the jury in the 1888 case, *US v. King*:

> The declarations of an individual made at the moment of a particular occurrence, when the circumstances are such that we may assume that his mind is controlled by the event, may be received in evidence, because they are supposed to be expressions involuntarily forced out of him by the particular event and thus have an element of truthfulness they might otherwise not have. . . . [But the principle applies only to a statement] made at a time when it was forced out as the utterance of a truth, forced out against his will or without his will, and at a period of time so closely connected with the transaction that there has been no opportunity for subsequent reflection or determination as what it might or might not be wise for him to say. They must be "spontaneous," "impulsive," "instinctive," generated by an excited feeling which extends without break or letdown from the moment of the event they illustrate.

In this description, the spontaneous declaration exception has been greatly elaborated, in large part by emphasizing the circumstances/event that caused a true utterance about the precipitating event to be blurted out. The event forces the spontaneous utterance out of the speaker "against his will." Such utterances are "true" accounts of "the event they illustrate." In this description, the thing that has agency is the event not the speaker, and the result is "truth."

In *Evidence in Trials at Common Law* (1st edition 1904), Wigmore reiterates much of the argument made in his edition of Greenleaf, refining the label and description further. In the 3rd edition (1940) of Wigmore's *Evidence*, we see the term *spontaneous exclamation* used with this definition, which quotes liberally from *Keefe v. State* (1937):

> This general principle is based on the experience that, under certain external circumstances of physical shock, a stress of nervous excitement may

> be produced, which stills the reflective faculties and removes their control so that the utterance, which then occurs, is a spontaneous and sincere response to the actual sensations and perceptions already produced by the external shock. Since this utterance is made under the immediate and uncontrolled domination of the senses, and during the brief period when considerations of self-interest could not have been brought fully to bear by reasoned reflection, the utterance may be taken as particularly trustworthy (or at least lacking the usual grounds of untrustworthiness), and thus as expressing the real tenor of the speaker's belief as to the facts just observed by him; and may therefore be received as testimony to those facts.

I quote extensively from Wigmore for a number of reasons. First, this text is still widely quoted, and indeed the Federal Rules of Evidence adopted by US Congress in 1973 are rooted in Wigmore's evidence. Second, the link here between evidence, admissible testimony, and the senses does two things; first it unpacks the *Trevanian* (1694, 90) justification for the admissibility of spontaneous speech which believes such speech to be unreflective, and second, it resonates with the deep trust of firsthand sensory knowledge that we find in Gilbert's work on evidence; an exciting "external shock" is observed and/or experienced by a person, stilling his/her reflective faculties and causing an utterance that is nothing more than an account of what happened, which lacks all self-interest, to erupt out of the speaker. A key concept in this discussion, and one that is repeated a number of times, is the importance of the role of the senses. A trustworthy utterance is grounded in firsthand sensory experience. Perceptions are trustworthy when they are the result of the senses themselves, "actual sensations" and "observations" of a person "under the immediate and uncontrolled domination of the senses." "Self-interest" and "reasoned reflection" distort sensory-based knowledge. A spontaneous exclamation, then, is like a snapshot of what the person saw unsullied by the wants and desires of the speaker. Such an utterance is granted an objective status. It is admitted as evidence without cross-examination the way an object would be.

Since the earliest moments in Anglo-American law, there has been a preference for evidence that the jury can see for themselves. Gilbert called this "best evidence," a phrase that has endured through many changes in legal lexicon (others like Starkie, for example, used terms like primary evidence or original evidence, which are not currently common). Witness testimony gave an account of events, behavior, and things that couldn't be seen by the jury. Testimony was given the status of secondary evidence. The hearsay rule is situated in an ideology in which the best evidence is objective, which the discussion of hearsay consistently pits against language, which is merely representational. That is, the hearsay rule is fitted into the law's objective preference for producing a language ideology that trusts language when it is rooted in firsthand experience of real things in the world. The legal dis-preference for hearsay is underpinned and supported by an empiricist language ideology that trusts objectively based, firsthand accounts. The exception for spontaneous declarations, which by the authoritative accounts (Gilbert 1791; Starkie 1833; Wigmore 1940; *Crawford v. Washington* 2004) can be located in very early English common law, supports and maintains the language ideology of the hearsay exclusion by functioning as primary and secondary evidence. The spontaneous exclamation is testimony (secondary evidence) that is made admissible through a process of treating the utterance like an object with an immutable semantic, pragmatic, rhetorical, and referential content. As an objective account of sense-based knowledge, the spontaneous declaration would mean the same no matter the context in which it was spoken, the co-texts that accompanied it, the interactional frame in which it was situated, or the speaker.

Hearsay in Modern US Law

The historical development of the hearsay rule and the spontaneous declaration are an important metadiscursive resource for the modern-day hearsay case law. The language ideology developed in this history and circulated through precedential citation is used to entextualize hearsay as admissible and inadmissible in ways that continue to adopt and reproduce the empirical language ideology developed during the seventeenth and eighteenth centuries. In hearsay case law and the law of evidence generally, there is a presupposition that some utterances are by their very nature superior evidence, more factual. For example, an "excited utterance" is more factual, because it indexes something—an event, speakers, objects—in the world, and because it sprang from the empirical event and is not the product of the speaker's reflective faculties. Such presuppositions are circulated in legal texts that become the discursive resources with which attorneys and judges in courtroom interactions and judicial opinions "entextualize" (Silverstein and Urban 1996) evidence—that is, to identify and label a bit of discourse as evidence (or not evidence, as the case may be). The assumptions made about why an excited utterance is admissible are established in statute and case law, where they function as discursive resources used to entextualize evidence during the trial and again in higher court opinions.

The language ideology circulated in the hearsay rule and its exceptions work to recontextualize something that happened in the world in the legal context in a process that ultimately labels it as admissible or inadmissible evidence. In the United States, the development of the hearsay language ideology has been impacted by the Constitutional right to confront one's accuser, promised in the sixth amendment to the US Constitution. As the Court put it in *California v. Green* (1970, 155), "Hearsay rules and the Confrontation Clause are generally designed to protect similar values, it is quite a different thing to suggest that [. . .] the Confrontation Clause is nothing more or less than a codification of the rules of evidence and their exceptions as they existed historically at common law." Here the Court draws a line between the historical developments of the law of evidence and the US Constitution. Still, such arguments are made by drawing heavily on Wigmore's *Evidence* (1940), and indeed, many of the features of the hearsay language ideology persist in the US Supreme Court's discussions of the constitutionality of admissible hearsay. The potential for hearsay to be admissible in evidentiary law sometimes comes into conflict with the constitutional right to confrontation. The US Supreme Court has ruled on such cases a number of times. Table 2 lists the most prominent[6] precedents.

The 1980 opinion, *Ohio v. Roberts* is partially overturned by the 2004 opinion, *Crawford v. Washington*, which works to substantially narrow the window of admissible hearsay. Hearsay is then broadened again in Michigan v. Bryant (2011). Through all of this narrowing and broadening of admissible hearsay, the artefactual language ideology that underpins the rule remains intact.

EMPIRICISM, RELIABILITY, AND TRUSTWORTHY UTTERANCES IN OHIO V. ROBERTS

In the late twentieth century, hearsay utterances are still deeply distrusted. As an out-of-court utterance, hearsay is presumed to be unreliable (cf. *Roberts*, 1980; *Bourjaily*, 1987) because it can't be cross-examined to test the firsthand knowledge that underpins the utterance and would make it reliable. Hearsay also doesn't provide an opportunity for the accused to confront those who give evidence against them. Still, some types of hearsay remain admissible. In *Roberts* (1980), the Court makes the admissibility of hearsay hinge on the criterion of reliability:

> [A] statement is admissible only if it bears adequate indicia of reliability; reliability can be inferred without more in a case where the evidence falls within a firmly rooted hearsay exception, but in other cases the evidence must be excluded, at least absent a showing of particularized guarantees of trustworthiness.

Thus when cross-examination isn't possible, the court must look at the reliability of the utterance, which is determined by looking at 1) which exception is being invoked and how "firmly rooted" that exception is; and 2) in the absence of such an exception, whether the utterance has other indicators of reliability. The test case in *Roberts* is testimony given in a prior legal situation that provided the opportunity for cross-examination. Only the criterion for "firmly rooted" has survived the tests of time, and indeed, the cases that distinguish and explain *Roberts*, have tended to focus on firmly rooted exceptions. As *Bourjaily* (1987: 200 explains, a firmly rooted exception "suggests that, through experience in its use, the exception has proved to promote the 'accuracy of the factfinding process.' (53 Ford. L. Rev., at 1306-1307)." That is, such an exception has shown

TABLE 2

Prominent US Supreme Court Cases

Case	Year	Type of Hearsay	Court's disposition
Mattox v. US	1895	Use of testimony given in a different trial between the same parties because the witness had since died.	Hearsay is admitted: "To say that a criminal, after having once been convicted by the testimony of a certain witness, should go scot free simply because death has closed the mouth of that witness, would be carrying his constitutional protection to an unwarrantable extent" (at 243).
California v. Green	1970	Trial use of prior testimony given at a preliminary hearing.	Hearsay is admitted: Testimony from a preliminary hearing is admissible because the previous courtroom encounter satisfied the accused's right to confrontation.
Ohio v. Roberts Develops *Green;* Broadens hearsay	1980	Trial use of prior testimony given at preliminary hearing.	Hearsay admitted: *Roberts* creates the rubric for evaluating hearsay used until 2004. "Firmly rooted exceptions" to hearsay are admissible, as are statements that "bare indicia of reliability," such as those made at a preliminary hearing.
Bourjaily v. US	1987	Co-conspirator statements: Statements about conspiracy to sell cocaine.	Hearsay admitted: Statements fall into firmly established exception to hearsay.
Idaho v. Wright Develops *Roberts*	1990	Statements made to a pediatrician: Statements made by young child to doctor regarding sexual abuse.	Hearsay not admitted: Statements didn't fall into a traditional exception to hearsay and lacked sufficient guarantees of reliability.
White v. Illinois Develops *Roberts*	1992	Spontaneous declaration or excited utterance exception and medical examination exception: Statements made by a child to mother, babysitter, doctor, nurse and police about aggravated sexual abuse.	Hearsay admitted: Hearsay is reliable and the Confrontation Clause does not require either that the declarant is present or that the prosecution prove that the declarant is unavailable.
Lilly v. Virginia	1999	Statements against penal interest exception: Tape recorded statements about the crimes committed by both the speaker and his brother used as evidence without speaker as witness.	Hearsay not admitted: Not a "firmly rooted exception." Tape-recorded statements made to police at the station are the type of *ex parte* statement the Confrontation Clause was intended to exclude.
Crawford v. Washington Partially overturns *Roberts;* Narrows hearsay	2004	Statements made during police interrogation in the formal setting of the police station.	Overturned the "particularized guarantees of reliability" standard in *Ohio v. Roberts*. Hearsay not admitted: Testimonial statements are inadmissible.

continued

TABLE 2
(continued)

Case	Year	Type of Hearsay	Court's disposition
Davis v. Washington, Hammon v. Indiana Follows *Crawford;* Narrows hearsay	2006	*Davis*, present-sense impression exception; *Hammon*, excited utterance exception: Statements to police about domestic assault. Women didn't testify.	*Davis*, hearsay admitted; *Hammon*, hearsay not admitted: Testimonial criterion developed. In ruling on two cases together, the court demonstrates the kind of hearsay that is admissible. Testimonial statements are inadmissible if there is no opportunity to cross-examine. Non-testimonial statements are admissible.
Giles v. California	2008	Forfeiture of rights exception by wrongdoing: Admissibility of statements made by woman who was killed by Giles, her abusive boyfriend.	Hearsay not admitted: The exception in question is not Constitutional "because it was not an exception at the founding" (at 2).
Michigan v. Bryant Develops *Crawford* and *Davis/Hammon;* Broadens hearsay	2011	Statements made to police by a shooting-victim who died from his wounds.	Hearsay admitted: Testimonial criterion further developed. Statements were not testimonial and thus admissible hearsay because their "primary purpose [was to] enable police assistance to meet an ongoing emergency" (at 2, quoting from *Davis* (2006)).

itself to consistently lead to accurate facts. *White v. Illinois* (1992) suggests that the firm roots of a hearsay exception are determined through age and common usage: "the exception for spontaneous declarations is at least two centuries old, may date to the late 17th century, and is currently recognized under Rule 803(2) of the Federal Rules of Evidence and in nearly 4/5 of the states." *White* (1992) uses a genealogical framework stretching from the Enlightenment to 1973, when the US Legislature ratified the Federal Rules of Evidence, which was followed (or preceded) by similar actions in the majority of state legislatures.

Definitions such as those found in *Bourjaily* (1987) and *White* (1992) indexically reference historical discussions of admissible and inadmissible hearsay that only trust empirically grounded language. The phrase "firmly rooted" is an indexical structure that links, over and over, current legal concepts, structures, and arguments with those from early common law, linking current legal-linguistic situations to ancient ones, while eradicating the need to comment on or even notice the changes in usage, sociopolitical environment, or geographical location. This is in part because the indexical structure of common law functions via benchmark cases; it doesn't simply reference the last opinion in a chain of similar opinions.

Not only is the historical citation not simply linear, it also doesn't simply accrete over time, where each opinion cites all that came before. There is simply too much case law at this point for that to be feasible. Indexical structure embedded in the concept of "firmly rooted" that is described in *White*, for example, takes an initial leap back two hundred years and then back nineteen years to the Federal Rules of Evidence, and then points at state statutes. The ideas about language produced and circulated in the Enlightenment are indexically referenced, couched in metadiscourse that sometimes doesn't reexplain the language ideology, which is instead treated as a foregone conclusion. However, at other times, these metadiscourses are explicitly repeated and updated, renewing the objective language ideology that positions the material world as distinct from, prior to, and more accurate than speech. Even more than it did in the eighteenth and nineteenth century treatises, in more recent judicial opinions, the explication of the language ideology largely happens in discussions of exceptions to the rule. Such arguments justify and solidify the indexical framework of hearsay. That is, the rule is proved by its exceptions. We see this in especially in discussions of excited or spontaneous utterances. Take for example, *Idaho v. Wright* (1990, 820), which uses Wigmore (1974 edition) to make the argument that

> . . . if the declarant's truthfulness is so clear from the surrounding circumstances that the test of cross-examination would be of marginal utility, then the hearsay rule does not bar admission of the statement at trial. The basis for the "excited utterance" exception, for example, is that such statements are given under circumstances that eliminate the possibility of fabrication, coaching, or confabulation, and that therefore the circumstances surrounding the making of the statement provide sufficient assurance that the statement is trustworthy and that cross-examination would be superfluous. (see, e.g., 6 Wigmore, supra, §§ 1745–1764; 4 J. Weinstein & M. Berger, Weinstein's Evidence ¶ 803(2)[01] (1988); Advisory Committee's Note on Fed. Rule Evid. 803(2), 28 U. S. C. App., p. 778.)

According to the Supreme Court, the circumstances in which an utterance is made, in particular, exciting circumstances, eliminate the possibility of falseness and render the resultant statement trustworthy without the use of the in-court safeguards of adversarial practice, which would be of "marginal utility." This is because, "the declarant's truthfulness is clear from the surrounding circumstances." That is, the court doesn't need to cross-examine somebody who is so obviously telling the truth, and this can be determined not by interrogating the speaker but by analyzing the circumstances in which the utterance was produced. *White v. Illinois* (1992, 355–356) makes a similar argument, again explaining that the circumstances in which an utterance is spoken, or blurted as the case may be, eliminate the potential for fabrication and produce an utterance that needs no further interrogation.

> We note first that the evidentiary rationale for permitting hearsay testimony regarding spontaneous declarations and statements made in the

> course of receiving medical care is that such out-of-court declarations are made in contexts that provide substantial guarantees of their trustworthiness. But those same factors that contribute to the statements' reliability cannot be recaptured even by later in-court testimony. A statement that has been offered in a moment of excitement—without the opportunity to reflect on the consequences of one's exclamation—may justifiably carry more weight with a trier of fact than a similar statement offered in the relative calm of the courtroom.

As I noted above, *White* also described the spontaneous utterance as admissible because it is firmly rooted. Here, *White* shows that such a "firmly rooted" exception also has "substantial guarantees of trustworthiness," which are provided by contexts. In fact, an exciting context that doesn't allow the speaker "opportunity to reflect on the consequences of [the] exclamation" may be more trustworthy than "a similar statement offered in the relative calm of the courtroom." In this construction, the context is what makes an utterance trustworthy and "cross-examination superfluous." Other opinions also use the same construction:

- "These circumstances go beyond a showing that Williams had no apparent reason to lie to Shaw. His statement was spontaneous, and it was against his penal interest to make it. These are indicia of reliability, which have been widely viewed as determinative of whether a statement may be placed before the jury though there is no confrontation of the declarant." (*Dutton v. Evans*, 1970, 89)
- "The circumstantial guarantees of trustworthiness on which the various specific exceptions to the hearsay rule are based are those that existed at the time the statement was made" (*Huff v. White Motor Corporation*, 1979: 609)

In all of these opinions, an utterance that is "presumptively unreliable" is made reliable by looking at the context in which it was made. Each opinion goes through a list of the features of an event that the law presumes will result in a trustworthy utterance—features that indicate that the subjective complications to trustworthiness that the speaker might bring with him/her have circumvented, leaving no mark on the resultant utterance. The criteria for trustworthy speech consistently point outside of the speaker to the circumstances (also called transaction and context) as the progenitor of trustworthy statements. Thus it is only an utterance that through this process the law establishes as essentially trustworthy that does not require adversarial testing. The presumed reality of the circumstances, the neutral objectivity and objective stability of things and events in the world, quite literally ground admissible hearsay in "what really happened," bypassing the lack of reliability of spoken language and the self-interestedness of the speaker.

"TESTIMONIAL STATEMENTS" AND "OBJECTIVE CIRCUMSTANCES" IN *CRAWFORD V. WASHINGTON*

The empiricism of the hearsay rule is further developed in the most recent US Supreme Court opinions concerned with hearsay embedded in the concept "testimonial" that is used as a criteria to determine when admissible hearsay is out of alignment with the confrontation clause of the US Constitution. The concept is introduced in *Crawford v. Washington* (2004), which overturned *Roberts* (1980). It is further developed in *Davis v. Washington/Hammon v. Indiana* (2006), and *Michigan v. Bryant* (2011). According to *Crawford* (2004: 51), "witnesses" "bear testimony," and so if an utterance is testimonial—is bearing testimony—it necessitates the right to confront the witness. In the context of hearsay, the person who made the testimonial statement in question is not in the courtroom, and so according to the confrontation clause, it should be inadmissible. Typically, a witness is called to the stand in-court and then anything he or she says is testimony. That is, the context of the courtroom has an available subject position called "witness," and when the speaker is in the context and the subject position, his/her utterances are testimony. Quoting from the brief for the petitioner, *Crawford* (2004, 51–52) reverses the relationship between witness and testimony:

> Various formulations of this core class of "testimonial" statements exist: "ex parte in-court testimony or its functional equivalent—that is, material such as affidavits, custodial examinations, prior testimony that the defendant was unable to cross-examine, or similar pretrial statements that declarants would reasonably expect to be used prosecutorially."

That is, some statements are the "functional equivalent" of in-court testimony, rendering the speaker of such an utterance a witness. Thus with hearsay it is the utterance that is evaluated, and after *Crawford*, if the utterance is found to be testimonial, then the speaker was necessarily filling the role of witness at the time of speaking. The subject position "witness" is brought into being when his/her utterance is evaluated, and if the utterance is testimonial, then the speaker is a witness. This is made explicit in the Supreme Court opinion that followed *Crawford* (2004), *Davis/Hammon* (2006). "Statements of this sort [that is testimonial] cause the declarant to be a 'witness' within the meaning of the Confrontation Clause." That is, when a statement is labeled "testimonial," the related subject position "witness" is also constituted. In this body of law, the pragmatic function of an utterance determines the subjectivity of the speaker. (I discuss this reasoning in some detail in Chapter 3.)

As it is described in *Crawford* (2004), the concept "testimonial" hinges on a set of assumptions about objectivity and the guiding role of circumstances. We see both in *Crawford* (2004: 52) which states (quoting from an *amicus* brief), "'statements that were made under circumstances which would lead an objective witness reasonably to believe that the statement would be available for use at a later trial.'" Circumstances play a controlling active role, actually working on the witness—leading him/her to a reasonable conclusion. Moreover, the witness is objective and can read the circumstances without bias or self-interest. A concurring opinion repeats the sentiment about circumstances, arguing, "Exceptions to confrontation have always been derived from the experience that some out-of-court statements are just as reliable as cross-examined in-court testimony due to the circumstances under which they were made." That is, there has long been a legal assumption that some circumstances produce reliable utterances. Cross-examination is satisfied if the circumstances in which a statement is spoken otherwise lead to the same results as in-court, cross-examination.

Objectivity and circumstances are explicitly interconnected in the 2006 joint opinion for *Davis v. Washington* and *Hammon v. Indiana* (*Davis/Hammon*) in the process of developing a more precise rubric for determining whether an utterance is testimonial. By contrasting testimonial and nontestimonial hearsay, a more detailed application of testimonial is developed by making the role of circumstances explicit and linking them to the concept of objectivity.

> Statements are nontestimonial when made in the course of police interrogation under circumstances objectively indicating that the primary purpose of the interrogation is to enable police assistance to meet an ongoing emergency. They are testimonial when the circumstances objectively indicate that there is no such ongoing emergency, and that the primary purpose of the interrogation is to establish or prove past events potentially relevant to later criminal prosecution. (*Davis/Hammon* 2006, 822)

When an utterance is about an ongoing emergency—in the case of *Davis*, the context of domestic violence in which a statement is made to end an episode of abuse—it is nontestimonial because the circumstances reveal that its purpose was to secure help. When an utterance is about a past emergency—in the case of *Hammon*, the police do not arrive to the homes until after the violent event has ended, and so they talk to Mrs. Hammon about things that had happened in the past—it is testimonial because the circumstances reveal that its purpose was to give evidence that could be used in a legal context. Here again, we find the imprecision of language ameliorated with references to the objective circumstances. Whether or not a statement is testimonial, or self-interested and/or spoken to use against the accused at some later time, is impossible to tell from the utterance itself; one can't tell if an utterance is factual or even neutral simply by hearing or reading it. The circumstances alone can point to the pragmatic purpose of an utterance.

The present sense impression, or utterance spoken as an event is unfolding, which is the progeny of the ancient *res gestae* exception, is admissible because it was nontestimonial—its pragmatic purpose was to get help not to be used later as evidence. This is contrasted to the excited utterance in *Hammon*. In that case, circumstances reveal that the utterance was not an excited utterance and that it was testimonial. "It is entirely clear from the circumstances that the interrogation was part of an investigation into possibly criminal past conduct" (*Davis/Hammon* 2006, 829). Excited utterances or spontaneous speech are the ideal for admissible hearsay because they are not only devoid of intention to testify, but they are forced from the speaker—they have no purpose at all. By contrast, a testimonial utterance is elicited and given to prove or give evidence to be used in prosecution. Mrs. Hammon is speaking in an interrogation situation, which, the Court argues, is a situation that a reasonable person would recognize as eliciting statements that could be used as evidence in a later legal proceeding. The point is also made in terms of past and present by contrasting the circumstances underlying the two utterances. "McCottry's present-tense statements showed immediacy; Amy's narrative of past events was delivered at some remove in time from the danger she described" (*Davis/Hammon* 2006, 832). That is, telling something as it happens is not a story, it is a report of what one sees; what the Court calls "telling a story" (*Davis/Hammon* 2006, 832) is an inherently textual and subjective account of something that happened in the past. The danger was over and the link between the circumstances and the utterance had been disrupted by the speaker's now repaired "reflective faculties." Statements that ask for accounts of the past "are an obvious substitute for live testimony, because they do precisely *what a witness does* on direct examination; they are inherently testimonial" (*Davis/Hammon* 2006, 830). That is, the Court is drawing a direct correlation between utterances that are always testimonial, inherently testimonial, and the speaker's ability to speak purposefully. Importantly, the utterance is evaluated first, and if it is inherently testimonial, testimonial in and of itself, then that implies that the speaker was acting as a witness.

Michigan v. Bryant (2011, 1156) makes the controlling role of objectivity even more explicit, even commenting on the number of times the word is used in *Davis/Hammon*: "no fewer than eight times." Making the connection between objectivity and the material world more explicit, when *Bryant* uses a version of the term "objective," it is paired with the term "circumstances." The following explains how the two work together (*Bryan*t 2011, 1155)

> An objective analysis of the circumstances of an encounter and the statements and actions of the parties to it provides the most accurate assessment of the "primary purpose of the interrogation." The circumstances in which an encounter occurs (e.g., at or near the scene of the crime versus at a police station, during an ongoing emergency or afterwards) are clearly matters of objective fact. The statements and actions of the parties must also be objectively evaluated. That is, the relevant inquiry is not the subjective or actual purpose of the individuals involved in a particular encounter,

> but rather the purpose that reasonable participants would have had, as ascertained from the individuals' statements and actions and the circumstances in which the encounter occurred.

Here we have a legal opinion that circumstances are "clearly matters of objective fact." That is, what happens in the world is objectively factual. Statements and actions are only assessed as objective or not by looking to the circumstances in which they are produced. As we saw in the eighteenth century texts, *Bryant* is openly concerned with the subjectivity that is inherent in speech. The "subjective purpose of the individual" can only be nullified by looking to the circumstances in which the speech is produced, which itself will reveal the "primary purpose" of the utterance. As it was in all of the previous centuries, *Bryant* (2011), following *Davis/Hammon* (2006), posits that the utterances that are made during an emergency are more objectively true, that is true in relationship to that which is "objective fact." *Bryan*t (2011, 1157) demonstrates the longevity of this reasoning by describing the excited utterance/spontaneous declaration exception.

> This logic is not unlike that justifying the excited utterance exception in hearsay law. Statements "relating to a startling event or condition made while the declarant was under the stress of excitement caused by the event or condition" (Fed. Rule Evid. 803(2); see also Mich. Rule Evid. 803(2) (2010)), are considered reliable because the declarant, in the excitement, presumably cannot form a falsehood. See *Idaho v. Wright,* 497 U.S. 805, 820, 110 S.Ct. 3139, 111 L.Ed.2d 638 (1990) ("The basis for the "excited utterance" exception. . . . is that such statements are given under circumstances that eliminate the possibility of fabrication, coaching, or confabulation. . ."); 5 J. Weinstein & M. Berger, Weinstein's Federal Evidence § 803.04[1] (J. McLaughlin ed., 2d ed.2010) (same); Advisory Committee's Notes on Fed. Rule Evid. 803(2), 28 U.S.C.App., p. 371 (same). An ongoing emergency has a similar effect of focusing an individual's attention on responding to the emergency.

Bryant (2011) presents the excited utterance as the ideal utterance in which circumstances create an objective link between the utterance and the material world, bypassing the subjectivity of the speaker. The idea of an "ongoing emergency" that is presented first in *Davis* (2006) and then in *Bryant* (2011) is rationalized in both opinions by likening it to the longstanding logic of the excited utterance: exciting "circumstances eliminate the possibility of fabrication, coaching, or confabulation" (quoting *Idaho v. Wright* 1990, 820). An emergency, according to *Bryant* (2011, 1157) "[focuses] an individual's attention on responding to the emergency," such that the resultant utterance is not subjective and thus admissible hearsay.

The Excited Utterance and Objectivity

By consistently indexing the circumstances in which an utterance is spoken, this body of case law creates a situation in which if an utterance is not subjective it is objective. This is the result of the consistent location of what *Bryant* (2011, 1156) calls "objective fact," which is supported by the oppositional logic of the law: A/not A. If something is subjective (self-interested, goal-oriented, or linguistic), then it is not an objective fact (a real thing in the world). Because of the presumption that language is subjective and subjects are self-interested, only an utterance that indexes objective fact by somehow circumventing the speaker is admissible as hearsay, because any link to the personal goals of the original speaker does not exist and thus does not need to be cross-examined.

The spontaneous declaration or excited utterance is often presented as the ideal type of admissible hearsay because it satisfies the requirements of objectivity via a close link to the circumstances themselves. Such utterances are objective, which necessarily implies their lack of subjectivity. It is an utterance that is forced from the speaker by an exciting event *that the utterance also reports*. This is a key, distinguishing feature of the excited utterance—that it reports the same event that forced it to be spoken. Whereas a deathbed statement is not necessarily about dying, or a medical statement isn't about the event of being examined by the doctor, an excited utterance is about the same event that caused the speaker to blurt out the utterance. According to *People v. Poland* (1961, 181), in addition to being spoken in response to exciting circumstances while the reflective faculties have been stilled, it must also directly "[relate] to the circumstances of the [exciting] occurrence." The circumstances in which the utterance was produced still prove it to be admissible or not, but in this case, that utterance is also an account of those circumstances. "Voluntary or spontaneous declarations [. . .] explain the conduct of the plaintiff at the time of the accident and the cause of the accident, and [are] made at a time so near the occurrence of the accident as to preclude the idea of deliberate design" (*City of Austin v.* Ritz 1888, 7). The spontaneous declaration accounts for the exciting event that caused the speaker to speak an utterance free of the goals and intentions of the speaker. Such a nonsubjective utterance is treated as objective and factual.

An excited utterance or spontaneous declaration is a kind of utterance that itself functions as objective evidence, much the same way that Gilbert's written documents did. The declaration is received as evidence alongside other physical evidence. Quoting Baron Wood, the 1840 decision for *The People of New York State v. Fulton Fire Insurance Co.* (1840, 223) explains, "Declarations to be receivable in evidence must have been the natural effusions of the mind of the party making them, and must have been made when his mind stood in an even position, without any temptation to exceed, or fall short of the truth." Here, even the word statement is avoided, instead using "effusions of the mind." Such spontaneously produced "effusions" are simply "the truth," because they avoid both the subjectivity of language and the self-interests of speakers. As Chief Justice Bleckley put it, the "will [of the speaker] must have become and remain[ed] dormant so far as any deliberation in concocting matter for speech or for selecting words is concerned" (qtd. in *The People of NY State v. Del Vermo* 1908, 486). That is, both the content and the words themselves must be the product of spontaneity rather than the speakers will; they must be "the impulsive or instinctive outcome of the act" (484). Greenleaf's evidence similarly argues that declarations are admissible "if they spring out of the principle transaction" (qtd. in *Price v. State of Oklahoma* 1908, 367). This idea is developed in *Price* (1908), which argues that with a spontaneous declaration, "It is the facts talking through the witness." Thus, with a spontaneous declaration, the facts are put in the subject position and the speaker is reduced to a conduit that transmits the truth for the speechless objective fact. *Johnson v. Southern Railway Company* (1943, 7–8) makes the relationship between spontaneity and event explicit: "The testimony showed that what the injured man said was a natural and spontaneous utterance directly connected with and arising out of the main event; that it was the event itself speaking through the man, and not the man speaking about the event." Here, utterances are connected with and arise out of the same event, which put the speaker in the position of a vehicle through which the event could speak. He was not "speaking about the event." The event is the agent, and the utterance itself is a fact.

The spontaneous declaration/excited utterance is thus assumed in hearsay case law to have a sort of objectivity that is granted by its relationship with the circumstances of its production. The circumstances counteract the need for cross-examination because the "statements were spontaneous declarations, depending for credence, not upon the veracity of the deceased, but upon their close connection with the immediate facts of the killing and the circumstances which negates the idea of premeditation or fabrication. [. . .] The connection between what he said and the main fact had never been broken" (*Price* 1908, 375). That is, the circumstances both make it impossible for the speaker to plan to lie and the indexical connection between the "fact" and "what was said" is so close that they are treated as unproblematically interchangeable—because of the circumstances of its production, the utterance functions as fact. In fact, the spontaneous declaration in *Commonwealth of Pennsylvania v. Werntz* (1894) was referred to as "the most material evidence" of the case. Quoting the American and English Encyclopedia of Law, *Werntz* (1894) argued for the admissibility of "spontaneous utterances of thought created by or springing out of the transaction itself, and so soon thereafter as to exclude the presumption that they are the result of premeditation and design." That is, a spontaneous utterance is the product of the event that caused it to be spoken, which is explicitly opposed to premeditated speech. Directly related to the event that it also reports, the spontaneous declaration has a sort of objective value: it is what happened.

As the US Supreme Court continues to maintain and update the reasoning that bars hearsay from in-court testimony, it is no surprise that it so often does so with reference to the spontaneous declaration/excited utterance case law, because this particular type of admissible hearsay reproduces central values of the law of evidence for common law: 1) knowledge should come from firsthand sensory experience, and 2) that truth is located in objective facts that ideally the jury should see and evaluate for themselves. The spontaneous declaration/excited utterance is controlled by the circumstances in which and about which it was produced in a way that maintains both of these values. *Idaho v. Wright* (1990), *White v. Illinois* (1992), and *Michigan v. Bryant* (2011) all comment on the spontaneous declaration, using it as archetypical admissible hearsay, and treating it as though it is inherently admissible, because of its close and apparently indelible relationship to the circumstances of its production. *Wright* (1990, 820) argues that the circumstances in which spontaneous/excited statements are given "eliminate the possibility of fabrication, coaching, or confabulation" and make "cross-examination superfluous." *White* (1992, 356) goes so far as to say that due to the circumstances in which they are uttered, excited utterances/spontaneous declarations "may justifiably carry more weight with a trier of fact than a similar statement offered in the relative calm of the courtroom." *Bryant* (2011, 1157) introduces the "ongoing emergency" standard to distinguish between testimonial and nontestimonial statements, justifying the new standard by likening it to the "logic" of the excited utterance to hearsay. As *Bryant* lays it out, with an excited utterance, an utterance "'relating to a startling event or condition made while the declarant was under the stress of excitement caused by the event or condition,' (Fed. Rule Evid. 803(2))" is free from "fabrication, coaching, or confabulation [quoting *Idaho v. Wright*, 1990]." Similarly, an "ongoing emergency" has the "effect of focusing an individual's attention on responding to the emergency." That is, the circumstances which an utterance is responding to can produce an utterance about the circumstances that is so correct that it is admissible as evidence, without being cross-examined. The link between the firsthand knowledge of the original out-of-court speaker and the event it references is such that the utterance is objective because it bypasses the subjectivity of the speaker. Like any other object, such evidence can't be, and indeed, doesn't need to be cross-examined, because its accuracy speaks for itself.

Legal Intertextualities

The language ideology of hearsay and early Anglo-American common law fundamentally values firsthand knowledge gained through sensory experience. In this language ideology, language, especially speech, is legally problematic because it is both subjective and context dependent—that is, it indexes the subjective desires of the speaker and the social contexts that make it meaningful. True language should only index the material world. This language ideology is readily apparent in the legal treatises and what we have of the case law of the eighteenth and nineteenth centuries. As Bauman and Briggs (2003) have noted, cleansing language of the subjective free will of the speaker and the social world and thereby strengthening the relationship between things and words was part of John Locke's language project in the early 1700s. The similarities between the early legal and early linguistic conversations stem not only from a shared episteme, but from the direct borrowing of Locke's ideas by Sir Geoffrey Gilbert, whose work on the law of evidence was and continues to be pivotal in Anglo-American common law. This history is circulated and updated intertextually in the precedential structure of common law. The language ideology circulated in the hearsay metadiscourses consistently emphasizes the guiding role of the circumstances and the value of objective facts and firsthand knowledge. Rooted in Lockean empiricism, objectivity is the locus of truth.

Language ideology is never just about the relationship between language and speakers; it is about the social meaning in which the relationship between language and speakers is developed and the impact that social meaning has on the speakers (cf. Irvine and Gal 2000; Gal 2005). In the context of the hearsay metadiscourses that make some utterances admissible and other utterances inadmissible, this means that some speakers' knowledge is more recognizable and others is less. The emphasis on firsthand knowledge creates filters that are co-articulated with expectations about speakers and make utterances hearable in particular ways. The language ideology of the law, which is clearly articulated in the hearsay rule, presumes that witnesses are at least potentially lying. That is why they must take an oath and be subjected to cross-examination. Such views about trustworthy and untrustworthy speech are developed socially in real cases involving real speakers. That is, the abstract discussion about language that I have reviewed and analyzed above arises out of real cases and legal analyses of real people's speech, through which it accretes social meaning. Such social meaning is suppressed, skirted by assumptions of legal neutrality. Of course, the social meaning is always there, working to authorize and deauthorize speakers. In the context of domestic violence that is at the center of the present discussion, the legal distrust of language and the presumption of witness self-interest and fabrication circulating in the hearsay rule are co-articulated with assumptions about the psychological state of domestic violence victims, which presupposed a fundamental inability to tell the truth. The excited utterance exception itself makes presumptions about hysterical and spontaneous speech. These two sets of social expectations work together with the hearsay rule and the excited utterance exception to consistently put domestic violence victims just out of reach of speech that is both true and purposeful.

3

Social Discourses about Domestic Violence and Hearsay: Interdiscursivity and Indexicality in the US Supreme Court

What we know as "law" is produced and reproduced linguistically in ways that perform, maintain, and align with legal values, but that also perform, maintain, and align with social values. The network of language events that does this work does so intertextually and interdiscursively by indexing both a legal history that sees itself as positively consistent over time and cultural norms and values that are deployed to make legal ideals and indeed legal outcomes seem natural (cf. Constable 2005). In the network of legal and social language events that makes up law, we come to find sets of discourses overlapping with and embedded in other sets of discourses, where the embedded discourse is not always called attention to, but is nevertheless intertextually present over and over. The intertextual mingling of social and legal principles and ideologies creates indexical forms that link social ideas and legal principles. Indexical forms serve as resources for the entextualization and circulation of legally salient evidence, while also being a consequence of legal entextualization. Indexicality links discursive events to social realities in which they are meaningful. Indexical forms can take the form of texts that are stocked with linguistic, interactional, and social meaning "'Realities' of meaningful social practices emerge from people's situated experience of indexical semiotic processes that constitute them" (Silverstein 1992, 314). Which is to say that indexicality emerges out of the same sociosemantic contexts that they also prefigure in the form of texts, performances, and contexts.

This chapter identifies and analyzes discourses about domestic violence and gender roles in intimate relationships that intersect with and are cited in legal discourses about hearsay and sociolegal intertextuality that are underpinned by and result in indexical formations. In the metadiscursive discussions of hearsay, we find a rehearsal of criteria about what makes speech reliable, intermixed with discourse about domestic violence and women's speech. I trace hearsay case law intertextually by following citations back to the late 1700s, and what I find is that a consistently negative commentary about the speech of women who have been the victims of domestic violence emerges in such points of overlap. Sometimes the reported speech of victims of domestic violence is admitted and other times it is not. What remains consistent is that the reliability of some aspect of the speech of victims of domestic violence is always questioned.

The hearsay utterances of victims of domestic violence are only deemed admissible in cases where the court finds that the original utterance wasn't intentional—that is, was not the product of reflexivity or self-interest as in the excited or spontaneous utterance exception. However, the point of issue here isn't that domestic violence victim's utterances are never or always admissible. Indeed, they are admitted, not admitted, and are reversed on appeal. The issue is how the arguments that make hearsay utterances admissible or inadmissible work to make the victims of domestic violence recognizable as unreliable, by evaluating their speech against a legal rubric that essentially distrusts them. In the opinions discussed here, the analysis of speech and the analysis of the speaker are organized around a story about the legality and social conditions of domestic violence, which over time, sediment into iconized forms that relate categories of speech and speaker types (Irvine and Gal 2000). That is, the process of entextualizing an utterance also translates the speaker into a legally recognizable category that brings her within the disciplining gaze of the law.

When the US Supreme Court hears a case regarding the admissibility of hearsay, constitutional ideology is added to the discussion of hearsay and domestic violence, further complicating the fraught relationship between law and victims of domestic violence and in some ways explicating the ways Anglo-American law accounts for domestic violence as a crime. The Supreme Court is concerned with the right to confrontation. The right to confrontation is an essential component of the US legal system, and so it is no surprise that the Supreme Court tends to prohibit hearsay when it hears such cases, with the exception of a few key cases, notably *Mattox v. US* (1895), *Michigan v. Bryant* (2011) and a number of co-conspirator cases (cf. *Lilly v. Virginia*). Nearly all of the cases that admit hearsay admit the speech of male speakers talking about nondomestic crimes. Only in *Davis v. Washington* (2006), analyzed above, is the speech of a domestic violence victim determined admissible by the US Supreme Court (see the introduction to Section 1 for more information). When discussions about the confrontation clause and the speech of victims of domestic violence are brought together, we find explicit and in many ways troubling arguments that are dismissive of domestic violence and protective of legal principles.

The Supreme Court opinions I analyze—*Crawford v. Washington* (2004), *Davis v. Washington/Hammon v. Indiana* (2006), and *California v. Giles* (2008)—combine legal history, briefs, textbooks, and treatises with common sense notions about the reliability of speech creating an indexical link between hearsay and domestic violence. I argue that in these recent Supreme Court opinions, the legal facticity of domestic violence (discussed in Chapter 1) is developed intertextually and interdiscursively when it is combined with and reinforced by discussions of the confrontation clause of the 6th amendment of the US Constitution. In these opinions, the evaluation of the admissibility of hearsay in the US Supreme Court has come to hinge on a determination of whether the hearsay in question was "testimonial" (*Crawford* 2004). According to *Crawford*, if a hearsay utterance is testimonial, then the speaker is deemed a witness. This definitional argument correlates with the confrontation clause in the Sixth Amendment of the US Constitution, which reads, "In all criminal prosecutions, the accused shall enjoy the right . . . to be confronted with the witnesses against him [or her]." That is, the US Constitution guarantees the accused the opportunity to see, hear, and cross-examine all of the witnesses against him or her. I will detail this reasoning in the following section.

In this chapter, I work chronologically through three US Supreme Court opinions: *Crawford v. Washington* (2004), *Davis v. Washington/Hammon v. Indiana* (2006), *California v. Giles* (2008). In these three opinions, we find a systematic development of the paired concepts of "witness" and "testimonial," embedded in implicit and explicit discussions of domestic violence. I follow the analysis of these opinions with an analysis of Supreme Court opinions that deal with non-domestic violence crimes, opinions that are cited in *Crawford* (2004), *Davis/Hammon* (2006), and *Giles* (2008). I argue that in the intertextual connections across and between these opinions, there is an indexical link between legal hearsay and domestic violence victimhood. "The concept of indexicality involves the creation of semiotic links between linguistic forms and social meaning" (Bucholtz and Hall 2010, 21). That is, some linguistic forms (phrases, genres, styles, etc.) index social values and expectations for those who use the linguistic form, producing and reproducing an indexical link that works to make the speaker and the utterance socially and linguistically meaningful. In the legal context analyzed here, semiotic links are established in precedents and operationalized in the language events of trials, and often again in the appellate process. In this chapter, I focus on the Supreme Court opinion and the ways this court's decisions manage and intermingle with social discourses and prior legal texts. In any case involving a hearsay utterance that a party is attempting to have admitted using an exception to hearsay, there is significant discussion of the hearsay utterance in question as well as the speaker, her emotional and mental state, her location, etc. The Supreme Court opinions analyzed here anticipate their impact on the social problem of domestic violence even as they look backward at prior legal texts on hearsay, creating an intertextual, interdiscursive text that connects legal principles with social meaning. When the speaker is a victim of domestic violence, social ideas about domestic violence, victim behavior, victim psychology, and the like tend to be included in the legal analysis of the potentially admissible hearsay. What we find is a discussion of domestic violence victims as a class of speaker, all of whom are assumed to have similar experiences and thus similar motivations and liabilities as witnesses that are rooted in their victimhood (cf. Trinch 2013 on the use of the term "victim"). Embedded in the hearsay text-artifact that is produced in the trial and reproduced in the appellate opinions is an account of the person said to have spoken the hearsay utterance, an account that fits social and legal expectations of such speakers. The result is that embedded in Supreme Court case law and its associated documents are the resources for making social sense of a domestic violence victim and her speech. In short, hearsay case law is an indexical form that relies on social expectations of domestic violence victim behavior to make legal claims about metadiscourse—the hearsay law thereby enabling the law to manage her speech. When the speaker of hearsay is not a woman, hearsay case law does not focus on emotional state to the same degree or using the same vocabulary.

Hearsay, the Right to Confrontation, and Witnessing

Let me begin by describing the relationship between hearsay and the confrontation clause by taking a close look at *Crawford v. Washington* (2004), which articulates this relationship and plays a pivotal role in redefining the concepts "witness" and "testimonial" in the context of hearsay case law. Hearsay is always brought into the court as reported speech. As reported, secondhand speech, hearsay is legally distrusted and typically inadmissible. As I discussed in Chapter 2, this is largely because the person in court giving testimony is not the person who saw or experienced the event being recounted in the testimony. The in-court witness is repeating an account of the event, a story that they only heard at some point after the event ended. The prohibition against hearsay has developed with several longstanding exceptions, types of utterances that are admissible. For example, utterances that are said by an excited speaker, responding to an exciting event that caused her to spontaneously erupt into speech that is not reflective of the interests of the speaker. Whether it is determined to be admissible or inadmissible, hearsay always involves two speakers: Speaker 1, who saw the event and has what Gilbert called the "original knowledge," and Speaker 2, whom Speaker 1 spoke to and who gives in-court testimony (I discuss this relationship in some detail in Chapter 4). When hearsay is included in in-court testimony and argued for using an exception to hearsay, it is the person to whom the knowledge claim is tied—the out-of-court speaker—who is the one whose emotional and mental states are evaluated. This happens by asking Speaker 2, who is giving in-court testimony, questions about the emotional state of Speaker 1. Thus, the emotional and mental state of Speaker 1 is elicited and entextualized in the in-court testimony of Speaker 2, because Speaker 1 is not in the courtroom and can thus not be cross-examined.

Any in-trial discussion of hearsay indexes a number of events: the criminal event in question that was witnessed by Speaker 1 and the event in which Speaker 1 said something to Speaker 2, who takes the stand in the trial. The long-running discourses about gender and emotionality are often embedded in discussions of hearsay because they play such a big role in most exceptions to hearsay, perhaps most notably in the excited utterance exception that in turn plays such a big role in domestic violence cases. Legal and social discourses thus become intertwined, creating an indexical link between women who have been the victims of domestic violence, expectations about their mental and emotional state, expectations about their reliability, and the hearsay utterance when it is entextualized during trial as admissible or inadmissible.

When the admissibility of hearsay reaches the US Supreme Court, the focus shifts from a discussion of hearsay law to a discussion of the confrontation clause in the US Constitution. The admission of hearsay potentially violates the accused's right to confront their accuser, because the person with the physical knowledge of the event—the person who spoke the hearsay in question—is not in the courtroom to be cross-examined. That is, hearsay evidence does not give the accused the opportunity to confront and cross-examine the person with evidence against him/her, which runs afoul of the constitutional guarantees of the Sixth Amendment. According to *Ohio v. Roberts (*1980), exceptions to hearsay that were in place when the US Constitution was written do not violate the confrontation clause. In 2004 *Crawford v. Washington* partially overturned *Roberts* (1980), arguing that even some exceptions to hearsay may violate the right to confrontation. *Crawford* (2004) argues that any hearsay that is "testimonial," whether or not it falls under a long-standing exception to hearsay, is inadmissible because the speaker of such an utterance is a "witness" for the purposes of confrontation. The person who accuses the person of a crime is acting as a "witness," according to *Crawford*, if the utterance that is spoken is "testimonial." This pair of concepts, "testimonial" and "witness," play a central role in the *Davis/Hammon* (2006) and *Giles* (2008) opinions that both deal with domestic violence directly.

According to *Crawford* (2004), Kenneth Lee had attempted to rape Mrs. Crawford. When she told Mr. Crawford, they went together to confront Lee. Crawford and Lee got into a physical fight, in which Crawford stabbed Lee in front of his wife. *Crawford* (2004) is a typical hearsay case involving male-on-male violence; the out-of-court utterance in question is produced by a wife about her husband who stabbed another man. The Crawfords were taken to the police station, where they were formally and separately questioned by the police, in interrogation rooms. In their individual interviews, Mr. and Mrs. Crawford gave slightly different accounts of the moment of the stabbing. Mr. Crawford claimed self-defense, saying that Mr. Lee had put his hand in his pocket and pulled out what Crawford thought was a knife just *before* the stabbing. Mrs. Crawford said that she thought Lee had put his hand in his pocket *after* the stabbing.

Mrs. Crawford could not be an in-court witness, because Mr. Crawford invoked his spousal privilege, "which [in Washington] generally bars a spouse from testifying without the other spouse's consent. (cf. Wash. Rev. Code § 5.60.060(1) (1994))." In lieu of Mrs. Crawford's in-court testimony the prosecution played the tape of the police interview during the trial. Because Mrs. Crawford was not on the stand to be cross-examined by the defense, the account was hearsay evidence, and was admitted, over the objection of the defense, using the long-standing "statement against penal interest" exception to hearsay.

When they ruled on *Crawford* (2004), the US Supreme Court determined that Mrs. Crawford's hearsay statements should not have been admitted by the trial judge, because they were testimonial and thus initiated the accused's right to confrontation. As *Crawford* (2004, 51) puts it, "An accuser who makes a formal statement to government officers bears testimony." Such a testimonial utterance is always inadmissible because it violates the requirements of the confrontation clause of the Sixth Amendment of the Constitution, whereas non-testimonial statements do not violate the right to confrontation and are therefore only governed by hearsay rules. If a non-testimonial statement fits into an exception to hearsay, then it is admissible. Remember that the type of utterance with which the court is concerned is an out-of-court utterance—in this case the recorded police interrogation. Thus, according to *Crawford* (2004), an utterance can be testimonial even if the original speaker is not under oath in a formal courtroom setting. Asking "whether a statement was testimonial is the same as asking whether the person who made the statement was a witness against the defendant at the trial" (Ross 2006, 162). That is, an out-of-court statement can be rhetorically and pragmatically identical to in-court testimony.

The US Supreme Court comes to the conclusion that an utterance can itself be testimonial, by analyzing the text of the confrontation clause. Keep in mind the relationship between witness and testimonial described above while reading this passage from *Crawford* (2004, 51).

> [The text of the Confrontation Clause] applies to "witnesses" against the accused — in other words, those who "bear testimony." (2 N. Webster, An American Dictionary of the English Language (1828)). "Testimony," in turn, is typically "[a] solemn declaration or affirmation made for the purpose of establishing or proving some fact." (*Ibid*). An accuser who makes a formal statement to government officers bears testimony in a sense that a person who makes a casual remark to an acquaintance does not. The constitutional text, like the history underlying the common-law right of confrontation, thus reflects an especially acute concern with a specific type of out-of-court statement.

Remember that the issue in the confrontation clause is that the accused is guaranteed the opportunity to see, hear, and cross-examine all of the witnesses against him or her. It is notable that neither the concept nor the definition of "testimony" comes from the Constitution or from prior cases, but from an 1828 version of Webster's dictionary definition of witness as "those who 'bear testimony.'" Testimony, according to the same dictionary, is "a solemn declaration or affirmation made for the purpose of establishing or proving some fact." In-court, sworn testimony produces facts, which are then scrutinized and tested by cross-examination. In introducing this definitional structure, the Court creates a discursive structure in which any declaration solemnly made that establishes or proves facts is by definition testimony, and the speaker of testimony is by definition a witness. This argument works, tautologically, beginning with the problem of unconfronted witnesses (in the Constitutional discourse), finding a definition of witness that introduces the concept of testimony, and then looking up the word testimony, which itself gives a definition of witness that stretches beyond the courtroom context. Thus, the metadiscursive analysis in *Crawford* begins and ends with the concept "witness." The rhetorical force of the utterance is determined by considering the speaker's goals when she spoke, but the speaker's status (witness/nonwitness) is also determined by the assessment of the statement in question. The speaker is caught up in the analysis of hearsay at every step. That is, even though the Court opines "statements are what they are," the speaker is both involved in determining what a statement is, and they are impacted by the assessment of the metadiscourse.

The process of evaluating the hearsay utterance results in an entextualized form that is either testimonial or nontestimonial, and along with it, the speaker is made recognizable as a witness or not a witness. When the standard developed in *Crawford* (2004) is applied later in cases involving domestic violence like *Davis/Hammon* (2006) and *Giles* (2008), the speaker is recognizable as either a witness-victim or not a witness and just a victim.

Witnesses and Victims in *Davis/Hammon*

Though *Crawford* (2004) is not a case involving domestic violence, it is a very important precedent in domestic violence adjudication. "While *Crawford* is relatively recent, evidence has already emerged that it has significantly undermined the prosecution of domestic violence cases" (Amicus Brief, NNEDV, *Davis/Hammon* 2006, 16). The prescient problem with *Crawford* (2004) is that it makes it difficult to admit prior, unconfronted "testimonial" statements. The relationship between *Crawford* (2004) and domestic violence cases is further developed in the Supreme Court opinion on hearsay and the confrontation clause that followed *Crawford* (2004), *Davis v. Washington* and *Hammon v. Indiana* (2006). *Davis/Hammon* jointly rules on two cases involving domestic violence in a single opinion. In this opinion, the concept "testimonial" is expanded and formalized, and in both the statement in question was a report of domestic violence made by a woman about a (former) domestic partner[1] to an authority (a 911 operator and police in *Davis* and a police officer in *Hammon*). Importantly, the person who reported the assault and gave the statement in question was also the only firsthand witness, *and* she did not appear in court. Her prior statements were admitted as hearsay. Because the speakers did not appear in court, their utterances could only be admitted to the court via an exception to the hearsay rule of evidence: the present sense impression exception (FRE 803.1) in *Davis* (2006), and the excited utterance exception (FRE 803.2) in *Hammon* (2006). In the case of *Hammon* (2006), the hearsay is deemed testimonial and thus inadmissible by the Supreme Court; in the case of *Davis* (2006), it is deemed non-testimonial and thus admissible.

In *Hammon* (2006), the police responded to a "reported domestic disturbance" at the home of Hershel and Amy Hammon. When they arrived, Amy was on the front porch where she told police "that things were fine" but invited them in nevertheless. Inside the Hammons' home, there was a broken furnace and glass was on the floor. Interviewed separately, Hammon told the police that though there was a fight, it "never became physical." Mrs. Hammon[2] told police that the argument with Hammon "became . . . physical after being verbal," and that "when it became physical he threw her down into the [broken] glass [from] the heater" that Hammon had broken during the course of the argument. Amy handwrote and signed a battery affidavit that said, "Broke our Furnace and shoved me down on the floor into the broken glass. Hit me in the chest and threw me down. Broke our lamps & phone. Tore up my van where I couldn't leave the house. Attacked my daughter" (*Davis/Hammon* 2006, 12). She was subpoenaed to give testimony about the events of the evening, but she did not appear in court, making her signed battery affidavit inadmissible as evidence. Using the excited utterance exception, Mrs. Hammon's statements to police were admitted by the trial judge as hearsay in a police officer's testimony.

Like *Hammon*, in *Davis* the statements in question were about a domestic assault, but the circumstances and interaction were somewhat different. In *Davis*, Michelle McCottry called 911, but the connection was cut. The 911 operator called back and McCottry answered and explained that her ex-boyfriend, Adrian Davis, was at her house hitting her: "He's here jumpin' on me again. [. . .] He's usin' his fists" (*Davis/Hammon* 2006, 817). The operator sent police and continued asking questions to ascertain who the assailant was, during which time he ran away from the house. When police arrived, McCottry was "frantic"[3] trying to gather her belongings and her children so that they could leave. McCottry had also previously gotten a no-contact order, which Davis had violated, making his attack a felony. McCottry didn't appear in court and so her statements to the 911 operator that identified Davis as her assailant were admitted as a present sense impression, or a statement about something happening concurrently with the statement (FRE 8.3).

Davis/Hammon (2006) contrasts the situations in the two cases in order to clarify and develop the evaluation for testimonial utterances from *Crawford*

(2004). The cases do so by adding the "primary purpose" criteria to determine whether an utterance is testimonial (2004, 822):

> Statements are nontestimonial when made in the course of police interrogation under circumstances objectively indicating that the primary purpose of the interrogation is to enable police assistance to meet an ongoing emergency. They are testimonial when the circumstances objectively indicate that there is no such ongoing emergency, and that the primary purpose of the interrogation is to establish or prove past events potentially relevant to later criminal prosecution.

The argument is that nontestimonial utterances, like those made by McCottry that are frantic and concurrent with the event, are made to help police in their responses to an ongoing emergency, while testimonial utterances, like those made by Mrs. Hammon that are reasonably calm and about past events, have the goal of being used later for legal purposes. If the primary purpose of the utterance is to be used in subsequent legal proceedings (or if a reasonable person would know that the statement would be used that way), then the utterance is testimonial and inadmissible. Note that the determination of the primary purpose is gleaned from "objective circumstances." That is, according to the Supreme Court, whether an utterance was intended to be used later in court or meant to get help can be objectively determined. That is, it is treated as a foregone conclusion that the rhetorical relationship between context and text is objective, stable, identifiable in the event.

The presupposition that both speaker intent and pragmatic meaning can be objectively identified is highly effective in this precedent, underpinning the heuristic used to determine whether an utterance is "testimonial" and forming the tautological relationship between "witness" and "testimonial." *Davis/Hammon* (2006) argues, "Statements of this sort [that is testimonial] cause the declarant to be a 'witness' within the meaning of the Confrontation Clause." The causal relationship is made explicit in the verb "cause." A testimonial statement, then, is special in that is has its own agency; it *does* something. It can cause an ontological state in the speaker, transforming her into a witness even when she is not in court. In a typical trial situation, a person is called as a witness; they take the stand; they take an oath; and *then* anything that they say will be testimony. That is, in the typical courtroom interaction, the category "witness" comes first, imposed on the speaker from the courtroom context with all of its discursive trappings. In the arguments about hearsay in *Crawford* (2004) and *Davis/Hammon* (2006), a person makes utterances that are deemed testimonial, and those utterances transform the out-of-court speaker into a legal witness.

In the process of determining the primary purpose and thus admissibility of hearsay, the interactional context of the original interaction between the victim and police in which the utterances were said is never evaluated.

The police who interviewed the Hammons were engaged in assessing and controlling a domestic assault and collecting facts about the case. They were not engaged in interviewing a witness in order to prove that a crime had happened. Mrs. Hammon was answering questions, yes, but they were about an event that had very recently ended and in which she had been pushed around, punched, and shoved into glass. Thus even though the threat and other variables are dramatically different between the on-scene interaction and the courtroom interaction, the *Davis/Hammon* Court assumes that situations are fundamentally the same. That is, the primary purpose criterion assumes that any utterance could possibly be made in circumstances that would mimic what *White v. Illinois* (1992) called the "relative calm of the courtroom." Furthermore, this opinion presupposes that talking to police is the same as giving testimony, and that any reasonable person would know that their words were going to used for later prosecution. Thus demonstrating the reasonableness of the speaker, or lack of excitement, can be used to present the utterance as purposeful rather than accidental, thereby making it testimonial and thus inadmissible.

Eliding the interactional space of police intervention in an episode of domestic violence allows the court to see an out-of-court utterance as equivalent to testimony, and this transforms the speaker into a witness. Therefore, arguing that such statements are "an obvious substitute for live testimony, because they do precisely *what a witness does* on direct examination; they are inherently testimonial" (*Davis/Hammon,* 2006, 830) is deeply tautological—it creates an utterance that must be spoken by a witness in order for it to function as evidence, evidence which is assumed to be inherently testimonial and thus always spoken by a witness. Remember that the relationship between testimonial statement and witness in *Crawford* (2004) was tautological. Via intertextuality, that prior discourse reperforms its tautology in *Davis/Hammon* (2006). Any opinion discussing hearsay will begin with an evaluation of the statement in question: was it testimonial or nontestimonial? Each type of statement indexes a particular kind of speaker: a testimonial utterance is spoken by a witness and a nontestimonial utterance is not. Moreover, the statement is given a sort of agency and life of its own. In *Davis/Hammon* (2006), the Court begins with an evaluation of the statement, asserting that a statement that narrates past events "is an obvious substitute for live testimony." That is, the testimonial quality of a statement is located in the statement, not in the context in which it was spoken or the speaker who spoke it. The category of "witness" is then layered into the claim about statements: "they [testimonial statements] do precisely what a witness does [. . .]; they are inherently testimonial." Testimonial statements can act as witnesses. Thus, testimony, acting as a witness, produces testimony. Testimonial statements act like witnesses, and so they are "inherently testimonial." This final key step, to determine whether an utterance is inherently testimonial, requires a sort of prior conception of witness as one who gives testimony in order to make the assessment that some utterances do the same thing. The definition of witness from *Crawford* (2004) anticipates an inherently testimonial statement that is founded on a definition of witness.

The discursive relationship between witness and testimonial statement laid out here traps the speaker, the witness, in a legal tautology in which statements that are testimonial are spoken by witnesses who speak inherently testimonial statements. The speaker is locked in the subject category "witness," in such a way that the subject category "victim" is diminished, undermined to the point that it can be dismissed. The speaker is subsumed by the legal category "witness," rendering the context of domestic violence in which she was the victim legally unimportant. That is, because of the tautological relationship between witness and testimony, this speaker is only ever speaking as a witness, and this presupposition ignores the ways in which the interaction with police is also about being the victim of a crime. Framing the speaker as a witness rather than victim allows for the conflation of a courtroom and a living room a few minutes after a violent and destructive act. Starting with an evaluation of the utterance to determine the subjectivity of the speaker puts the victim of domestic violence in an impossible situation. She is in a position where her utterance can transform her into a witness regardless of, and in some cases in opposition to, her explicit goals and/or actions.

Intertextuality and Domestic Violence in *Giles*

At the end of *Davis/Hammon* (2006), the Court explicitly discusses the admissibility of hearsay in the context of domestic violence. The Court anticipates the usefulness of exceptions to hearsay in future domestic violence cases. In particular, they name the forfeiture by wrongdoing exception (*Davis/Hammon* 2006, 833). Forfeiture by wrongdoing admits hearsay statements if the person incriminated by those statements makes it impossible for the witness to appear in court to testify against the accused, through intimidation tactics or even murder. This exception seems useful in domestic violence contexts, because it allows for the use of hearsay in situations when the speaker has been intimidated or threatened if they testify. Such an act would mean forfeiting the protections of the confrontation clause. However, as we will see in *Giles* (2008), the forfeiture by wrongdoing provision isn't as easily applied in intimate violence cases as *Davis/Hammon* (2006) insinuates, even when the violence culminates in a murder. In fact, in his dissent in *Giles* (2008, 405), Justice Breyer goes so far as to say, "To the extent that it insists upon an additional showing of purpose, the Court [in *Giles*] breaks the promise implicit in [*Davis/Hammon*] and, in doing so, grants the defendant not fair treatment, but a windfall." That is, according to Justice Breyer, the protections granted to the accused in *Giles* (2008) go beyond the expectations of the confrontation clause.

In *Giles* (2008), Dwayne Giles shot and killed his ex-girlfriend, Brenda Avie, during an argument outside of Giles's grandmother's house. The trial judge admitted statements that Avie had made about Giles to police who were responding to a domestic violence call about three weeks prior to the shooting. Avie told police that in addition to choking and punching her, Giles had taken a folding knife out and threatened to kill her if she cheated on him. Because she had been killed, Avie could not testify at Giles's trial, but the prior statements to police were admitted as hearsay, using an exception stipulated in the California rules of evidence, which admits "out-of-court statements describing the infliction or threat of physical injury on a declarant when the declarant is unavailable to testify at trial and the prior statements are deemed trustworthy" (Giles 2008, 2682). On appeal, the California Supreme Court affirmed the admissibility of Avie's statements, arguing that Giles had forfeited his right to confrontation when he killed Avie and made her unavailable to testify.

The Supreme Court determined that the forfeiture by wrongdoing exception does not apply in *Giles* (2008). This argument is founded on legal notions of intentionality: Did the murder happen with the express intention of quieting the witness? The Court's opinion in *Giles* (2008) hinges on two arguments. One is that the murder was not designed with the express purpose of stopping Avie from testifying. The other is that Avie's statements to police were testimonial, and thus she was a witness. These two arguments are intertwined. Indeed, the first premise that the murder is designed to quiet a witness presupposes that Avie is always already a witness, or at least potentially a witness.

The Court considers the problem of intentionality by again referencing the 1828 Webster's Dictionary, other historical dictionaries, historical "cases and treatises," which all "indicate that a purpose-based definition" should be applied when determining if rights have been forfeited (*Giles* 2008, 2683–2684). The forfeiture by wrongdoing exception only applies when "the defendant ha[s] engaged in wrongful conduct designed to prevent a witness's testimony" (366). That is, the abusive partner has only forfeited their right to confrontation if it can be shown that he killed his partner with the express purpose of stopping her from giving testimony. If, as is the case in *Giles* (2008), death is the result of a separate instance of abuse, then the forfeiture of confrontation doesn't apply, because the purpose of the murder was something other than stopping the witness from giving testimony.

The *Giles* (2008, 2684) Court argues that in the hearsay case law, "prosecutors do not appear to have even *argued* that the judge could admit the unconfronted statements because the defendant committed the murder for which he was on trial" (emphasis in original). That is, historically, nobody ever tried to admit statements of the person who had been murdered during the trial of their alleged murderer by using the forfeiture by wrongdoing exception. For one reason, such an argument would circumvent the presumption of innocence that is so fundamental to common law. The forfeiture by wrongdoing exception presumes that the witness was silenced by the person on trial for the express purpose to stop the witness from testifying against the defendant. If the crime that silenced the witness is the same as the crime that the accused is on trial for, then the accused's innocence is not presumed but rather his/her guilt. Furthermore, it is the judge and not the jury who determines that admissibility of hearsay, and so according to *Giles* (2008) admitting hearsay in such a situation would require the judge to determine whether or not the defendant was guilty and to do so even before the jury had presented a verdict. The Court supports its argument about the inadmissibility of the hearsay statements of murdered women, by turning to historical cases in which women were killed by their intimate partners. The majority of the historical cases detailed in *Giles* (2008) are not key precedents that are commonly used for hearsay cases or forfeiture by wrongdoing cases. Instead, the Court handpicked cases that discuss the statements of women who died at the hands of their husband, most of which are about the dying declaration exception to hearsay.

One such eighteenth century case is *King v. Woodcock* (1789), which is cited in *Giles* (2008) and *Crawford* (2004). *Woodcock* (168 English Reports: 352–354) is also about a statement made by a dying woman in which she describes her husband as her murderer. Mrs. Sylvia Woodcock was found bleeding to death in a ditch. She was taken to a poorhouse, where she received medical attention and made a report, under oath, to a magistrate identifying her husband as her attacker. She died within forty-eight hours of the report, and though it was clear to the doctors that she would not live, Mrs. Woodcock herself didn't express any knowledge of her impending demise. As the Chief Baron Eyre explained to the jury, in order for a dying declaration to be admissible, "the deceased herself [must apprehend] that she was in such a state of mortality as would inevitably oblige her soon to answer before her Maker for the truth or falsehood of her assertions" (168 English Reports: 354). Because there was not clear evidence that she did know she would soon die, the judge did not allow her utterance. In so doing, he commented directly on wife battery: "Great as a crime of this nature must always appear to be, yet the inquiry into it must proceed upon the rules of evidence" (168 English Reports: 352). The *Giles* (2008) Court directly quotes the last point, reiterating the hierarchy between law and the individual crime established in a 1789 English case in a 2008 US Supreme Court opinion. That is, the historical claim is updated intertextually and interdiscursively when the Supreme Court reaches back into legal annals in order to anticipate future applications of law. This claim is not much different from those given in *Davis/Hammon* (2006), discussed above. The rules of evidence then and now require that testimony must be given after the witness has taken an oath, in the courtroom where they are visible by the judge and jury, and that the accused must have the right to question the person giving testimony. Without these prerequisites or a successful use of an exception to hearsay, no statement is admissible as hearsay.

A similar argument is made when *Giles* (2008) cites *King v. Dingler* (1791), which used *Woodcock* (1789) as a precedent. Dingler was accused of stabbing his wife multiple times. She lived in the hospital with the wounds for twelve days, and during that time, a magistrate interviewed her "under oath" but not in front of Dingler. When the prosecution attempted to admit Mrs. Dingler's statements as testimony, using *Woodcock* (1789), the defense argued that they were not dying declarations because they were voluntary, which implies self-consciousness and thus may reflect the interests of the speaker. Additionally, the statement didn't suggest that the speaker knew she was going to die. Nor were they admissible under the Marian statutes (which would have required the presence of the accused when the deposition was taken). Thus, the judge did not admit the signed statement into evidence.

Yet another case cited and described in *Giles* (2008), *Smith v. State* (1848), involves a husband who poisoned his wife with arsenic. The trial court admitted the dying wife's statements, but the Tennessee Supreme Court overturned, arguing that they did not qualify as dying declarations. This time, the argument further narrowed the criteria necessary to qualify as a dying declaration. The speaker didn't only have to know that she would die. She had to be "under the impression of almost immediate dissolution," not simply "that she was satisfied she could not live" (*Smith* 1848, 21). In *Smith*, it wasn't enough for the speaker to know that her wounds were mortal; she had to believe that she was going to die immediately. Over and over we see the law interpreted in such a way as to exclude the statements of women dying at the hands of their abusive husbands. Over and over we see arguments that value the stability of the law, while dismissing the voluntary testimony of women who can't possibly appear in court.

As we move through the argument in *Giles* (2008), we see that exceptions to hearsay become a bit of a moving target when prosecuting domestic crimes. The criteria shift slightly with each iteration, but in so doing, the alignment between the social and legal approval of a husband's control over his wife and any violence that maintains that control is affirmed. What we find in the analysis of hearsay in *Giles* (2008) is an argument that defends legal principles, and it does so by citing cases in which women have been abused by their domestic partners. The historical cases are lined up, it seems, to show that the forfeiture by wrongdoing principle wasn't used historically in cases similar to *Giles* (2008), and indeed, as the preceding analysis has shown, the cases that are explicated are contextually similar not only legally similar. That is, we expect appellate opinions to comment on the rule of law by drawing similarities between different crimes in which the same law has been applied. What we find in *Giles* (2008) is a heavy reliance not on legal analogy but on similarity, as case after case is presented in which a man kills his intimate partner. The focus on the specific type of crime in addition to the legal principles creates an interdiscursive point in this case law, in which discourses about the law are interwoven with discourses about domestic violence and its victims. The dissenting opinion argues, and shows, that it is far more typical to admit the speech of murdered people. There is substantial case law that supports this reading. However, it is the cases involving murdered wives that are available for the primary argument made in *Giles* (2008). That is, the cases in which the speeches of murdered people have historically been found inadmissible have been those in which the speech was made by women against their abusive partners.

Giles (2008) describes multiple episodes of domestic violence, spanning three hundred years and two continents, intertwining legal and social discourses about domestic violence. The result is a presentation of the legal facticity and everyday matter-of-factness of domestic assault. The statements in *Giles* (2008) and those given under oath to a magistrate that we find in *Woodcock* (1789) and *Dingler* (1791) are produced and entextualized in quite different legal circumstances. The utterances in *Giles* lack the hallmarks of testimony that the historical cases have. Nevertheless, *Giles* explicitly draws an equivalency between itself and the cases from the late eighteenth century That is, the Supreme Court argues that the women in these various contexts—whether in a hospital under oath in 1791 or at home while crying to police officers in 2002—are all said to be speaking as witnesses because their statements are all equally testimonial. These arguments about the speech of victims of domestic violence are used to reinforce the inadmissibility of hearsay. That is, these arguments about domestic violence are used to prove a legal point about hearsay, reported speech, and in the process, all domestic violence is flattened into one identifiable category. Domestic violence serves as the backdrop for a discussion of hearsay, in judicial opinions that entextualize accounts of domestic violence as unauthoritative nonevidence. This (re)produces an indexical form in which women are not related to authoritative accounts of domestic violence, which remains only marginally criminal anyway. Even when abusive partners are prosecuted, the legal result reinforces the legal privilege of the husband, who has, after all, had legal sovereignty for significantly more time than his wife has.

The indexicality that interconnects discussions of domestic violence and legal hearsay is stabilized by the concepts "witness" and "testimonial" developed in *Crawford* (2004), creating a situation in which *Giles* (2008) produces a similar witness—one who can give testimony without being in the courtroom. Remember the issue in *Giles* (2008) is that the witness-victim, Avie, cannot give testimony in court because she was shot and killed by her estranged boyfriend, Giles. The prosecution tried to admit prior statements to police that included a threat against her life. The trial court and state Supreme Court admitted those statements. Even though all courts decided that based on *Crawford* (2004) the statements were testimonial, they decided that Giles had forfeited his right to confrontation by shooting Avie. The Supreme Court undoes that decision when they rule that her prior statements to police were testimonial, and thus she was a witness, for the purposes of confrontation.

In *Giles* (2008), Avie's status as a witness is strengthened by the intertextual use of *Woodcock* (1789), *Dingler* (1791), and other similar cases that were woven together in order to evaluate the statements made by Avie to police after a previous incidence of abuse by Giles. The statements were about Giles threatening to kill Avie at knifepoint, and they were made to a police officer while she was "crying" and right after the assault had ended (2008, 2682–2683). By drawing an equivalency between Avie's statements to police and the testimony of murdered wives in *Woodcock* (1789) and *Dingler* (1791), *Giles* (2008) effectively argues that Avie was a witness. In this way, Avie cannot be an in-court witness because she has been shot and killed, but because she was a witness nevertheless, her testimony can't be used. The intertextual network made-up of *Crawford* (2004), *Davis/Hammon* (2006), a set of historical cases, and even legal treatises and textbooks entextualize her out-of-court statements as inadmissible hearsay, and in so doing, they make Avie recognizable, in the Butlerian sense, as a witness. To put it another way, Avie cannot be a witness because she is dead, but she is always already a witness because her statements are entextualized as inherently testimonial. Caught between these two definitions of witness, nothing she has said about her abusive boyfriend is admissible. Entextualized as a witness-victim, the mortal crimes are against her body, and she is unconfrontable, and so her testimony is lost. What we find in *Giles* (2008) is a rehearsal of arguments involving hearsay spoken by women dying at the hands of their husbands. The result is a laundry list of reasons *not* to admit the utterances of victims of domestic violence who died as a result of the abuse.

Non-Domestic Violence Precedents

What this chapter has argued is that the facticity of domestic violence is written into the fabric of hearsay case law. When that case law is used by the US Supreme Court to create arguments intertextually and interdiscursively it rarely rules in favor of admitting hearsay testimony of domestic violence victims, with the exception of *Davis* (2006), and McCottry's frantic call to 911. Because hearsay is typically inadmissible, this may seem to make legal sense. However, there are commonly cited hearsay precedents evaluating the speech of men who were murdered in non-domestic assault. Without the space to go into them all, I will focus on *Mattox* (1895), which has been positively cited thousands of times since 1895, and the recent case, *Michigan v. Bryant* (2011). In both cases, the speech is deemed admissible. Indeed, *Crawford* (2004), *Hammon/Davis* (2006), and *Giles* (2008) all use *Mattox* (1895) as the positive standard to prove that hearsay is inadmissible. One important thing to note from the outset of this analysis is that none of these witnesses has an intimate relationship with their assailant, though two of them are victims of the crime that their statements recount.

MATTOX V. US

In *Mattox v. US* (1895), Mr. Mattox had been convicted of murdering John Mullen. The case had already been to the Supreme Court, who remanded for a new trial. The second trial also delivered a verdict of guilty, which Mattox again appealed. This opinion was delivered for the second appeal. One key contention in this appeal is that between the two trials, the key witnesses had died. Their testimony in the initial trial was read at the new trial, which constitutes hearsay. In *Mattox* (1895) the court takes quite a different stance on hearsay, in particular on the relationship between legal principles and society. Recognizing the importance of the right to confrontation, they go on to say:

- "But general rules of law of this kind, however beneficent in their operation and valuable to the accused, must occasionally give way to considerations of public policy and the necessities of the case."
- "The law in its wisdom declares that the rights of the public shall not be wholly sacrificed in order that an incidental benefit may be preserved to the accused."
- "A technical adherence to the letter of a constitutional provision may occasionally be carried farther than is necessary to the just protection of the accused, and farther than the safety of the public will warrant."

Each of these quotes clearly argues that the Constitution wanted to protect those accused of crimes from ex parte evidence, give him/her the opportunity to confront the witness, and give the jury the opportunity to "judge by his demeanor upon the stand and the manner in which he gives his testimony whether he is worthy of belief" (1895, 242–243), but that sometimes these principles will need to be sacrificed out of "necessity" and for the public good. Compare these to *Davis/Hammon* (2006) and *Woodcock*, both of which argue that the rule of law should not be breached for any reason. Taken alongside the reasoning presented here in *Mattox* (1895), we find an argument that the rule of law should not be put aside for the "trifling" crime of domestic violence (*State of North Carolina v. Rhodes*, 1868; cf. *Giles* dissent).

Such statements in *Mattox* come after a rehearsal of English and US case law, more than fifty cases, all of which rule to admit hearsay of deceased witnesses. For example, in *Kendrick v. State*, cited in *Mattox,* "testimony of a deceased witness taken before a committing magistrate was held to be admissible testimony" (*Mattox* 1895, 243–244). Moreover, *Mattox* (1895) gives the dying declaration as the *sine qua non* of admissible hearsay:

> From time immemorial they have been treated as competent testimony, and no one would have the hardihood at this day to question their admissibility. They are admitted not in conformity with any general rule regarding the admission of testimony, but as an exception to such rules, simply from the necessities of the case, and to prevent a manifest failure of justice.

This description of the dying declaration is unqualified, lacking demarcations of time or the speaker's knowledge of her impending demise.

All of these examples from *Mattox* (1895) are claims that can be read as directly opposing those used in cases about domestic violence victims' speech, either before or after, even when *Mattox* (1895) is cited. Recall that *Woodcock* and *Dingler* both argue that the statements given under oath to a magistrate are inadmissible, and they qualify the parameters within which the dying declaration can be admitted with increasingly stringent analysis of the speaker's knowledge of her death and how soon it would come. *Giles* (2008) uses the reasoning from the seventeenth century English cases that exclude the hearsay rather than the closer US case that is also a benchmark precedent, *Mattox* (1895).

MICHIGAN V. BRYANT

Like *Mattox* (1895), *Michigan v. Bryant* (2011) admits the speech of the murdered speaker who is a man. This stands out against the ruling in *Giles* (2008) that doesn't admit the speech in otherwise similar legal context. *Bryant* (2011) is a case in which Anthony Covington was shot by Richard Bryant. Covington got into his car and drove to a gas station where police responding to a 911 call about a shooting in the area found him lying by his car. Five individual police officers arrived and asked him what had happened, to which Covington responded either "I was shot" or "Rick shot me" (2011, 1163). Other questions allowed the police to ascertain that Covington had just spoken with Bryant through his back door, though all of the police officers said that they did not know what the conversation was about when they set off to locate the shooter. When Covington turned to leave, Bryant, recognized by his voice, shot him through the back door. Covington died in the hospital within hours of the shooting and thus couldn't testify in court.

The trial court admitted his statements identifying the person and location of his shooting. The various appeals the case went through reversed the trial court and then reaffirmed the ruling a number of times. The Supreme Court affirmed Bryant's conviction, ruling that Covington's statements to police the night of his death were nontestimonial. They used the so-called "primary purpose" test primarily developed in *Davis/Hammon* (2006). Recall that the primary purpose test is used to determine whether an utterance is testimonial or not. *Bryant* (2011, 22–23) quotes *Davis/Hammon* (2006):

> "Statements are nontestimonial when made in the course of police interrogation under circumstances objectively indicating that the primary purpose of the interrogation is to enable police assistance to meet an ongoing emergency. They are testimonial when the circumstances objectively indicate that there is no such ongoing emergency, and that the primary purpose

> of the interrogation is to establish or prove past events potentially relevant to later criminal prosecution." *Davis*, 547 U.S., at 822, 126 S. Ct. 2266, 165 L. Ed. 2d 224.

That is, if the primary purpose of the hearsay is to assess and deal with an ongoing emergency, and as such is nontestimonial, which it is found to be in *Davis*. If instead the primary purpose is to produce evidence that can be used later during a trial, as they argue was the case in *Hammon* (2006), then the hearsay is testimonial. Testimonial statements are inadmissible, whereas nontestimonial statements are admissible. The Court in *Bryant* (2011) uses *Davis* and *Hammon* (2006) binarily, analogizing the circumstances in *Bryant* (2011) with the testimonial statement in *Hammon* (2006) and the nontestimonial statement in *Davis* (2006). In *Davis*, McCottry called 911 and "frantically" described an abusive event that was happening right at the time. In *Hammon*, the violent assault on Mrs. Hammon had ended, Mrs. Hammon was in a separate area from her husband, and when police questioned her, she seemed only "somewhat frightened." In *Bryant* (2011), Covington is alone in a parking lot, lying on the ground, obviously injured, no shooter in sight. The Court argues that Covington's speech is more like McCottry's, and that the primary purpose of the interaction with police was to allow them take control of the situation rather than to gather evidence to be used later in court. That is, it was nontestimonial rather than testimonial.

The analysis in *Bryant* (2011) hinges on the way that a shooting, a male-on-male crime, is different from domestic battery crimes in *Davis/Hammon* (2006), and *Giles* (2008; in *Giles*, Avie was killed with a gun, but it was her speech directly following a physical assault that was the hearsay in question). As *Bryant* (2011, 1158–59) puts it, in *Davis* and *Hammon* "the assailants used their fists," whereas "the emergency here [. . .] involved the use of a gun." The weapons are different, fists in the domestic cases and a gun in *Bryant* (2011). This is translated into a public/private distinction. "Domestic violence cases like Davis and Hammon often have a narrower zone of potential victims than cases involving threats to public safety" (*Bryant* 2011, 1158). To determine whether there is an ongoing emergency, *Bryant* (2011, 1159) argues, the court should take into account whether the incident is "a public threat" or "actually a private dispute." A public threat will indicate a longer lasting ongoing emergency and one with a broader physical scope—a neighborhood rather than a home. This may be the case. What is striking here is how the shooting in *Bryant* (2011) is described as a public incident.

> Because *Davis* and *Hammon* arose in the domestic violence context, that was the situation "we had immediately in mind (for that was the case before us)." (547 U.S., at 826, 126 S. Ct. 2266, 165 L. Ed. 2d 224). We now face a new context: a nondomestic dispute, involving a victim found in a public location, suffering from a fatal gunshot wound, and a perpetrator whose location was unknown at the time the police located the victim. Thus, we

> confront for the first time circumstances in which the "ongoing emergency" discussed in *Davis* extends beyond an initial victim to a potential threat to the responding police and the public at large. (1155–1156)

While it is nice to see the Court take context so seriously, this view of context essentializes domestic violence as merely a private issue and thus not dangerous to "the public at large." In the discussion of *Hammon* (2006), domestic violence is downplayed, as it always has been, as between intimates and as a crime with less social consequence than a male-on-male shooting. Though the dispute between Bryant and Covington is cast as a potentially public issue, in fact, the shooting in *Bryant* (2011) was particular. Bryant shot Covington, somebody he knew. This shooting did not involve, as one of the hypothetical and hyperbolic examples gives as an analogy, a sniper who is shooting strangers (2011, 1164).

The shooting in *Bryant* was a private crime, as the Court has defined it in this very opinion. The victim and assailant knew each other, as indicated by the use of the name of the shooter, Rick. The shooter may have been at large, but the attack on Covington was a personal attack—Rick was targeting Covington. That is, the attack on Covington wasn't random; it was based on the fact that he was Covington. The same could be said of *Hammon* (2006). It was a targeted attack based on the prior relationship between the Hammons. Of course, the relationship is different in a number of important ways. But as we've seen elsewhere in the case, the differences such as these are easily overlooked by focusing on the law rather than the specific details, facts, of the case. Interestingly, in the analogy between *Hammon* (2006) and *Bryant* (2011), the similarities are ignored and context is hightened in order to frame *Bryant* (2011) as a public crime and *Hammon* (2006) as a private one. The fact that the shooting in *Bryant* (2011) was between men and did not involve intimate partners seems to be sufficient to assume both that the crime was public and that the speech is reliable enough to admit. That is, by reading the crime as public, the Court is able to make the argument that the emergency was still going on—a shooter was at large and a risk to the general population—and thus that any hearsay reporting what had happened woud be both reliable and nontestimonial. Such reasoning is underpinned by the long-held treatment of the public domain as dominated by men and male issues as public (cf. Gal 2002, 2005; Lerner 1986; Olsen 1983). Crimes involving non-intimate individuals, often men, are assumed to have public consequence, whereas domestic incidents, only recently criminal, are assumed to always be merely private affairs.

Using the authoritative, patriarchal discourse of the law, *Bryant* (2011) creates a bright line between public and private that reinforces the patriarchal sanctity of the home. According to Gal (2005, 24), "the ideology of public/private divides spaces, moralities, types of people, activities, and linguistic practices into opposed categories." For centuries, domestic crimes were private and by virtue of the binary logic of Anglo-American law, thus not public and not within the purview of the law. Crimes between husbands and wives are pushed behind the veil of domesticity, which limits their public visibility, underestimates their public consequences, and trivializes their criminality. According to Gal (2005, 24), there "is a circulatory or feedback process" between public and private. "The interactional *effect* of publicness or privateness is created through contrasting interactional practices that are themselves interpreted through a language ideology that formulates (presupposes) the values and cultural images identified as characteristic—emblematic, iconic—of public and private" (emphasis in original, Gal 2005, 24). That is, the determination whether something is public or private is a product of interaction, which is underpinned by presuppositions about what is public and what is private. In social and legal language ideologies, domesticity is tantamount to private, and so it is no surprise that domestic violence is assumed to be a private event, even after it has been legally redefined as a public crime. The public/private distinction is thus developed interdiscursively in *Bryant* (2011) by contrasting it to *Hammon* (2006), and the result is the social and legal minimization of domestic violence.

Compare the treatment of Covington's speech in *Bryant* (2011) to that in *Giles* (2008) and *Hammon* (2006), described earlier. With about as much evidence about the nature of the relationship between the victim and assailant, the assault with a gun in *Giles* (2008) is never discussed as anything but domestic and the hearsay is not admitted.[4] That is, *Giles* (2008) is cast as entirely about an intimate relationship even with the presence of a gun. Without the idea of an intimate relationship coloring the interpretation in *Bryant* (2011), its interpersonal dimension is completely overlooked. In *Hammon* (2006), Mrs. Hammon's speech is excluded using *Crawford*'s reasoning because she "'deliberately recounted, in response to police questioning, how potentially criminal past events began and progressed'" (*Davis/Hammon* qtd. in *Bryant*, 2011, 1954). That is, she spoke willfully about the event that had already ended. Similarly, Covington answered police questions about how a past criminal event began and progressed. Two elements are key. First, the context in *Bryant* is presupposed to be public, while *Hammon* is always already private in nature. Bryant uses "domestic" to characterize *Hammon* and *Davis* thirteen times.

Second, whereas Mrs. Hammon is characterized as speaking "deliberately," Covington is characterized this way: "He was obviously in considerable pain and had difficulty breathing and talking" (2006,1165). Michelle McCottry was characterized as "frantic": "McCottry's call was plainly a call for help against a bona fide physical threat" (*Davis/Hammon* 2006, 827). McCottry also had visible "fresh injuries" (819). Part of the positive analogy between McCottry and Covington is that both were visibly affected both physically and emotionally by the encounter. Mrs. Hammon by comparison was deliberate and rhetorical. Characterizations of emotion and speech are very common in hearsay cases, especially those involving the excited utterance exception to hearsay, which admits the speech of somebody who is so excited that their reflective faculties have been stilled, rendering the resultant, blurted speech reliable and admissible. Indeed, by highlighting the role of "emergency," *Bryant* (2011, 1157) weaves together confrontation clause case law and hearsay case law that is concerned with emotional state.

> Implicit in *Davis* is the idea that because the prospect of fabrication in statements given for the primary purpose of resolving that emergency is presumably significantly diminished, the Confrontation Clause does not require such statements to be subject to the crucible of cross-examination. This logic is not unlike that justifying the excited utterance exception in hearsay law. Statements "relating to a startling event or condition made while the declarant was under the stress of excitement caused by the event or condition" (Fed. Rule Evid. 803(2)); see also Mich. Rule Evid. 803(2) (2010), are considered reliable because the declarant, in the excitement, presumably cannot form a falsehood. See *Idaho* v. *Wright*, 497 U.S. 805, 820, 110 S. Ct. 3139, 111 L. Ed. 2d 638 (1990) ("The basis for the "excited utterance" exception . . . is that such statements are given under circumstances that eliminate the possibility of fabrication, coaching, or confabulation . . .").

According to *Bryant* (2011), then, the reasoning behind the excited utterance exception that makes such an utterance admissible, namely that exciting circumstances "eliminate the possibility" of self-interested or coerced falsehood, is the same as the reasoning why statements made during an emergency are not testimonial and thus do not violate the confrontation clause. A statement made in the midst or wake of an emergency can be admissible as long as the speaker seems to still be suffering from it. *Bryant* (2011) thus explicitly aligns the testimonial/nontestimonial evaluation and confrontation clause case law with hearsay case law and the time-honored exceptions to hearsay that identify some speech as inherently reliable. Emergencies produce statements that don't need to be "subjected to the crucible of cross-examination." The implications of this claim, however, can divide a speaker from her own speech. The excited utterance exception, in particular, grants agency over speech production to the emergency, the exciting circumstances, which has the effect of dividing the speaker from her own accounts of her experiences (more on this in the case study on *US v. Hadley* (2002, 2005), which makes up the second half of this book).

While *Bryant* (2011) is willing to see that meaning is context dependent, its assertion that context can be "objectively identified" refuses to recognize the ways that meaning can be a) more than merely referential, and b) the ways that it is slippery, emerging in interaction rather than existing prior to interaction. That is, *Bryant* (2011) argues that statements are context-dependent within a language ideology that views the material world as stable and always prior to speech. The result is that the language that references such a stable world is itself treated as though it is stable, a very Lockean perspective. This perspective is mingled with social presupposition about women's speech, especially women who are reporting domestic violence. The result is that the paternal paradigm of the law recognizes the reliability of men's speech. What we see in both *Mattox* (1895) and *Bryant* (2011) is that the same reasoning that makes women's speech inadmissible makes men's speech admissible when it is applied to the public domain of male-on-male violence. To put it another way, law developed to manage the public domain historically concerned with male experience finds any excuse to not recognize the criminality of domestic violence. Indeed, it typifies and reifies domestic experience in ways that continue to misrecognize women's accounts of violence against their bodies.

Judicial Commentary on Domestic Violence

As I've discussed above, in the Supreme Court case law, the legal history this case law cites, and the briefs that support it and are referenced in the resultant opinions, we find presuppositions about domestic violence victims that are developed implicitly in evaluations of secondhand speech. Embedded in these cases, we also find very explicit, *ad hominem* discussions about victims of domestic violence, their trustworthiness, and the seriousness of the crime. Such overt discussions of victims of domestic violence directly are often deployed in arguments regarding the necessity of protecting legal principles over and above the needs of individual victims. We find a lot of this talk in both *Davis/Hammon* (2006) and *Giles* (2008). For example at the end of the *Davis/Hammon* (2006, 832–833) opinion, the Court takes the opportunity to comment on domestic violence directly:

> This particular type of crime [domestic violence] is notoriously susceptible to intimidation or coercion of the victim to ensure that she does not testify at trial. When this occurs, the Confrontation Clause gives the criminal a windfall. We may not, however, vitiate constitutional guarantees when they have the effect of allowing the guilty to go free.

This brief commentary on domestic violence doesn't seem to take the crime particularly seriously. The specifics of domestic violence aren't discussed beyond a passing commentary on the fact that victims are "notoriously" coercible. Moreover, the part the law has played in perpetuating domestic violence is completely absent. Indeed, the law is presented in the last sentence as the thing that must be protected over and above the victim. The constitutional guarantees must not be invalidated; the positivity of Anglo-American case law must not be shown to be ineffective. Further, this claim that explicitly undermines the position of the victim-witness is a part of this discourse with which hearsay is entextualized and reentextualized.

The rhetoric of this passage from *Davis/Hammon* (2006) interdiscursively echoes the ideas presented by Blackstone (1766), who condemned (certain forms of) domestic violence but would not go so far as so say that it is illegal because such a ruling isn't supported by either case law or social norm. Some 250 years later, Justice Thomas uses the at best agnostic perspective attributed to the Constitution's authors to exclude domestic violence complaints: "today's understanding of domestic abuse had no apparent significance at the time of the Framing, and there is no early example of the forfeiture rule operating in that circumstance" (concurring opinion in *Giles* 2008, 2695). From his so called "originalist" orientation to law, Thomas not too discreetly asserts the legal invalidity of domestic violence complaints within the context of the Constitution. The opinion in *Giles* (2008, 2693) explicitly states that domestic violence is a serious crime but ultimately protects the law over and above the victim:

> Is the suggestion that we should have one Confrontation Clause (the one the Framers adopted and *Crawford* described) for all other crimes, but a special, improvised, Confrontation Clause for those crimes that are frequently directed against women?

This somewhat sarcastic rhetorical question not only assumes that the consistency and maintenance of the rule of law is of supreme importance, but it also indexes domestic violence obliquely, avoiding the language of violence or the context of the home that worked to shield this specific violence from legal scrutiny and, indeed, that the law itself protected. ("We will not inflict upon society the greater evil of raising the curtain upon domestic privacy, to punish the lesser evil of trifling violence" [*State v. Rhodes*, 1868, qtd. in dissenting opinion in *Giles* 2008, 2704]). The sarcastic tone is dismissive of women's legal status and the ways the law has long harmed women. These explicit statements along with more presuppositional strategies discussed in detail here continue to facilitate the legal facticity of domestic violence, even as such presuppositions position the victim of domestic violence as an unreliable speaker. That is, the past legal approval of domestic violence continues to function interdiscursively in the texts and contexts that are used to rule on current cases, working to produce a speaker who is untrustworthy.

Another presupposition running through the cases analyzed here is about what it means to be a victim of domestic violence. This discourse creates a category of domestic violence victim that is stocked with stereotypical characteristics—for example, that she can't help herself, won't or can't leave, has been coerced or intimidated to the point that she cannot make good decisions, and is childlike. These arguments lump experiences together and pathologize the victim. We find a corollary to the argument by Carine Mardorossian (2002, 770) about rape that suggests that too often "victims [are] [. . .] cast as a uniform group of individuals driven by an emotional and incapacitating response to their own experience." Being a victim of violence is seen as a "psychologized inner state," a perspective that downplays that fact that such violence is an "external reality imposed on someone" (770). Such presuppositions run through legal and advocate discussions of domestic violence. We see this in the quote from *Davis/Hammon* (2006) above in which victims are described as "notoriously susceptible to [. . .] coercion." Similarly, in *Davis/Hammon* (2006), the amicus brief written and submitted by The National Network to End Domestic Violence, et al. (NNEDV) consistently describes the abused wife in terms that assume a reduced ability to respond appropriately to an abusive partner. "Domestic violence inexorably obstructs victims' efforts to escape abuse and achieve safety" (Amicus Brief, NNEDV, *Davis/Hammon* 2006, 5). The phrase "inexorably obstructs" presumes that the effects of domestic violence cause a (more or less) permanent state in the victim that she can't escape. Such claims problematically place the husband in a power position while the wife is in a position of object who is "subject to the control and coercion of the accused" (Amicus Brief, NNEDV, Davis/Hammon 2006, 3).

The focus on the victim as essentially controllable by an abusive partner pathologizes her (cf. Lamb 1999). The amicus brief argues that violence can "profoundly disable a person's ability to lead a normal life and can short-circuit their emotional and psychological functioning" (Amicus Brief, NNEDV, *Davis/Hammon* 2006, 12). Claims of short-circuited psychological functioning unequivocally allow the abuser agency in his abuse, while suggesting that the victim's agency is "inexorably" damaged. That is, the abusive husband is assumed to be a sovereign agent who is always framed as active, while the abused wife is situated as passive by virtue of having been abused. And, indeed, the idea that her psyche is short-circuited figures centrally in arguments that victims of domestic violence are unreliable witnesses. That is, legal and social presuppositions about domestic violence victims indexically link them to a set of ideas about the victim's ability to speak reliably and act appropriately. For example, in *US v. Hadley* (analyzed in detail in Chapters 4 and 5), PH, who spoke the hearsay in question, is described as being false by the prosecution and as willing to lie for her husband—essentially coerced—by the judge, and as a liar by the defense: "Well [PH] is coming in and lying. [. . .] Obviously her truthfulness is in question" (last day of sentencing, 54: lines 8–13). That is, both the defense's and the prosecution's arguments claim that PH's speech can't be believed.

When hearsay case law is deployed, domestic violence victim and legal witness are collapsed and along with them, the legal and social assumptions about truthfulness linked to each. Though it is not always or even mostly the case, there is an assumption operating in social and legal discourses that abused wives are willing to lie for their abusive husband. As a victim-witness, layers of arguments are brought together, which ultimately construct this speaker as essentially unreliable. Her hearsay is only admissible when it can be shown that her damaged, coerced psyche and self-interest have been bypassed in some way.

Intertextuality, Interdiscursivity, and Indexicality

As the foregoing analysis has shown, Anglo-American law is structured intertextually—it explicitly draws on rules, principles, and precedents that precede any given interaction. In a trial, such rules and precedents govern courtroom behavior and the admission of evidence, among other things. In an appellate opinion, they are used to make arguments about the law itself, ruling on the correctness of the prior court's interpretation of the law (cf. Scheppele 1990). All of these processes require sifting through a huge number of prior texts—previous cases, rulings, and rules—and using them to make arguments about the case at hand. The use of precedent, *stare decisis*, is one of the things that sets Common Law apart from other forms of law, most explicitly Continental or Canon Law. "*Stare decisis* demands that courts conform their decisions to decisions reached by previous courts" (Peters 1996, 2033). The arguments that animate and intertwine precedents present the resultant arguments as though they are a natural outcome of the accretion of legal texts. But in fact as Patricia Williams argues, *stare decisis* "filter[s] [. . .] certain types of systemic input" (Williams 1991, 7). Even with the guidance of precedent, there are various ways of interpreting prior opinions, a fact that is demonstrated in the consenting and dissenting opinions that are increasingly common in Supreme Court opinions. Sometimes justices will come to the same conclusion but via a different reasoning process and/or different set of prior texts, and at other times justices will use the same set of prior texts as the majority opinion, but they will draw a different conclusion for their aggregate argument. Texts are combined and recombined to draw legal conclusions, and the vast number of legal texts to choose from means that the arguments, although they may be based on precedent, are anything but obvious legal outcomes.

Legal outcomes aren't necessarily simple consequences of the correct interpretation of a textual accretion (case law, historical cases, briefs, legal text and treatises), but rather the law is what Foucault (1972, 38) would call a "discursive formation," or "a system of dispersion, [. . .] [of] objects, types of statements, concepts, or thematic choices." A discursive formation "determines a regularity proper to temporal processes; it presents the principle of articulation between a series of discursive events and other series of events, transformations, mutations, and processes" (1972, 74). That is, the relationship between events, processes, and discourses are organized and explained/explainable only as and within a discursive formation that relates the parts to each other and to the whole. A discursive fact is thus not a product of linguistic structure or grammatical and semantic function. Instead, it emerges as a part of a discursive formation. Thus, when analyzing a discursive fact, the question to ask is "how is it that one particular statement appeared rather than another" (Foucault 1972, 130). In the context of law, the question is important. It asks us to question positivity and precedent, asking, "of all of the possible texts that could be recombined to make this argument, why were these selected, and how did they come to form this particular intertextual statement?" That is, when analyzing legal intertextuality, as I have done here, we need to consider the sociocultural and linguistic goals and values that are animated in and through the precedents and echoed in legal discursive events.

Intertextuality is not simply backward looking; it anticipates future discursive events, which according to Bauman and Briggs (1990, 61) are made up of "performativity, text, and context" and any text or utterance "is tied to a number of speech events that precede and succeed it (past performances, readings of texts, negotiations, rehearsals, gossip, reports, critiques, challenges, subsequent performances, and the like)." That is, speech events, or discursive events, both index past events and anticipate future uses of the speech event; discursive events cannot be reduced to text alone, but will always include context and the cultural norms and values that impact the re/performance of a text.

Legal discourses like those analyzed here create texts with the purpose of making them citable in future legal discourses. This happens by intertwining layers of legal text archeologically, thereby maintaining the force and focus of particular legal texts (those that are indexed in the current textual process) while making each element available for reiteration in future cases. This process is interdiscursive as Silverstein imagines it, as is the resultant text. Interdiscursivity is underpinned by "indexical relationships between a stretch of discourse that is actually experienced in the here and now and some other discourse, or feature of discourse, to which the current discursive event indexically points" (Agha 2005, 2). Law works in just this way. Legal discourse proves itself correct by pointing back to other instances of law, which are combined to make an argument that also anticipates future uses of the same texts. Supreme Court precedents perform interdiscursivity explicitly, actively citing past cases, ruling on the present case at hand, and writing guidelines for how the opinion should be used in the future.

Legal texts are thus produced via intertextuality and interdiscursivity; multiple texts, representing different genres (legal briefs, higher court opinions, historical cases, legal treatises, and textbooks) are brought together with discourses from multiple social and institutional domains (legal principles, governmental goals, popular culture media such as movies, etc.) to entextualize law, from the trial case to the Supreme Court opinion. Intertextuality is a choice, at some level, in that the person who creates the legal text chooses which texts to reference. At other levels, however, intertextuality is a product of interdiscursivity, in which cultural discourses come together to point to particular textual choices in order to create and maintain alignments with social norms. This process creates indexes, or "linguistic forms that evoke and/or construct [. . .] what is sometimes called 'social meaning,' a concept that encompasses matters such as register (in the narrower sense of situational appropriateness), stance (certainty, authority, etc.), and social identity (class, ethnicity, interactional role, etc.)" (Johnstone, Andrus & Danielson 2006, 81). That is, a bit of language can point to or (re)constitute a set of socially meaningful identification points, and the two become more or less formally associated with each other. A particular accent, for example, may evoke a particular style of dress, ethnicity, gender, etc. The correlation between the style of dress and gender/ethnicity does not need to result from an overt performance of the feature, nor does the person for whom the index is socially meaningful need to be fully aware of the effect.

Early stages in which linguistic and social features become correlated often go fairly unnoticed by those engaged in the interactions in which they are meaningful. Silverstein (1992, 2001) refers to the early correlative stage of indexicality as "n-th-order indexical," which Johnstone, et al. (2006, 82) defines as "a feature whose use can be correlated with a sociodemographic identity (e.g., region or class) or a semantic function (e.g., number-marking)." Such correlations underpin social interaction, providing the patterns that can be used to more explicitly organize sociolinguistic meaning. In a typical social interaction, people can come to explicitly perform an indexical form to do social or identity work. In this legal setting, the indexes produced and reproduced in the law can be used to make legal sense of a bit of speech spoken in a completely different social situation by a person who isn't legally trained. Thus, in this situation, the "n-th-order indexical" is used to make arguments that correlate the social identity with a bit of speech in the process of entextualizing that speech into a legally recognizable text. The result is that the speaker is made intelligible at the same time that her speech is and that social values and expectations play an important role in the whole process. The process of entextualizing legal hearsay of a domestic violence victim thus productively feeds back into assumptions about victims while it entextualizes her speech in accordance with the historical legality and social legitimacy of wife abuse. The result is that ideas about women, ideas about domestic violence victims, and ideas about speech are correlated within a discourse about witnesses, victims, and testimonial speech, and that the women this indexical form points to are constituted as untrustworthy.

Conclusion

In US Supreme Court opinions we find a discussion of domestic violence that treats victims as a class of speaker who all have similar motivations and liabilities as witnesses that are rooted in their victimhood. The same discourses about domestic violence victims are used regardless of whether the hearsay is deemed admissible or inadmissible. When an utterance is inadmissible, it is because it is entextualized as purposefully uttered and intentional, what *Crawford* calls testimonial. When an utterance is determined to be admissible hearsay, it is because it is entextualized as spontaneous, not purposeful, what *Crawford* calls non-testimonial. Willful, testimonial speech is inadmissible, and accidental non-testimonial speech not attributed with the speaker's agency is admissible. Whether the utterance is included or excluded, the reasoning finds fault with the victim of domestic violence.

In *Davis/Hammon* (2006), *Giles* (2008) and the legal history and precedents that they cite, there is an intertextual network in which the victim of domestic violence is positioned in opposition to the rule of law, specifically the protections of hearsay. In some cases, the needs of the victim are argued as insignificant to the logic of common law. In other cases, the victim is positioned as a hindrance to the successful application of law and even to her own safety. Both arguments occur within a discussion of secondhand speech. That is, the metadiscursive hearsay rule and its exceptions (and primarily three of its exceptions: the deathbed utterance, the excited utterance [spontaneous declaration], and the present-sense impression) develop an intertextual double bind for domestic violence victims. *Davis/Hammon* and *Giles* both work out of a distinction between testimonial and non-testimonial speech that is developed in the 2004 Supreme Court opinion, *Crawford v. Washington*. By analyzing *Crawford,* the two post-*Crawford* opinions, *Davis/Hammon* and *Giles*, and the historical precedents that inform them, this chapter has argued that the speech of women who are constructed as absent witnesses is inadmissible, while the speech of women who are constructed as victims is admissible, sometimes against the express wishes of the speaker herself. This sub-set of opinions on the confrontation clause works in concert with a set of opinions about admissible hearsay that circumvent the victim to admit the out-of-court speech of women who either aren't willing or aren't called to testify (see Chapters 4 and 5). Taken together as a precedential body, these opinions create a double bind. When an utterance is inadmissible, it is because it is entextualized as purposefully uttered and intentional, what *Crawford* calls testimonial. When an utterance is admissible hearsay, it is because it is entextualized as spontaneous, not purposeful, what *Crawford* calls non-testimonial. Thus, the domestic violence victim is denied a purposeful speaking position within the law.

The fitting of old law to new contexts tends to still focus on the positivity of the law and ignore contextual issues such as the gender and power dimensions of domestic violence. As such, these issues are often elided, filtered out as inconsequential. Applying law, divided from context, ignores the ways that social discourses about gender find their way into courtrooms and sidesteps the very real bodies risked in legal discussions of domestic violence. Moreover, the application of common law filters out the ways in which the law has explicitly accounted for and entextualized violence against women's bodies and experiences in the historical development of the Anglo-American law of evidence, specifically in the development of the hearsay rule and its exceptions.

The discourse circulated in this case law produces one side of the double bind, the side in which legal principles are protected and supported by legal history. One result is a kind of legal victim-blaming that assumes that all victims can be witnesses, ignoring the complexities of intimate violence and the fact that victims are often not called as witnesses. We would hope and even expect that the discourse sensitive to the complexities of intimate violence found primarily in legal briefs and dissents would give a more positive view of women who have been the victims of domestic violence, but in fact these discourses emphasize victimhood and tend to pathologize and advocate for structures that bypass the victim altogether. Both assume that victims of domestic violence are recalcitrant and can't be trusted to show up in court, let alone make reliable and trustworthy statements if they do.

PART TWO

The Excited Utterance Exception in *US v. Hadley*

In order to fully understand the effects and effectiveness of the language ideology of hearsay and the excited utterance exception, we have to look at the kind of work they do in an actual trial. This section uses the trial *US v. Hadley* (2002–2003) and its appellate opinion (2005) as a case study to describe the application of the precedent and black-letter law and to understand the ramifications of the language ideology when it is used to evaluate an individual's real speech.

The original trial, *US v. Hadley,* was heard in the United States District Court for the Eastern District of Tennessee, where it was heard by a Chief District Judge. Because the offense in *Hadley*, felony possession of a gun, is a Federal felony, there was no state trial or appeal and the case heard in the Federal District Court was a jury trial. The jury in the trial found JH guilty. The decision was appealed to the Sixth Circuit of the US Court of Appeals in 2004 on the basis of the admission of PH's excited utterances in the testimony of Officer 1 and Officer 2. During the trial and again in the appeal, the defense argued that the only evidence that JH ever held a gun comes from PH's statements. Because those statements were admitted as excited utterances, they are evidence—evidence that is solid enough to lead to and affirm a conviction. I have chosen to work with *Hadley* because the appellate opinion came out just after *Crawford v. Washington* (2004), the Supreme Court opinion that changed the admissibility of other types of hearsay. Due to this timing, the appellate opinion goes painstakingly through the reasoning behind the hearsay ban and the admissibility of the excited utterance. It is also a case in which the speaker chose not to testify against her husband regarding domestic assault. As I explained in the introduction, the use of the excited utterance in cases of domestic violence is a relatively recent change, most prevalent in the last twenty years. The situation of domestic assault changes the relationship between the speaker, the utterance, and the event:

- The event of domestic violence takes place in a private rather than a public space;
- The speaker is the victim of the crime rather than a witness to an accident or crime;
- The speaker is not an anonymous bystander, but rather an intimate partner of the assailant;
- The speaker is available but chooses not to testify;
- The speaker disowns the excited utterance or claims that it is partly or entirely false.

Such changes make apparent the effects on discursive agency embedded in the rule. The effects on discursive agency have been embedded in the excited utterance over its history, but they become apparent and performative in cases such as *Hadley* in which the role of the speaker is complicated by the context of domestic violence. The potential for discursive agency is visibly altered in situations when the court uses an utterance when a speaker does not to testify and even more if they have explicitly chosen not to testify, as is the case in *Hadley*. I also focus on *Hadley* because as Figure 4 shows, it is integrally connected in the web of excited utterance case law produced between 2005 and the present.

Figure 4 illustrates just how web-like legal citation is. When a case is used as a precedent, the cases used as precedents in that case are also cited implicitly and sometimes explicitly, thereby strengthening the chain of citation that links the current excited utterance to the "firmly rooted" history of the rule. The Supreme Court cases listed in the figure 4 are also the most cited Supreme Court cases in the US Court of Appeals on the issue of an admitted excited utterance. *Hadley* is a central case in this web of citation. It cites all of the key Supreme Court cases, as well as many from the Court of Appeals, and it is cited by cases that follow it. Again, due to its timing with regard to Supreme Court opinions, *Hadley* also provides a thorough reading of these cases and an extended argument rationalizing the decision of the court.

According to court record, the events in *Hadley* go like this: In May of 2002, PH and JH had some friends and family over for a cookout. Around midnight, the couple began fighting and went into their bedroom. The fight escalated, which involved JH holding a gun to the head of his wife. After being told to wait by JH's brother and another male friend, a female friend of PH's called 911. Another anonymous person called within a few moments asking the police to "hurry up." The 911 dispatcher advised police officers of a "domestic disturbance with a gun" and classified it as "Priority 1." The 911 operator also kept an "open line" and the operator "could hear the incident

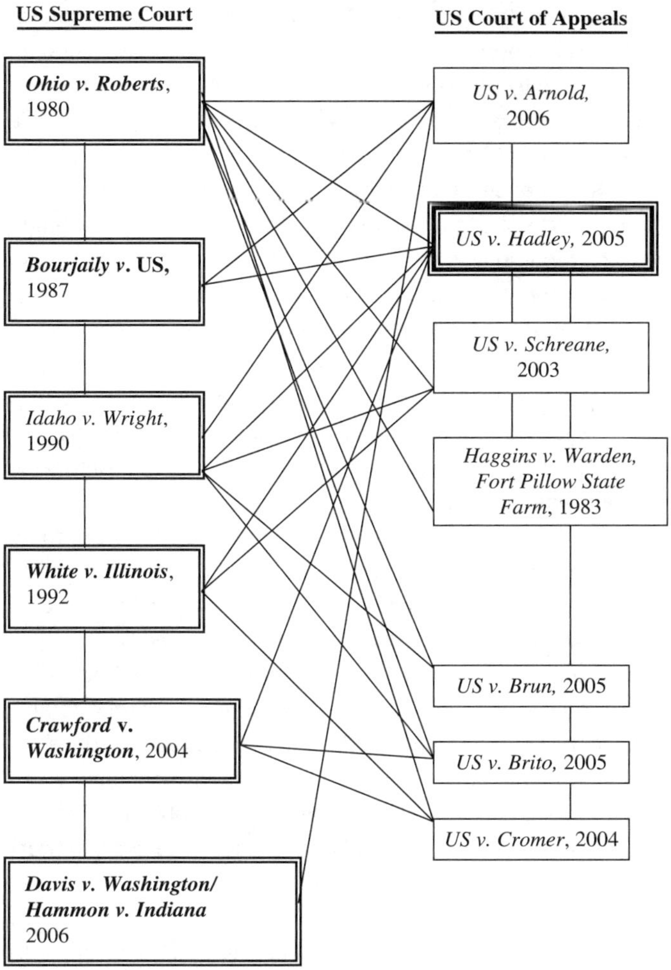

Note: The opinions included in this figure have been cited three or more times in *Hadley* (2005). Lines indicate citation. A line linking Supreme Court cases to US Court of Appeals cases means that the Supreme Court case was cited by the case in the lower court. *Schreane* and *Haggins* are used together to discuss the excited utterance, and *Cromer*, *Brun*, and *Brito* are used together to explain *Crawford* in order to determine whether the utterances in *Hadley* were testimonial.

FIGURE 4 Intertextuality in *US v. Hadley*(2005).

in progress over the telephone" (Officer 1, 2002: 6). Two police officers arrived at the home of the PH and JH within two minutes of the first call to 911. Officer 1 arrived first, followed closely by Officer 2. Officer 2 testified that when they pulled up, PH ran out of the house to the police, "hysterical" and "in a state of panic." She made comments to them that she was afraid of her husband and that he had a gun. Officer 2 also recalled her saying that "he put a gun up to her head." Officer 1 testified that PH ran out of the house and immediately said "[H]e has a gun" and "he's going to kill me." The police were responding to an assault in progress (Officer 1, 2002: 20), and indeed the initial charges that were brought against JH were for aggravated assault. In Officer 1's words, "I initially arrested [JH] for the assault that occurred on [PH]. [. . .] The firearm was in addition to the assault itself, because she told me it was used in the assault" (Officer 1, 2002: 23). As I will discuss in the following analysis, the utterance that becomes the key excited utterance in both the trial and the appeal was the excited utterance given in the testimony of Officer 1. Officer 2's testimony is far more narrative, fleshing out the scene of the domestic dispute. Her more narrative version of PH's statements is brought in line with the excited utterance given in Officer 1's testimony during direct examination.

PH was not called to testify during the trial on the charges of felony possession of a gun. She had testified during the hearing for the original assault charges, and she was asked to take the stand during the sentencing procedures, where she was only willing to comment on the testimony she had given during the original hearing concerning the assault. It is important to note that the charges she was willing to testify about, aggravated domestic assault (domestic assault in which a gun was an aggravating factor), were dropped after only a few days, even with her first-person testimony. The charges JH was convicted on involved felony possession of a gun. The conviction was based on the excited utterance about a gun attributed to her in the secondhand testimony of the police officers. The excited utterance used in the trial contained the same information given in PH's testimony regarding the charges of aggravated assault. However, her subjective (agented) account given in testimony was ineffective and those charges were dropped. When she was a non-agent reporting an exciting event in an excited state, her statements led to a felony conviction.

Because the only evidence that JH had a gun is PH's excited utterance, the status of the utterance is the foundation for the arguments built by both the attorneys for the government and the attorneys for the defense. The defense spends a great deal of time establishing the lack of actual proof linking JH to the gun that night, filing a motion for dismissal based on the fact there was no in-court testimony by somebody who had actually *seen* the gun in JH's possession. However, the excited utterance is stronger evidence than PH's testimony would have been, because with it, a direct link is established between the event in which PH saw the gun in JH's possession and the utterance made in an excited state. As it is constructed in the language ideology of the rule, the excited utterance represents first-hand knowledge of sensory experience. The language ideology that trusts language that indexes the original event is embedded in the discourse of the excited utterance that is used to deem such an utterance inherently trustworthy. Thus the fact that PH's sensory knowledge puts the gun in JH's possession is all that is needed as evidence as long as the utterance that reports the knowledge is an excited utterance. As the attorney for the government, Prosecution 2 (2002: 140) explains: “The whole reason that [utterance] is admissible is because – as an excited utterance as an exception to the hearsay rule is because it carries guarantees of truthfulness and reliability because of the circumstances surrounding the giving of the statement.” However, these are the rules that the law operates under, not those that speakers in interaction operate under. When PH ran out of her house to speak with police, her utterances were not about the law; they were about her husband and her relationship with him that night, in the past, and in the future.

4

Making the Excited Utterance Legally Intelligible: Shifting Audiences, Contexts, and Speakers

> "There are obvious differences between texts and events, but these differences are minimized in trials. In the courtroom, we don't have the event before us, but instead we have verbal accounts of events (whether orally or in writing) or sometimes trace evidence from which inferences may be drawn. . . . At a trial, actions and harms are converted into accounts and claims. Events are made into texts." Kim Lane Scheppele (1990, 44)

The events that cause a victim or witness to call the police and those that lead up to an arrest after police arrive on the scene are only available in a courtroom context as texts: statements to police, police reports, testimony during trial, and the like. As Kim Lane Scheppele (1990, 44) explains, legal processes and discourses work to minimize the "obvious differences between texts and events." As early Anglo-American legal scholars such as Starkie, Greenleaf, and Wigmore noted, events are always in the past of the legal proceeding, and as such, they are only available via testimony—linguistic accounts of what happened. Accounts of what happened are at the center of any legal proceeding. And as Bauman and Briggs (1990, 61) argue, an event doesn't erupt as a fully formed "single, bounded social interaction" that can be easily captured and represented as a narrative. Interaction is bounded as a discursive event when it is narrated in a sort of after-the-fact process, like a trial, during which the interaction is plucked out of ongoing discourse and labeled a text, or "entextualized." The process of giving an account of what happened, which often includes repeating previously spoken utterances, "entextualizes" evidence (cf. Bauman and Briggs 1990; Silverstein and Urban 1996). "Entextualization" occurs when a bit of discourse is extracted from ongoing discourse when it is appropriated by or made useful in a new context; such "recontextualization" renders the bit of discourse as a discrete "text-artifact" (Silverstein and Urban

1996). Forming the text outlines the boundaries of the event of which it gives an account. "[Entextualization] is the process of rendering discourse extractable, or making a stretch of linguistic production into a unit—a *text*—that can be lifted out of its interactional setting" (Bauman and Briggs 1990, 73). That is, when something is entextualized, the resultant text-artifact and its meaning are made to seem independent of the stretch of ongoing interaction in which it was produced. The now decontextualized text can be easily moved into new interactional settings and contexts with clearly demarcated boundaries. Entextualization decontextualizes a text thereby making it available for use in future contexts, future discursive events.

The law practically runs on this process of recontextualizing, thereby entextualizating bits of discourse (fragments of context, text, and performance) as Bauman and Briggs (1990) describe it, forming evidence and making it available for future legal use. Any event that is brought into the courtroom is brought in through language—or in the case of photographs and physical evidence, they are identified, explained, and linked to the case with language. Evidence that doesn't fit into an explanatory narrative is speculative, merely circumstantial. This process of recontextualization "render[s] diverse realms of cultural experience in a common language" Mertz (1998: 149) argues, that "[T]he act of translation into legal language is one in which linguistic and social regimentation mesh." This process pulls social interactions, stocked with myriad layers of presupposition and norm, into a legally recognizable text. In translating an event into a crime, the criminal event is bounded with identifiable beginning and end points within which evidence can be located, cataloged, and used in legal proceedings. The legal text/context minimizes, or in many cases obscures, its own involvement in the production of the event cum text (cf. Scheppele 1990) in part with the help of the Enlightenment-based empirical language ideology that underpins modern Anglo-American common law (see Chapter 1). The empiricist language ideology that hearsay law circulates and maintains presupposes that events are fully formed and stable and thus precede both language and the law.

In a legal context, events, descriptions of objects and individuals, explanations of actions, etc., are entextualized when discourse from a prior event is recontextualized during the trial in testimony. Entextualization is not natural or neutral, but rather it is guided and constrained by the discourses circulating in the recontextualizing context. In the trial, the rules of evidence, courtroom protocols, and I argue, language ideology give shape to the entextualized account as it emerges via trial interaction. For example, through direct- and cross-examination, inconsistencies between accounts are obscured and some aspects are foregrounded while others are backgrounded (Matoesian 2000). Trials also impact prior speech, "decontextualiz[ing] speech from one speech event and recontextualiz[ing] it in a new one" (Matoesian 2000, 879). The appellate process "magnifie[s]" the entextualization process (Scheppele 1990, 44), or as Ehrlich (2007) argues, works to re-entextualize the account, making it available as a part of case law (Andrus 2011). Importantly, as Ehrlich (2007) argues, institutional processes of recontextualization at the trial and appeal levels don't only affect the resultant text, but the recontextualization and re-entextualization that takes place in a trial also constitutes the identities of participants. That is, the co-processes of entextualization and recontextualization also determine the role and identity of the speaker, making speaker subjectivity a product of the process of entextualizing evidence. Indeed, speaker roles are entextualized as a part of the resultant utterance, traveling with the text as it is recontextualized in future legal contexts.

Because it is speech that both gives an account of an event and is recontextualized during the trial as evidence, the excited utterance gives insight into the process and effects of legal entextualization. The ways in which a text is made to function like an event are highlighted in the entextualization of an excited utterance. By positing the trial as the moment of entextualization, rather than some prior interaction[1], we also gain insight into the language ideology of the excited utterance exception to hearsay and the relationship between the legal entity "excited utterance" and the "original utterance," made in a prior context that the excited utterance is said to repeat. That is, a bit of reported speech is entextualized as original speech and attributed to an absent speaker.

By taking the trial as the moment of legal entextualization, the moment when the excited utterance becomes a legal text-artifact, I identify and comment on the relationship between the two utterances and the quite different interactional spaces in which each is produced. The legal language ideology that is embedded in the excited utterance exception to hearsay has multiple interrelated affects: 1) it manages the relationship between events and accounts of events; 2) it provides the discursive resources that produce textual accounts; 3) it rationalizes the processes of entextualizing reported speech such that the legal process of repetition is seen as invisible or ineffectual; 4) it allows the excited utterance to function as surrogate events in court, by diminishing the distinctions between events and texts; and 5) it creates an indexical link between the text and the subjectivity associated with the text that is also decontextualized, making it applicable to future speakers and utterances.

The language ideology of the hearsay rule, reiterated in the excited utterance exception to hearsay, presupposes that spontaneously produced speech is objective—not originating from the subjectivity of the speaker. This idea produces the excited utterance, which is treated as though it is formally, pragmatically, rhetorically, and semantically the same as the original utterance, spoken by the person who is not in the courtroom, often many months before the trial interaction even takes place. That is, because it was not produced subjectively, it remains functionally the same no matter who says it or in what interactional space. This presupposition is highly effectual, in that it strips away the interactional effects of context and speaker roles (police encounters, interviews with attorneys) through which the utterance passes and those in which it is ultimately entextualized (the courtroom).

The subjectivity of the speaker to whom the excited utterance is attributed is also established in the process of entextualizing the excited utterance. The language ideology of the excited utterance presumes an utterance that is not the product of the speaker's reflective faculties. As such, it treats the speaker as a conduit for the trustworthy excited utterance. The metadiscourses that are used to entextualize an excited utterance thus impact the legal intelligibility of the speaker. Judith Butler (1990, 23) calls such discourses "norms of cultural intelligibility," which "institute and maintain coherence and continuity." Ideas about language are articulated with social and institutional assumptions about truth and authority, where they work together to make language, interaction, and participants meaningful. The process of "entextualization both reflects and constitutes asymmetrical social relations" (Silverstein and Urban 1996, 4). That is, the same discourses that recontextualize a bit of discourse thereby creating a text-artifact, also (re)produce social relations, making the speaker associated with an excited utterance legally recognizable.

In the trial and appellate opinion of *US v. Hadley* (trial, 2002; appeal, 2005), we can see both entextualization of evidence and the ways in which this process impacts the speaker and her relationship to her utterance and by extension, her story. *US v. Hadley* (2002) entextualized and admitted the excited utterance "He has a gun! He's going to kill me!" as the primary evidence in the trial. In *Hadley* (2002), this excited utterance was initially established in the testimony of the two police officers who gave testimony. The trial court admitted the utterance as an excited utterance, over the hearsay objections of the defense. PH did take the stand during JH's sentencing, but even when she was asked to, she refused to repeat the statement in court and to accept the excited utterance as something she had said. The language ideology developed historically and reproduced intertextually in case law is used in trial to entextualize an utterance as an excited utterance, granting it a status as artifact and making it function as an account of an event that is referentially true in and of itself. Such an utterance is delinked from the actual speaker and interactional context and linked instead to a simplified, legally intelligible speaker role. Legal metadiscourses are self-fulfilling in that they don't simply go into an event and locate evidence, perhaps especially spoken evidence such as an excited utterance. Evidence is not a natural state; it is not simply laying around an event as evidence merely waiting for that status to be recognized by a court of law. Rather, as Peter Brooks and others have argued, evidence is a product of legal discursive processes. The excited utterance is a type of spoken evidence that is entextualized as evidence. As speech, the process of entextualization necessarily impacts, even constitutes, the role with which the speaker of the excited utterance will be recognizable. The speaker role, which in this case of domestic violence analyzed here is "victim," becomes a feature of the utterance once it has been entextualized as an excited utterance.

Entextualizating the Excited Utterance in Trial

Like any legal process, admitting an excited utterance is not a neutral fact-finding process, but rather it is one in which the process recontextualizes speech in a legal setting thereby constituting, via entextualization, a form of evidence called the excited utterance. In fact, it is analytically useful to think about two utterances, the original utterance, spoken long before the trial, and the excited utterance, entextualized during the trial. On their own, texts "are relatively empty of meaning: they are invested with meaning 'as part and parcel of the shaping and reshaping of social and political practices'" (Ehrlich, 2007, 468, quoting McConnell-Ginet). The social interactions that result in the original utterance are different than the institutional contexts through which the excited utterance is entextualized. Indeed, according to Silverstein and Urban, not only are texts open to reiteration and reuse that will necessarily change the text pragmatically and semantically, there is nothing natural about the parameters of the text itself. They argue that a "text-artifact" is formed, or "entextualized," when it is pulled "from its infinitely rich, exquisitely detailed context," and isolated and named a text within another context (Silverstein and Urban 1996, 1). Entextualization is thus a product of recontextualization, a metadiscursive process that involves the uptake of a moment of discourse in new texts and contexts, which often occurs in the process of identifying a text as such, and considering and commenting on its "meaning and structure." During the process of "enquiring into its structure and meaning" (Silverstein and Urban 1996, 1), the depth and richness of the ongoing discourse is truncated—taken out of the context that it was in (whether or not that context was "original" in some sense), inserted into a new set of contexts—and bounded as a text-artifact. The contexts used to evaluate and comment on the content, structure, context, correctness, rhetorical adequacy, etc. of the discourse entextualize it as a text with an apparently stable meaning and discrete referential content, with a beginning and end.

When it is formed, a text is "despatialized" and "detemporalized" and thus available for transmission "across social boundaries" (Silverstein and Urban 1996, 1). As such, a text seems "durable" and mobile; it is available for use in different contexts; it is "transmittable" (Urban 1996, 21). The utterance entextualized as an excited utterance can be moved from speaker to speaker, from context to context, and from speech to writing within a language ideology that assumes that such movement has no effect on the referential and non-referential value of the utterance. "[Entextualization] is the process of rendering discourse extractable, or making a stretch of linguistic production into a unit—a *text*—that can be lifted out of its interactional setting" (Bauman and Briggs 1990, 73). That is, when something is entextualized, the resultant "text-artifact" (Silverstein and Urban, 1996) and its meaning are made to seem independent of the stretch of ongoing interaction in which it was produced.

The now decontextualized text can be easily moved into new interactional settings and contexts with clearly demarcated boundaries. To put it another way, entextualization decontextualizes a text, thereby making it available for use in future contexts, future discursive events. Indeed, "the decontextualization from one social context involves recontextualization in another" (Bauman and Briggs, 1990, 74). That is, the process of decontextualization necessarily involves another context, the one into which the newly formed text is pulled, and which provides the vocabulary and other discursive resources used to call attention to some aspect of the interaction as text and other aspects as context and labeling features of the text (cf. Silverstein and Urban, 1996). And of course, the resultant text will carry with it some elements from its prior context(s) and some elements from the recontextualizing context. The result is a text that indexes any number of contexts, but not all at the same time, and not all in every interaction for every speaker. The possible number of contexts creates semiotic variability.

The excited utterance is narrative—it is about something that happened—which adds a layer of contextual complexity. Not only is an utterance recontextualized in a context that renders it a text, the utterance is itself an account of a prior situation, which means that recontextualization not only impacts texts but contexts. Thus the process that bounds and labels the excited utterance also determines the beginning and end of the context indexed by the utterance. Contexts and texts are produced in the same process: the constitution of a text also constitutes the contexts to which it is linked (after the fact) (Andrus 2011). Per Linell (1998, 144) explains that "any discourse or text is embedded in a matrix of contexts made up from an array of different contextual resources: prior discourse, concrete physical environments, people (and assumptions about people) with their interpersonal relations, various kinds of background knowledge, situation definitions (frames), models of topics talked about, etc." Context is irreducible to any single aspect of interaction, nor is it analytically prior or supplemental to text. Context is not "the scenery to which language and interactive structures are related once they have been 'objectively' defined on other grounds, linguistic or sociological" (Hanks 1996, 196). That is, the relationship between text and context is not unidirectional. A text doesn't enter a context (whether it emerged in that context or was moved there by a speaker or some other medium) after both text and context are fully formed. Texts and contexts are co-produced in an ongoing process of entextualization and recontextualization.

The excited utterance is in a complex relationship that creates and sometimes obscures linkages between multiple texts and contexts.

- Context A—The Trial: The excited utterance is entextualized in the trial context, where it is elicited from a police officer during cross-examination. This context comes stocked with language ideology, values, goals, technical vocabulary, and specialized definitions not necessarily shared with the accused or the victims and witnesses.

- Context B—Speaking to a third party: The excited utterance is blurted to someone—in the case analyzed here, police officers—and it is about something that happened recently and deeply affected the speaker.
- Context C—The thing that happened: The moment in which JH holds a gun to the head of PH. The excited utterance is about this context, which overlaps with the interaction in Context B, but is not identical to it.

The utterance spoken in Context B is about Context C. It only becomes an isolated, distinct "text" called an excited utterance when it is elicited in Context A, the trial. In *Hadley* (November 2002, 8), the excited utterance is elicited and entextualized during the direct-examination of Officer 1 by the prosecution:

Q: How long did it take you to get there?
A: Probably a couple of minutes.
Q: When you say "a couple," you mean two, or ten?
A: Probably two minutes.
Q: What happened when you arrived?
A: As I arrived on the scene and got out of my patrol car, I observed [PH] running from the front door. Seemed to be in a state of panic. And at that—
Q: Why do you say that?
A: She was crying, very upset, shaking, just really didn't have any control of her emotions at that time.
Q: Okay. What happened next?
A: At that time she was yelling something—
DEFENSE 1: Objection, Your Honor. Hearsay.
THE COURT: Overruled.
A: At that time she was yelling to me and another officer that "He has a gun."
DEFENSE 1: Objection. Hearsay again.
A: And said, "He's going to kill me."
THE COURT: What's the objection?
DEFENSE: He's basically stating that she was yelling that "He has a gun." And that is hearsay, Your Honor. He's basically stating what somebody else is stating in this case, Your Honor.
THE COURT: [Prosecutor 2]?
[PROSECUTOR 2]: Judge, we are offering it as an excited utterance.
THE COURT: Okay. [Defense 1], the government argues that these statements are admissible pursuant to Federal Rules of Evidence, Rule 803(2).

[PROSECUTOR 2]: Yes, Your Honor. But I believe at that time—I mean, it's basically more of a statement. She was coming out of the house, is what the testimony is. I don't think the incident was going on at that time. Therefore I don't think it falls into the scope of excited utterance.

THE COURT: Objection is overruled.

Q: I'm sorry, [Officer 1]. What did she say as she came out of the house?

A: She stated to me that "He has a gun," and she said, "He was going to kill me."

In this exchange, the questions are constrained and enabled by the requirements of the excited utterance case law and definitions, which are presupposed in the questions directing Officer 1 to be specific about the time that begins the lead-up to the elicitation of the excited utterance. There are also questions that get at the location of PH when the police arrived, who spoke first, and the emotional state of the speaker, all of which are requirements of the exception. These questions are underpinned by the language ideology of the excited utterance, which presupposes that the blurted, spontaneous speech of a hysterical speaker spoken soon after the event in question and not in response to police interrogation is an excited utterance and thus admissible hearsay.

Beyond the discourse specific to hearsay law, a trial excerpt shows the ways that the trial context itself shapes the resultant text (cf. Gewirtz 1996). The attorneys ask questions that witnesses must answer. The questions request information that will establish (and challenge) the "facts" and chronology of events, and create a narrative that puts the facts in relationship for the jury's consideration (Bruner, 1991). Attorney-led questions also establish a way of talking about the facts using a legal vocabulary that constrains the potential answers (cf. Conley et al., 1979; Ehrlich 2001; Erlich and Sidnell 2006). Officer 1 is directed to recount events in a particular order, using a legal vocabulary rather than a lay one.

In this way, the legal discourses, circulating in the trial context (Context A) give a particular legally useful meaning to the utterance blurted in the interaction with police (Context B), which is about the domestic assault that has just occurred (Context C). The utterance is pulled out of Context B and recontextualized in Context A as the text-artifact—called an excited utterance—that is about Context C. Once that text is formed in Context A, the shape and dimensions of Context C are also made legally intelligible. Further, this process makes the participant roles involved in entextualizing the excited utterance legally intelligible, perhaps nobody more so than the speaker to whom the utterance is attributed, PH.

In the legal discourse with which an excited utterance is formed, the process of forming the text/context relationship strips away details of context and participant roles presumed to have no legal relevance. This process is facilitated and in many ways obscured by the special role of circumstances established in US Supreme

Court opinions concerning admissible hearsay. In recent opinions such as *Crawford v. Washington* (2004), *Davis v. Washington/Hammon v. Indiana* (2006), and *Michigan v. Bryant* (2011), circumstances are granted a status of objectivity, which is stable. Indeed, it is argued that circumstances objectively indicate what an utterance means and what its pragmatic goals are. Such discourses call attention to particular aspects of the context of interaction while ignoring others within a discourse that explicitly argues that contexts are objective—that is tangible, stable, and durable. Yet these contexts are only available in court record as entextualized accounts produced within the constraints of Anglo-American jurisprudence. The excited utterance is thus produced within a discourse that trusts non-linguistic, objective events that are only available to the court as linguistic accounts. Because linguistic accounts are untrustworthy, they can only be admitted without cross-examination, as with the excited utterance, if the entextualization process makes the resultant utterance seem as objective as the event that it reports. This process thus circumvents the speaker as it diminishes the value of any aspect of the context of interaction that might disrupt the apparent stability of the excited utterance.

Participant Roles: Who Speaks and to Whom

As hearsay, the excited utterance is repeated in multiple contexts and by multiple speakers and contexts. Participants behave according to the implicit and explicit constraints of the context of the interaction. Both participant roles and contexts impact the resultant text in important ways. The interaction between a police officer and a victim is suffused with expectations of police officer and victim roles as well as the urgency of the situation. A potential excited utterance is blurted out in this context, but the excited utterance is entextualized as legally recognizable evidence when it is recontextualized in the trial context. In the trial, prior legal discourses are operationalized in face-to-face interaction, in which "participants' understandings of social identities and categories" are also at work (Ehrlich 2007, 455). That is, legal metadiscourses are co-articulated with the "norms of intelligibility" that the judge, jury, and attorneys necessarily use to make sense of the interaction. "Judges and other legally trained officials use their legal knowledge to orient their narratives" as well as their social knowledge (Scheppele 1990, 63). Thus, the highly authorized members of the court, who are the addressees of the excited utterance when it is offered in court in the testimony of the police officers, are not passive; this group actively processes the utterance and the context in which it was produced as it is entextualized as the excited utterance. Susan Philips' (1998) work regarding judicial politics shows that judicial reasoning is permeated by the ideology of the judge, because judicial reasoning is a product of the cultural norms and expectations that serve as prior texts for the judge and jury. Figure 5 illustrates the range of contexts that converged when the police interacted with

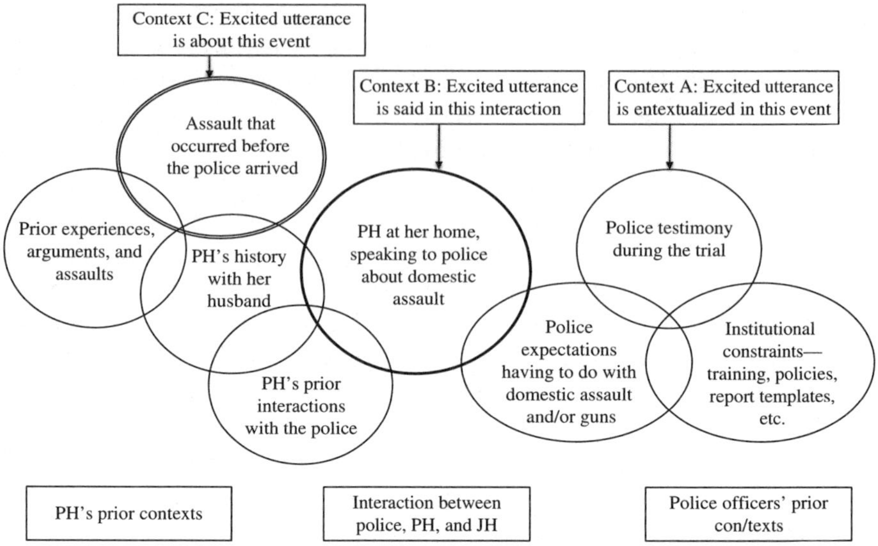

FIGURE 5 Prior Texts and Contexts and Entextualizing the Excited Utterance in *US v. Hadley* (2002).

PH on the front lawn of her home, minutes after a domestic assault, and the overlapping interconnection between texts and contexts.

INTERACTIONS WITH POLICE OFFICERS

We only have access to the interaction between police and PH as it is entextualized in the trial transcript. The police interact with PH in Context B, during a discussion of Context C. The police then give testimony in Context A (see Figure 5). The police and the texts and contexts they bring with them to the interaction thus play a pivotal mediating role in the recontextualization of an utterance as the excited utterance. With an excited utterance, the addressee in one situation is the speaker in the next. The police officer auditor who is not a speaker in Context B becomes a speaker in Context A. The court never hears PH speak the utterance. Importantly, the utterance that is transcribed and will be cited and attributed to PH as a direct quote in future legal documents is never spoken by her, but is in fact spoken by Officer 1. Further, the role the officer inhabited when he was the auditor in Context B or the effect that role inhabitance might have on the statement produced in Contexts A and B are apparently considered to be neutral, having no effect on the utterance that will be entextualized as the excited utterance in Officer 1's testimony. Finally, the role of the police officer is assumed transparent, leaving no rhetorical trace on the utterance. The police are represented as passive; they merely arrived and heard the spontaneous exclamation of a hysterical woman, which they repeat. By ignoring the role of the police officer in the initial interaction and in the in-court interaction, the law is able to ignore the differences between the original utterance, produced for a very real audience—the police—and the excited utterance, also produced for a very real audience—the courtroom.

Whether or not they asked questions or explicitly interrogated a witness or suspect, it is impossible to imagine a scenario in which the police presence itself would not impact their interactions. As a culture, we are inundated with discourses that conflate police force and police valor in television programming such as the incredibly popular *CSI* series, the long-running reality show *COPS*, and the news media generally. As the person on the ground who arrives—in blue suit, with badge, gun, and over-filled belt—the police officer strikes a figure of authority loaded with assumptions about what he or she is on the scene to do (cf. Lewis 1992). As Bonnie McElhinny explains, "appearances embody and reinscribe notions about who police officers are and what they do" (McElhinny 1995, 239). The police officer embodies authority and discipline, and the potential for arrest always accompanies them. "The weapon, the uniform, all of these trappings make the police look invincible" (Lewis, 1993: 3). The police officers themselves also recognize their institutional authority. In her work on police officers and gender, McElhinny quotes one female police officer as saying "'it's never just a fight between a man and a woman—it's a fight between a man and a police officer'" (McElhinny, 222). This comment implies that the officer understands their role in terms of institutional authority and their ability to gain control in a situation even when they may not have comparable physical strength (cf. Susan Martin, 1999).

In a situation of domestic violence to which the police are called, the reaction of the participants is informed by the prior texts that authorize police action and other texts, for example regarding gender. McElhinny argues that in responding to police, victims respond to both the police and to "the person inside the police uniform" (231). In her fieldwork in which she went on "ride-alongs" with police who responded to domestic violence calls, she recounts that victims interacted with the male officers differently than female officers. When the officer was female, the victim wanted affirmation that she had been wronged by the abuse; when the officer was male, the abused woman wanted him to say that he would never hit his girlfriend. When she was with male officers, the victim wanted female affirmation from McElhinny herself. Thus, in interacting with police, speakers recognized and responded to multiple layers of institutionally and culturally inscribed discourses, in terms of both gender and policing.

Like the women in McElhinny's ethnography, PH responded to the police as police; that is, she spoke to them fully aware that they were there to and could help her. According to the testimony of Officer 1 and Officer 2, when she saw them arrive, she ran out to them to request assistance and to get help, responding to them from her position in the assault—victim. Her statements to the police were necessarily influenced by her participation in the events, and the way she understood the role of the police officers who had been called to her house. That is to say that the utterances she initially spoke to police were not simply or neutrally referential (an account of the event), but they drew on prior expectations and texts, and were contingent on the situation at hand and the needs and goals of the speaker.

The officers' accounts of events also reveal interactional contingency that is based on prior interactions and expectations. The two officers who responded to the 911 call and who gave testimony about the events of the evening each related to PH[2] differently, revealing that the police officers were not merely the auditors of the excited utterance, but people who heard and responded to PH and the things she said from institutional and personal standpoints. When he recounted the events of the evening in his testimony, Officer 1 tended to focus on the gun—he only discussed the issue of domestic violence when he was pressed to in cross-examination by the attorney for the defense. He gave answers to questions using short answers that focused on the "facts" and positioned him as a person outside of the scene he was observing and trying to control, but of which he was not a part. For example, "PH seemed to be in a state of panic" (Officer 1, November 2002: 7) is merely descriptive, and "Based on what PH had told us, we believed the weapon to be in a dresser drawer." (November 2002: 11) positions PH as the person with knowledge who is speaking to silent officers. In his testimony, Officer 1 positioned himself as a spectator, a person outside of the scene that he is observing and trying to control. In offering the excited utterance, given above, he used a quotative style that maintains him as an outsider who was spoken to: "she stated to me that 'he had a gun,' and she said, 'He was going to kill me'" (Officer 1, November 2002: 8). Though this was not the only (para)phrasing of the "original utterance," it is no surprise that the excited utterance offered here was the excited utterance reiterated over the course of the trial, in the appeal, and when the appeal was cited by later cases, because it explicitly uses a quotative style that keeps the focus on the empirical details, original speaker, and original context.

Officer 2's testimony is noticeably different from Officer 1's, although, as we will see, the differences between the two are not accounted for in the appellate opinion. Most of Officer 2's account of the event focused on the domestic context and the assault on PH. When asked to continue with her testimony, Officer 2 narrated her initial encounter with PH, giving more detail about the interaction than Officer 1 had.

> Basically—It was hard to get anything out of her. Like I said, she was hysterical. She was weeping, and, you know, I was doing my best to try to get her to talk. And basically she kept talking about a gun, how he put a gun up to her head, and how he was going to kill her. (Officer 2, November 2002: 30)

Compare this to Officer 1's version of the excited utterance (discussed above). As it was narrated by Officer 2, the initial interaction between police and PH was far more dialogic and contextually situated. The event in this account was not a situation in which a single utterance about a gun was blurted out. Officer 2 narrates a discursive event—an event that took place in contextually dependent dialogue. She doesn't merely reiterate a statement, but gives a representation of interaction between PH and herself. In so doing, Officer 2's account makes PH's reaction to the violence the focal point of the event (". . . she was hysterical. She was weeping, and, you know, I was doing my best to try to get her to talk."), and situates the gun as a feature but not focal point of the scene. In other words, the context narrated by Officer 2 involved a gun, but it does not revolve around the gun; it revolves around PH's reaction to assault. The information about the gun that Officer 1 focused on is given toward the end of Officer 2's narrative, after she has established the scene of interaction, including dialogue between the police and PH: "So basically I was, like, pleading with her, 'Look, I'm going with you. I'm—You know, I will be there. I will be in between you. You know, there is nothing he can do to you'" (Officer 2, November 2002: 33). In her retelling of the event, she appears to understand herself as an active participant in the interactional context, and she sees PH's central concern as a structure of violence.

Officer 1's testimony is used by the attorney for the government, Prosecutor 1, to interrupt and refocus Officer 2's testimony on the issue of the gun (November 2002: 32).

> Q: I want to back up just for a minute. You stated earlier—testified earlier about PH running out of the house and stating to you, or yelling to you, "He has a gun. He's going to kill me."
>
> A: Yes, ma'am.

Importantly, Officer 2 did not make those statements, Officer 1 did. As I quoted above, Officer 2 gave an account of the things PH "talked about." From one perspective, it may seem like the meaning packaged in both statements is the same, and perhaps that is what led Officer 2 to reply in the affirmative. However, the two ways of linking JH to the gun presuppose different ways of contextualizing the utterance: one in which the primary event is domestic violence and the other in which the primary event is felony possession of a gun, which are the charges that JH was convicted on. "He has a gun" thus becomes the authoritative account, simplifying the context it was about, and making many aspects of the context in which it was uttered, namely police expectation, seem irrelevant. When Officer 2 discusses herself as a participant, she is redirected to repeat the correctly entextualized account, which focuses on a gun. Thus the trial context, expectations of the judge, the goals of the attorney asking the questions, the charges brought against JH, and the prior discourses of law are also involved in the recontexutalization of both the excited utterance and the event it indexed.

Officer 2's testimony also included another excited utterance—one that is not contested on appeal, but one that revealed the complications of the event on scene.

PH said[3] "[. . .] that she did not want to come back in the house because she was afraid of what he was going to do to her" (Officer 2, November 2002: 13). This utterance did not reference a gun, and thus it was not an excited utterance brought up by JH in his appeal. This excited utterance does show that she was afraid of her husband, a point that JH is apparently not contesting. In the appellate opinion, this excited utterance was used as evidence that the event was exciting enough to make PH hysterical, thereby stilling her reflective faculties. The fight becomes the reason why PH was excited, and in the appeal it will be used to prove that her utterances were excited utterances. Once the excited utterance is invoked, the issue that seemed to be central to PH's experience of the night's events, her fear of her husband, is conflated with her hysteria. Indeed, the issue on scene that night was the domestic assault in which a gun had been drawn, not the mere fact that he held a gun in his hand. As Officer 1 says in response to cross-examination, "I initially arrested [JH] for the assault that occurred on [PH]. [. . .] The firearm was in addition to the assault itself, because she told me it was used in the assault" (November 2002: 23). It is not until the charges against JH change that the gun becomes central. When that occurs before and during trial, the constraints on the utterance change and what will count as an excited utterance changes.

The event and participant roles to which the original utterance is linked affect the entextualization of the excited utterance that occurs after the event has ended: one set of charges brought and dropped, and another set of charges brought against JH leading to a trial. These shifts affect the production of the excited utterance and reveal differences in what the original utterance and the excited utterance were "about." That is, what the original utterance was about is a product of the interactional relationship between participants who coproduce the original utterance; what the excited utterance is about is a product of institutional rules. The story of the event and the attendant (excited) utterance was about something different for Officer 1 and Officer 2, and it was even about something different depending on who was asking questions in court and what their goals were. Thus, when the utterance is reproduced as an excited utterance in court, what the utterance is about changes again. The situation in which people are standing in the same place, witnessing and hearing the same things, talking to each other about the event in front of them, is different from an institutional setting mediated by a highly rule-governed institution.

In recounting the excited utterance in the legal context, embedded in legal co-texts, the rhetorical direction of the utterances shifts. The utterance becomes an accidental accusation of gun possession rather than a purposeful narrative told to police about an assault that involved a gun. The discourse of the excited utterance that presumes the spontaneity of the utterance elides the role of the legal discourse in entextualizing the excited utterance as a legal text-artifact. The function of the idea of spontaneity in the language ideology of the excited utterance makes the utterance appear as though it erupted from PH as a fully-formed, self-cohesive text—an excited utterance. By conceiving of the utterance as having erupted spontaneously, without reflection, the contextual messiness of discourse can be sidestepped.

Domestic assault is particularly contextually complex, because it is rooted in the historical trajectory of an intimate relationship and the economic and gendered factors that underpin domestic relationships. The fact that PH has demanded to testify in defense of her abusive husband points at these complexities. Recognizing this complexity would fundamentally disrupt the inherent trustworthiness of the excited utterance. Thus even though in her dialogue with police PH's narrative indexed a domestic assault in which a gun was used, the intimacy of the violence is stripped out of the event when it is entextualized in the excited utterance "he has a gun." In the application of excited utterance law, the event is effectively reduced to a gun in the hand of a felon, and PH is effectively reduced to a hysterical speaker. During this entextualization, her narrative, translated into an excited utterance, is linked to an isolated moment involving a gun rather than the contextually complicated relationship with her husband that extends beyond the single moment entextualized in the excited utterance.

As I discussed above, the account given by Officer 2 is a narrative of an interaction between a police officer and an abused woman in which violence rather than the gun alone was the topic of conversation. Again, her narrative is more dialogic, she tends to quote herself and others in dialogue saying things such as:

> As soon as you walked in the door, there was a holster laying there. And I said, "Well, there's a gun somewhere." Most people don't have just a holster laying around. (November 2002: 31)

and

> I made observations to other officers, as well as to them, the house was immaculate. It was so—It was clean. Everything was in place. It was—The furniture was actually, I believe white or something. (November 2002: 31)

In testimony like this, Officer 2 creates a setting of interaction and participants involved in the event that she reports. Such narrative tangents give significant context for the whole interaction. Compare this to Officer 1's: "Based on what PH had told us, we believed the weapon to be in a dresser drawer" (Officer 1, November 2002: 11). In fact, Officer 1's testimony is used by the attorney for the government, P1, to interrupt and refocus Officer 2's testimony on the issue of the gun (November 2002: 32).

> Q: I want to back up just for a minute. You stated earlier—testified earlier about PH running out of the house and stating to you, or yelling to you, "He has a gun. He's going to kill me."
>
> A: Yes, ma'am.

Importantly, Officer 2 did not give those statements, Officer 1 did. As I quoted above, Officer 2 gave an account of the things PH "talked about." From one perspective, it may seem like the meaning packaged in both statements is the same, and perhaps that is what led Officer 2 to reply in the affirmative. However, the two ways of linking JH to the gun presuppose different ways of entextualizing the event: one in which the primary concern is domestic violence and the other in which the primary concern is felony possession of a gun. In offering Officer 2 the more direct and quotative excited utterance from Officer 1's testimony, Officer 2's version of PH's original utterance is disciplined and decontextualized—brought under the umbrella of legal discourse and entextualized as an excited utterance.

Officer 2's narrative was far too dialogic and contextual and did not serve the purposes of the court, and thus it had to be brought in line with the discursive constraints of the excited utterance. Indeed, because the excited utterance must be *the* utterance that PH made under the stress of the event, it should be the same across speakers and contexts. The discourse and context of this legal setting demands that the discontinuity be rectified and all of the admissions of excited utterance be the same. Any actual difference in the wording of the excited utterance is whitewashed by the legal presupposition that the excited utterance is substantively, functionally, and rhetorically the same as the original utterance.

ATTORNEY PRESUPPOSITION

Like judges, "Jurors [also] use cultural knowledge, background knowledge available in the social world, to orient and guide their narratives about what happened" (Scheppele 1990, 63). The jury is not "a blank slate but rather a multiple inscribed stele bearing all the impressions and prejudices of the society in which they function" (Lewis 1992, 1). The jury uses their prior knowledge: expectations of justice, crime, criminals, victims, the courtroom, and courtroom drama gleaned from television dramas, news, etc., all saturated with political views and ideological assumptions about race, gender, ethnicity. Recent studies have further complicated the picture of juries, by showing the level to which police procedurals on prime time television affect the expectations of jurors (cf. Tyler 2006; Cole and Dioso-Villa 2007). "The 'CSI effect' is a term coined by prosecutors and the mass media to describe the influence that television crime dramas like *CSI: Crime Scene Investigation* have on jurors. . . [who] now expect to witness the same sleights of evidentiary magic in real life trials" (Tyler 2006, 73). During redirect examination of ATF agent Harper by the attorney for the government, the following exchange took place that exemplifies the prior texts with which the witness understands the question asked and constructs an answer.

P1 Q: And at this point, Agent Harper, is there anything—other than what you've done as the case agent in this case, is there anything else you can do about finding prints on that weapon, that holster, or that ammunition?

TSA AGENT A: No. It's been processed for latent prints. You can only do what you can do. And I just stress, again, it's not always like you see on TV. You don't always get fingerprints on everything and wrap it up in 60 Minutes. (November 2002, 64)

P1, the attorney for the government, elicited this response from the TSA agent after the attorney for the defense spent a great deal of time establishing the lack of physical evidence in the case. The TSA agent links the emphasis on physical evidence to the pervasiveness of the television crime drama. In getting to this point on redirect, P1 is anticipating that jury members will hold such assumptions, and so she has a person speaking with authority problematize those assumptions. Because the only "actual evidence" in *Hadley* is PH's excited utterance, P1 needs the jury to see forensic value in evidence that may not immediately seem physical. And indeed, the language ideology of the excited utterance positions this particular utterance as a sort of eyewitness testimony of things seen, which falls in line with juror expectations of solid forensic evidence.

During trial examinations, attorneys elicit the most important information multiple times, which of course is done for the judge and the jury to hear. The excited utterance is elicited from Officers 1 and 2 or said by the attorneys themselves during questioning, multiple times, as Figure 6 shows.

As we can see, the answers to attorney questions establish (and challenge) the "facts" and chronology of events, and they establish a way of talking about the "facts" using a legal vocabulary.

The key "fact" in this case is the excited utterance elicited from the first witness questioned during the trial. The resultant utterance is shaped by the presuppositions of what counts as an excited utterance already circulating in legal discourse. These allow the defense attorney to object to hearsay, after only hearing: "At that time she was yelling something—". They also allow the judge to provide the statute citation when the prosecution says that they are presenting the utterance as an excited utterance: "Okay. [Defense 1], the government argues that these statements are admissible pursuant to Federal Rules of Evidence, Rule 803(2)," after which he overrules the objection. The excited utterance is the result of this in-court exchange: "She stated to me that 'He has a gun,' and she said, 'He was going to kill me.'" When viewed embedded in trial language, its indebtedness to the rules and discourse of the legal system becomes apparent. The excited utterance is the result of in-court entextualization that stripped away the traces of context and participant roles that were involved in the context in which the "original" utterance was spoken to police.

As is the case for any utterance made in the real world, PH's utterances were made as a part of dialogic ongoing discourse. The prior discourses of the courtroom undo the discursive nature of the utterance. When it is repeated in court by the person to whom it was originally said, it is divided from the world to

Testimony of Officer 1 November 2002	· Officer 1: "At that time she was yelling to me and another officer that 'He has a gun.'" [...] "And Said, 'He's going to kill me.'" (pg. 7: lines 17-20) · Defense 1: Hearsay Objection: "He's basically stating that she was yelling that 'He has a gun.' And that's hearsay." (7: 22-23) · Officer 1: "She stated to me that 'he has a gun,' and she said, 'He was going to kill me.'" (8:18-19) · Defense Attorney: Q: "That [JH] had a gun and everything, correct?" (19: 5-6) · Officer 1: A: "That he had a gun, that he said he was going to kill her." (19: 17-18). · Defense 1: Q: "And so when [PH] When you first came up, that's when [PH] came out and said, "He's got a gun. He's going to shoot me?'" (26: 10-12) · Officer 1: A: "She said, yes, 'He has a gun. He said he was going to shoot me in the head.'" (26: 14-15)
Testimony of Officer 2 November 2002	· Officer 2: "She said that he was going to kill her, that he had- Do you want me to continue? [...] Basically- It was hard to get anything out of her. Like I said, she was hysterical. She was weeping, and you know, I was doing my best to try to get her to talk. And basically she kept talking about a gun, how he put a gun up to her head, and how he was going to kill her." (30: 8-15) · Prosecution 1: Q: You stated earlier- testified earlier about [PH] running out of the house and stating to you, or yelling to you, 'He has a gun. He's going to kill me.' That was your testimony?" (32: 6-9) · Officer 2: A: "Yes, ma'am." (32: 10)

FIGURE 6 Entextualizating Hearsay in the Trial, *US v. Hadley* (2002).

which it refers, the people involved in the domestic violence, and the statements that came before and after it. In the elicitation of and ruling on the excited utterance, the constraints of the excited utterance assumed in the case law—time, excitement and spontaneity—are presupposed in the questions asked by the attorney that lead up to the production of the excited utterance. Such presuppositions truncate the rich context of discourse, limiting it with the ideology of spontaneous speech that makes the excited utterance exception operative.

JUDGE AND JURY

The legal presumption that the excited utterance is the utterance made during the exciting event is also apparent when the Judge admits an utterance made out of court using different reasoning. While eliciting an explanation from Officer 1 regarding the reasons why they went into the bedroom to search for the gun, an objection to hearsay is called. The following exchange illustrates the knowledge of excited utterance rules held by both the attorneys and the judge which includes ideas about using exact words as well as the time between event and utterance and the demeanor of the speaker (Officer 1, November 2002: 10).

Q: Okay. What happened?
A: She told me that he had—
Q: Objection, Your Honor. Hearsay.
THE COURT: [Prosecutor 2]?
PROSECUTOR 2: Excited utterance, Judge.
DEFENSE 1: I think we're past the excited utterance now, Judge.
THE COURT: This appears to be in response to a question by the officer, and not an unsolicited statement.
PROSECUTOR 2: That's true, Judge.
THE COURT: I don't know, but it appears to be.
PROSECUTOR 2: That's true. I believe he asked her for consent to search, is what he said. I mean, of course I didn't ask him what her demeanor was. I can do that, Judge. But I also think that we're not really offering it for the truth of the matter asserted. we're offering to show where he went inside the house and why he went there.
THE COURT: Well, you can do that, though, without bringing out the specific words that she said, though, can't you, if that's what you're trying to do?
PROSECUTOR 2: I can do that, Judge, yes, sir.

In the beginning, the attorneys jump to the excited utterance exception to hearsay that has worked for them up until now. The judge does not merely overrule, however, as he could have. He helps Prosecutor 2 get to the fact that this is non-hearsay because it was not being offered "for the truth of the matter asserted,[4]" but rather to show where and why the officers moved through the house. In establishing that this information was admissible but not as an excited utterance, Judge says, "Well, you can do that, though, without bringing out the specific words that she said" (November 2002: 11). The insinuation here is that an excited utterance consists of direct quotation, and that direct quotation is fundamentally different from indirect quotation—specific words do different work than a paraphrase does. Direct quotation gives the illusion that what the court, in particular the jury, is hearing is what was said during the original event. The use of direct quotation that links the now legally entextualized excited utterance to PH bypasses the roles of the police officer and members of the court in the coproduction of the excited utterance.

Re-Entextualization in the Appellate Opinion

During the trial, when the judge overruled an objection to hearsay by accepting an argument that called the hearsay an excited utterance, the proffered utterance became a legal fact. "[Facts] are considered to be virtually fixed at trial, and only issues of law can be raised on appeal" (Scheppele 1990, 42).

The appellate court is not supposed to confront or alter the facts of the case established in the jury verdict; rather, they are tasked with the job of evaluating legal interpretation. Of course, "there are no 'pure' descriptions of the facts of 'abstract accounts of legal rules. Statements of fact come already infused with legal judgment and legal rules come already fact-laden" (61). The appellate court is built out of the trial transcript, measuring the trial procedure and verdict against the measurement of precedent and statute. The layer of recontextualization makes the excited utterance portable and suitable for application in other cases concerning felony possession of a gun. In the 2005 appellate decision for *US v. Hadley*, the excited utterance is reified as substantively and effectively the same as the original utterance. With each reiteration of the excited utterance in the appellate opinion, "he has a gun" is further decontextualized and delinked from the context of domestic assault that PH references when she speaks to police. As it is moved from the trial to the context of the appellate circuit, the excited utterance in question is evaluated and judged using more legal texts. Recontextualized in this legal discourse, the utterance is abstracted away from the circumstances of the utterance and the expectations and history of the people involved in *Hadley* and toward the discourse of excited utterance case law of which it has become a component.

In the evaluation of the excited utterance that takes place in the appellate opinion, the court applies the legal discourse developed in three hundred years of common law to rationalize their decision. The analysis that takes place in the appellate opinion breaks the excited utterance into its constitutive parts and evaluates each in the service of evaluating the whole—was there an exciting event? Was the speaker under the stress of the event? In the process of evaluating each component of the excited utterance, the excited utterance attributed to PH is recontextualized with different co-texts from the trial and from US law based on the section of the appellate opinion and the argument being made in that section. Each time the excited utterance, "he has a gun" is reiterated, it is used as a part of the argument that the appellate court is making, and thus it does different rhetorical work. Figure 7 shows that depending on the place that it appears in the text of the appellate opinion as a whole and the words and phrases that it collocates with, the excited utterance has a different rhetorical force because it is entextualized and recontextualized within different sets of discursive resources and for different persuasive purposes.

At this stage in the lifecycle of the excited utterance, the original utterance and the excited utterance have been so conflated in the discourse of the law that the excited utterance is eventually given in the appellate opinion as stating in no uncertain terms that JH had a gun. The event to which the excited utterance was a response has been so constrained, that the only legal issue and thus the only indexical relationship the court recognizes is between the utterance and the gun. When it is first reiterated in the appellate opinion, the excited utterance is distinctly situated in testimony and the transcript of the trial: "According to

Section II of the Appellate Opinion,	II.A The Events Leading to Defendant's Arrest "According to officers, [PH] yelled that 'he has a gun' and 'he's going to kill me.' (Id. at 7-8, 30, J.A. at 29-30, 43)"
"Factual and Procedural Background"	II.B The Trial Proceedings and Challenged Evidentiary Rulings "The Government called [Officer 1] as a witness, and sought through his testimony to introduce [PH]'s statements that 'he has a gun' and 'he's going to kill me.'"
	II.C Defendant's Sentencing Hearing "In advocating this increase, the Government pointed to the evidence admitted at trial, including [PH]'s hearsay statements to the police that 'he's got a gun' and 'he's going to kill me.'"
Section III of the Appellate Opinion, "Analysis"	III.A.1 The Impact of *Crawford* upon "Testimonial" Out-of-Court Statements "Moreover, whatever additional evidentiary purposes [PH]'s statements might have served, it is clear that the Government's principal objective in offering these statements was 'to prove the truth of the matter asserted' — specifically, that Defendant 'ha[d] a gun,' in violation of the federal prohibition against the possession of firearms by convicted felons. Thus, the challenged testimony could be admitted only if it fit within a hearsay exception, and the district court invoked the exception for 'excited utterances,' Fed.R.Evid. 803(2)."
	III.A.2 The District Court Did Not Abuse Its Discretion in Determining that [PH]'s Statements Qualified as Excited Utterances "In Defendant's view, the proof of a startling event rests too heavily upon [PH]'s own statements that 'he has a gun' and 'he's going to kill me.'"
	III.A.3.b [PH]'s Statements were not 'Testimonial' "According to the uniform testimony of [Officer 1] and [Officer 2], [PH] volunteered the statements that 'he has a gun' and 'he's going to kill me' as she ran out of her home upon the officers' arrival, and before they could even begin to question her about the evening's events. Initially, at least, the officers did nothing to elicit any 'testimonial' statements from [PH] about her husband's activities that night."
	III.C Defendant is Entitled to Resentencing in Light of Booker "When the police arrived, [PH] ran out of the house and made statements to the effect that 'He is trying to kill me,' or 'He's going to kill me. He has a gun.' […]So she comes running out of the house, and she has thought that 'What I have to say is that he has a gun, because that will achieve my new goal, not my old goal.' So she tells the police officers that '[h]e has a gun,' that '[h]e is trying to kill me.'" (Quoting Chief District Judge).

FIGURE 7 Reentextualizing Hearsay in the Appellate Opinion, *US v. Hadley,* (2005).

the officers, PH yelled that 'he has a gun' and 'he's going to kill me.' (Id. at 7-8, 30, J.A. at 29-30, 43)" (*US v. Hadley*, 2005: 487). The discursive complexity of admissible hearsay is clearly apparent in this statement: an excited utterance must accurately recount the facts as they were established in trial; reference the police speakers who were authorized speakers during the trial; and link the utterance directly to PH, the only person in a position to be so startled by the event that the resultant utterance could be an excited utterance. Because of the complexity of the discursive situation of hearsay, the discourse markers point in multiple directions. The use of parenthetical citation lets the reader know that this information was obtained from the trial transcript, the first written version of the utterance. The fact of hearsay is clearly established in calling attention to the role of the officers with the introductory quotative clause "according to the officers." Next the indirect quotation marker "that" is used, signaling a paraphrase but not a direct quotation. Nevertheless, the utterance is still marked with quotation marks which link the utterance to the original event and the original speaker.

Again in the next iteration of the excited utterance, given in the description of the legal background: "The Government called [Officer 1] as a witness, and sought through his testimony to introduce PH's statements that 'he has a gun' and 'he's going to kill me' " (*US v. Hadley*, 2005: 488). Because this is the place in the appellate opinion in which the procedural background is given, the attorney's action in calling for a witness and providing him opportunity to introduce the excited utterance is included in this reiteration of the trial excited utterance. But again, the use of the quotation marks, an indicator of an exact quote, are used along with "that," an indicator of indirect quotation or paraphrase.

The use of direct and indirect quotation helps conflate PH's speech with the police citation of that speech during the trial. Linking the excited utterance directly to the event does three things: first, it makes the excited utterance appear to have been produced fully formed as an excited utterance; second, it elides the effects of the context of domestic assault and the police officer; and finally, it ignores the effects of the legal context in which the utterance is elicited and evaluated. By following the citation in the appellate opinion back to the trial transcript, we can see that the word "that" was said by Officer 1 when he first introduced the excited utterance. The appellate opinion (*US v. Hadley* 2005: 488) is explicitly quoting from the trial transcript, marking the quoted text with a parenthetical citation:

> The Government called [Officer 1] as a witness, and sought through his testimony to introduce PH's statements that "he has a gun" and "he's going to kill me" (Id. at 7–8, 30, J.A. at 29–30, 43.).

In the trial transcript (Officer 1, 2002: 7), we find this quote:

> At that time she was yelling to me and another officer that "He has a gun." (omitted line 19) And said, "He's going to kill me."

When the appellate opinion quotes the excited utterance testimony, the word "that" should have been a part of the quote—inside the quotation marks, indicating that the officer was paraphrasing not quoting. When Officer 1 says the utterance in his testimony, he uses indicators of both indirect and direct quotation. He uses the word "that." Because the quote is directly attributed to the officers in the parenthetical citation, the word "that" should be marked as coming from Officer 1's speech. Additionally, in the two consecutive talk turns in which the excited utterance is produced and reproduced, Officer 1 uses both the present tense "has," which would be direct quotation, and the past tense "had," which would indicate indirect, after-the-fact quotation. In the appeal, only the present tense is quoted, and in fact, when the appellate opinion uses the past tense form, had, it is marked with square brackets, "ha[d]," indicating that this change was made in the appellate opinion (*US v. Hadley*, 2005: 492). Thus the fact that Officer 1's testimony ambiguously uses direct and indirect quotation indicators at the same time calls attention to the fact that quoted speech will bear features that index the different speakers and contexts through which the utterance is filtered.

Additionally, Officer 1's paraphrasing is structurally erased in the appellate opinion. According to the excited utterance exception, a paraphrase cannot be an excited utterance, because a paraphrase is the product of the person paraphrasing. An excited utterance is bound by legal rules that link it directly to the person who saw the event, and these rules treat the excited utterance as though it is linguistically and semantically the original utterance. Moreover, the legal context in which the utterance is embedded presupposes an excited utterance will be a direct quotation. What we see in *Hadley* (2002/2005) is that when the spoken is transcribed, the expectations of the court, the presupposition embedded in the legal concept itself, and the conventions of writing lead to the use of quotation marks even when the speech is in the form of paraphrase.

These competing conventions mark the utterance as a quotation of PH, and in so doing they elide the consequences of the context. In other words, the evaluation of the utterance in the appellate opinion shapes, simplifies, and places the utterance, fully formed, in the mouth of PH. In the shaping of this referential utterance—making it simply about a gun—the context it indexes and the contexts it passed through (police report, trial, etc.) are all given shape, and some information is excised as irrelevant while other bits of information are highlighted. For example, some aspects of the police and trial contexts are ignored completely. It is in the interest of the law to accurately represent the speakers through whom the excited utterance is transmitted, because the police were the authorities on scene to witness the aftermath of the incident with the gun, witness the hysteria of PH, and create an authoritative account of the event. However, including the "that" inside of the quotation marks would call too much attention to the police officers' discursive agency, and deemphasize the attribution of the statement to PH, the only person who saw the event and would have been sufficiently excited by it. The police officer bringing this event into the courtroom is working between the spoken and the written contexts, and he uses indicators of both. The court reporter who transcribes the utterance is especially aware of the interplay between the two language systems, and as she translates the spoken into the written, she necessarily disciplines the spoken (adds quotation marks), but without upsetting the fidelity of the transcript (she doesn't omit "that"). And thus both the police interaction and the trial are indexed in the trial transcript, a point the appellate opinion seems to ignore.

Reiterating that face-to-face interaction of the encounter between the PH and JH and between the couple and the police in the institutional and textual context of the courtroom divides the texts out of contexts in such a way as to preserve the causal relationship that is required by the legal rule: an exciting context causes a particular speaker to make a spontaneous and thus trustworthy exclamation. In other words, the presuppositions of the court, which supersede individual interaction, assume a causal relationship between context and text, thereby entextualizing that relationship in the artifactual excited utterance "he has a gun" and making it perfectly available to any speaker at any time.

The combination of "that" and quotation marks has to do with the shift from spoken to written language. It is a moment in which we can see entextualization because we can see the difference between the two language systems—differences that the legal system minimizes. According to Andreea Ritivoi (2006, 89), "when discourse is inscribed in writing, meaning is deferred, and the particular reality that would conceivably be more easily recognizable to two interlocutors, that reality to which a speaker and hearer could point their finger, is bracketed, or suspended." That is, the trial transcript brackets the face-to-face interaction between a handful of people and the event that they could all see at the time. In the reiteration of that face-to-face interaction in an environment that is highly rule governed and that produces a written transcript, the discursive interaction changes. The police officer bringing this event into the courtroom is working between the spoken and the written, and he uses indicators of both. The court reporter who transcribes the utterance is especially aware of the interplay between the two language systems, and as she or he translates the spoken into the written, she necessarily disciplines the spoken (adds quotation marks), but without upsetting the fidelity of the transcript (she doesn't omit "that"). And thus, both language systems are marked.

In the section of the appellate opinion in which the sentencing was evaluated, "that" is removed in order to use the excited utterance to make a statement of fact. "…Defendant 'ha[d] a gun." No longer given in the form that calls attention to PH, this statement unequivocally presents the excited utterance as the thing that happened. PH is not referenced though her words are again marked using quotation marks. This construction marks the fact that JH "had a gun," not just according to a hearsay statement, but in fact—he had a gun. In this context, the excited utterance is obliquely cited in order to give a description of the event as it "was" when PH made the statement to police. At this point in the opinion, JH's conviction has been affirmed, and thus the language of the law need no longer presume his innocence. The excited utterance "he has a gun" establishes the fact that JH had a gun, but it is only a fact if PH said it, and so it remains in quotations until the end—even when it is cited in future opinions.

The more the excited utterance is treated as though it is the original statement uttered under circumstances that make it inherently trustworthy, the more decontextualized it becomes. The utterance and PH are evaluated in the appeal in order to establish whether the utterance was in fact made while PH was excited and to determine whether it was testimonial. At each move in the argument in the opinion, the excited utterance case law is used to reiterate some aspect of a true excited utterance. The utterance in question is then shown to properly fall within those criteria. Each time it is measured against a different criterion, the utterance is used to prove something different: the event was exciting; the speaker was excited; the utterance was spontaneous. These were the same issues brought up in the precedent cases used to evaluate the utterance in question in *Hadley* (2005). When the prior case is cited, the chain of citation is set off that positively establishes the utterance under analysis as excited utterance. Each time the evaluation of some aspect of the utterance is positive, the reasoning that translates an utterance in an excited utterance—an utterance that is not semantically dependent on interlocutors, history or prior texts—is strengthened.

Reiteration of the Entextualized Excited Utterance

The entextualized excited utterance is placed in the mouth of PH during the trial, and as it is moved deeper into the metadiscourse of the case law in the appellate opinion, a decontextualized version of the speaker is entextualized along with the excited utterance, becoming a part of the case law of the excited utterance. We see this when *Hadley* (2005) is used in cases such as *State of Ohio v. Johnson* (2006). The excited utterance from *Hadley* (2005) is quoted, attributing the utterance to "a wife" speaking in a "dispute between a husband and wife." No longer even a particular person, this utterance could have been said by any wife involved in any dispute. Nevertheless, it is still marked by quotation marks that bind the utterances to the sensory experience of an individual close enough to the event to be startled by it. The reason the police were called to the home of PH and JH is gestured to in *Johnson*(2006), but the case itself is about two anonymous statements made about a gun in the possession of a person they did not know. That is because the case as it is cited has nothing to do with the intimacy of the domestic situation; as it is reiterated in future cases, the contextual issue of domestic dispute that was central to PH becomes even more ancillary to the gun. The other cases that use *Hadley* (2005) are also cases in which an excited utterance is the primary evidence of gun possession (cf. *United States v. Mitchell* (2007) and *United States v. Newsom* (2006)), but have nothing to do with domestic violence. As her utterance is repeated, domestic violence and PH's concerns, fear, and story are effectively removed from her utterance. The end result is the construction of an excited utterance about gun possession.

The fundamental cause-and-effect relationship in the true excited utterance is between the spontaneous situation and the stilled reflective faculties of the speaker. This relationship creates a speaker with firsthand knowledge, but no (or limited) discursive agency. As the original utterance is further entextualized as the excited utterance, PH, as an agency-less speaker, becomes entextualized as a part of the excited utterance. In so doing, she too is delinked from her own history and her very real concerns and rhetorical response to a violent altercation with her husband. She is translated into a hysterical woman, just like any other hysterical woman. The excited utterance must continually be related to PH, the person victimized with the gun (though not PH as a subject with discursive agency), and thus the only person who could have been made sufficiently hysterical to give an inherently trustworthy excited utterance.

Agency and the Speakers of Excited Utterances

The language ideology circulated in the hearsay rule and the excited utterance exception presupposes that the blurted, spontaneous, excited utterance has a stable indexical, mimetic relationship with the event that forced the utterance to be spoken and that this relationship will not be affected by reiteration. When an utterance is found to be an excited utterance in the after-the-fact evaluation of the utterance in the courtroom, it becomes an artifact of the court rather than a story told by an individual. The ideology of spontaneity reiterated in the discourse of excited utterance case law is used to produce the idea that blurted, unintentional speech is inherently trustworthy, self-cohesive (that is, not intertextual), and thus movable from site to site and speaker to speaker. The mobile excited utterance is not the product of a discursive agent. Mobility is not a product of spontaneity but rather of the entextualization process in which the value of spontaneity is entextualized as a part of the excited utterance. Entextualizating the value of spontaneity into the excited utterance renders it "detachable from its local context," making it mobile across texts and contexts (Urban 1996, 21), as well as divesting the speaker of the utterance of discursive agency.

Since it is said after the reflective faculties of the speaker have been stilled, the law conceives of the excited utterance as a blurt—the thing one says unintentionally, without thinking. I have argued that as an utterance embedded in a legal discourse, it has been thoroughly decontenxtualized and delinked from the history or context in which it was made. The application of excited utterance case law shores up the truth value of the statement and effectively controls authority in the legal context and co-texts. Intertextuality and the link between that event and the statement that becomes the excited utterance culminate in the assumption that the statement entextualized as the excited utterance is the same statement that was uttered on scene. The event entextualized in the excited utterance is not the same event entextualized in the original utterance, because the interactional spaces in which each utterance is produced are different, as are the participants (speakers, addressees) and rhetoricity of the utterances.

In this legal context, the reality of the event is no longer even associated with two interlocutors. In the process of entextualizing the utterance made in real time, the text-artifact, "excited utterance," is constructed, and in the process of rendering it co(n)textually mobile, its link to the pasts and futures of the speaker and the spoken about are broken. "That reality" that existed for the interlocutors is lost to the abstract and artificial "reality" of case law. The Hadleys are made into spectators of their own story. What PH was talking about with the police was a fight with her husband, of which a gun was a part, but the gun was not the only part. She was speaking to police officers in an attempt to get help. Her rhetorical position was complicated, saturated with history and back story and context—she wanted help in the situation, but also wanted to remain married to her husband. Context and history are stripped away when the utterance is entextualized as an excited utterance. Assuming that the gun alone was what was traumatic about the event and the only reason to call the police only serves the purposes of the court, not the purposes of PH. PH's own purposes, of course, are surreptitiously dismissed in the course of evaluating the utterance. In admitting her statement as an excited utterance, she is established as having spoken spontaneously and not with purpose, and with that legal ruling any purpose that she might have actually had is institutionally erased, a point I will elaborate in the following chapter.

I have explained the metadiscursive process by which a speaker is delinked from a statement in the process of creating an essential link between the event and the statement. The end result of this statement is an artificially stable event and statement that has rendered the intertextual nature of the event, statement, and legal discourse invisible, as well as the speaker, who is dismissed by the legal discourse early in the process of constructing the excited utterance. This speaker is the central concern of the next chapter. I will consider the effects on the discursive agency of the speaker when the excited utterance is effectively delinked from the speaker and linked instead to the event. The speaker, in turn, is linked to a subject position that is either silent (has no utterance associated with it because the utterance is associated with the event), or is false (associated with an untrue statement).

5

The Attribution and Disattribution of Agency in the Excited Utterance Exception

In the context of domestic violence and the law, agency is complicated by individual actions, social ideas and perceptions, and institutional structures. In fact in many ways, domestic violence places a spotlight on agency, as questions ranging from "Why does she stay?" to "Can she leave?" position agency as something that an individual has, recognizing the victim of domestic violence as at least potentially capable of agentive action. Legal and psychological concepts such as abused woman's syndrome tend to explain the inability to leave as the fracturing of the potential of agency. The law too presumes a fully agented individual who makes purposeful, individual choices for which they can be held accountable. The hearsay rule, for example, bans reported speech based on a legal presumption that speakers have at least the potential for purposeful, self-interested action. The flip side is the admissibility of the excited utterance, which hinges on the belief that exciting events can still reflective faculties, thereby eliminating the agency to make purposeful speech. Individual agency in a legal context is all the more complicated by the fact that the law is a site with explicit and relatively unavoidable asymmetrical power relationships. The law is highly structural and self-sustaining, and it has significant power to sanction speech and discipline the body of witnesses (via direct- and cross-examination) and the accused (via rulings and sentencing). The law thus presupposes individual sovereign agency even as it acknowledges its own power to alter or disrupt such agency. Victims of domestic violence are caught within a matrix of assumptions about the agency of abused women as well as the law's ability to produce powerful disciplinary effects and its presumption that individuals are sovereign agents.

Legal language ideology as one of the mechanisms that works to constrain agency, producing what Butler (1997) calls "discursive agency," which is not or not only associated with an individual. Butler's definition of discursive agency as a linguistic "act with consequences" avoids the false binary between agency and constraint, while still allowing for the consideration of the legal contextualization of domestic violence victims and their speech and the ways in which victims negotiate the legal context. While it is undeniable that people make purposeful decisions, it is also undeniable that such decisions are constrained from the outset by sociocultural and institutional discourses. When we conceive of agency as discursive agency, we recognize that first and foremost, agency is interactional, emerging in context and between people (cf. Bucholtz & Hall 2005; Ochs 1992; Eckert and McConnell-Ginet 1999). What I show here is that discursive agency is deeply affected by language ideologies and that it emerges during the processes of entextualization. That is, the co-processes of recontextualization and entextualization create texts that are strongly linked to subject positions, such that the latter is a byproduct of the production of the former. Like the text-artifact, agency is a product of recontextualization, open to reformulation in new texts and contexts, and thus never totalizing or complete. Arguing that agency is a product of entextualization acknowledges the ways in which subject positions are formed and reformed as they move and are moved between contexts based on the discourses valued in that context and the subject categories that are already available. It also acknowledges individual negotiation of powerful discourses without slipping into discussions of speaker intentionality.

The language ideology of the hearsay rule and the excited utterance exception to hearsay constrain and enable discursive agency via the three language ideology processes described by Irvine and Gal (2000): iconization, erasure, and fractal recursivity. These processes work together to laminate ideology onto language, one effect of which is the discursive regulation of discursive agency. Iconization naturalizes ideological relationships between speech and speakers; erasure explains away or ignores inconsistencies; and fractal recursivity relates a binary opposition that is integral in one part of the ideology onto other parts. Here, I focus on the process of fractal recursivity to understand the binary construction of the excited utterance exception to hearsay, analyzing how the legal language ideology embedded in the US Federal Rules of Evidence (FRE) creates structures that control courtroom interaction, filtering out accounts and utterances deemed untrue or irrelevant, and producing a discursive agency that is associated with deceitfulness.

As I have noted earlier, there are two speakers involved with examples of hearsay such as the *excited utterance*: 1) Speaker 1 who purportedly made the "original" utterance ("That car hit him!"), and 2) the witness who heard the original utterance and repeats it in court (She was very excited and crying when she told me, "That car hit him!"). This analysis is concerned with the assumptions made in legal rules and precedents about Speaker 1, the person to whom the *excited utterance* is attributed, especially when Speaker 1 is a victim of domestic violence. In the trial analyzed here, *US v. Hadley* (2002), the language ideology of the excited utterance exception to hearsay allowed the utterance in question to be repeated, even though the speaker said to have originally uttered it is in the courtroom arguing that the excited utterance is untrue. Indeed, I'm interested in understanding how this secondhand attribution of utterance to a prior event and a different speaker constrains and alters the discursive agency of the speaker of the "original" utterance. In the context of domestic violence, Speaker 1 is the witness and the victim, and though she may be present trying to explain the original utterance, she is ultimately unsuccessful because of the indexical power granted to the *excited utterance* that she is told she said.

The utterance spoken to police the night JH was arrested for assaulting his wife was used in the trial as an excited utterance[1]. According to trial transcript (*US v. Hadley*, 2002) and the appellate opinion (*US v. Hadley*, 2005), the event that led to JH's arrest is as follows. In May 2002, JH and PH were having a party at their house. During the party, JH. and PH began to argue. As the argument escalated, they moved into their bedroom, where JH, a twice-convicted felon, removed a gun from a drawer and held it to his wife's head. Although the people at the party could not see JH and PJ, they could hear the fight, leading a friend of PH to call 911 twice. The 911 operator radioed to police that there was a domestic assault with a gun in progress, and in his testimony, Officer 1 estimated that he arrived at the Hadley home within two minutes of the first call to 911, followed closely by Officer 2. According to Officer 1, when he arrived, PH ran out of the house to the police (without provocation from police) and blurted out "He has a gun. He's going to kill me" (Officer 1, 2002: 8). After locating the gun, Officer 1 arrested JH on charges of aggravated domestic assault. Those charges were soon replaced with new charges of felony possession of a gun, a felony "third strike" for JH. PH gave testimony to the grand jury in the days following JH's arrest, testimony that she later claims she was tricked into giving. As she put it (PH, March 2003: 22): "I did not want to be there. And you told me I had no choice but to be there. That's what you said."[2] During the trial, she was not called to testify, but she came to the sentencing and demanded that she be allowed to give testimony in defense of her husband.

In the trial, the excited utterance, "He has a gun. He's going to kill me!" was introduced in the testimony of Officer 1 (2002: 8). The excited utterance was established in the testimony of Officer 1 on the first day of the trial (2002: 1–8). During sentencing, the attorneys for the government, Prosecution 1 and Prosecution 2, the attorney for the defense, Defense 1, and the Judge all used and debated the legal discourse of the excited utterance exception in order to determine which of PH's accounts was true: the excited utterance (which was attributed to her in police testimony during the trial), or the version of events she gave on the stand during sentencing. Defense 1 asserted that everything PH had ever said was a lie, and so all of her utterances had to be discarded. That argument ultimately failed, because Defense 1 did not engage the substance of the excited utterance rule—the circumstances that make the excited utterance inherently truthful. I focus my analysis on the exchange between Prosecution 1, the lead attorney for the government, and PH during sentencing. The terms of debate set within excited utterance legal discourse position PH within a binary framework, or what I will discuss as a fractal recursion, in which she can either be giving an excited utterance or making (legally) false statements.

The hearsay rule and the excited utterance exception to hearsay entextualize utterances as either admissible or inadmissible, either excited utterance or mere hearsay. The admissible excited utterance is a valid, factual utterance, but in the context of domestic violence, that does not necessarily mean that the speaker is validated. The discursive structures of the hearsay rule and the excited utterance exception validate one version of events (those that are labeled an excited utterance) and invalidate any others that PH speaks; by extension PH is invalidated as a speaker. Social discourses about domestic violence are co-articulated with those that render some utterances factual, constituting a subject who only speaks truth when she is out-of-control in her speech—when the event speaks through her. She is caught between two sets of her own utterances, both of which are entextualized as they are recontextualized in legal discourse. The process of managing accounts of events, entextualizing some kinds of spoken evidence as legitimate, also produces discursive agency.

Agency, Discursive Agency, and Language Ideology

Agency is slippery, difficult to define, and contentious, a term that has been at the center of much theoretical debate during which time it has been defined and redefined multiple times. This is in part because, as Bucholtz and Hall (2005, 606) point out, ". . . agency is vital to any [research] that wants to consider the full complexity of social subjects alongside the larger power structures that constrain them." Much of the sociocultural and poststructural theory of the last two decades or more has worked against the notion that agency is something that individuals have and toward a view of agency as something constrained and enabled discursively. In response to this, and perhaps because we feel as though we are purposefully acting and making decisions every day—what to wear, which cereal to buy, which career to go into—there are scholars and theorists who are concerned by this view because it positions the individual as acted on by powerful discourses, ignoring the ways individuals resist against them (cf. Bucholtz 2001). From still another perspective, there are those who crave a positive formulation of agency: not an agency of resistance against, but an agency of ability to act (Magus, 2006). Gender has often been caught at the center of this debate, pulled between a false and not altogether productive dichotomy between full, sovereign agency on the one-hand and entirely-discursive, constrained agency on the other.

Most social theories of language—from sociolinguistics, linguistic anthropology, and discourse analysis—take a middle point in the debate, understanding gender to be produced, at least in part, through discourse, but caught up in the (sometimes romantic) fully sovereign agency to both resist powerful institutions and discourses and to make positive, purposeful decisions. For example, Blommaert (2005, 99) does not deny agency—people do make individual decisions—but agency is always accompanied by structure, those institutional and cultural forces that constrain choice and linguistic creativity. Laura Ahearn (2001, 112) echoes this balance between choice and determinacy in her definition of agency as "the socioculturally mediated capacity to act." Though she admits this definition is vague, it calls attention to the ways in which agency emerges in and through interaction, and the ways action is discursively, socially, and institutionally mediated, both of which lead to an agency that is neither internal to the individual nor static across situations. Working out of the idea of "language as social action" (2001, 110), Ahearn moves away from the false opposition between purposeful, individual action and constraint by moving agency outside of the individual and away from intentionality. Bucholtz and Hall (2005, 606) develop such ideas to argue that agency is not something that one has, but rather it is an accomplishment that is the result of social relationships. Agency from this perspective is "intersubjective" (ibid, 606), distributed across individuals, or what Eckert and McConnell-Ginet (1992) call a "joint activity" (qtd. In Bucholtz and Hall, 2005, 606). Bucholtz and Hall (606–607) further argue that agency can't be isolated to one cultural or social process. It "may be the result of individual action," "distributed across several social actors," or "ascribed through perceptions and representations of others or assigned through ideology or social structures."

Language figures centrally in the form of agency under interrogation here. Duranti (2004, 451) is careful not to reify language as an agent—language as the thing that acts—but he does point to the ways that language is pivotal in the "definition and enactment of (past, present, and future) realities." This view recognizes language's socioculturally mediated capacity to be effectual (cf. Ahearn 2001). And importantly, it avoids the conflation of speaker intention[3] with agency, because it gives significant weight to the role that interactional context and audience play in communication. Similarly, Butler (1997) argues that language is always in excess of speaker intention. In fact, according to Butler, language, while not a sovereign agent in the romantic sense, has its own kind of agency—its own capacity to produce effects. According to Butler (1997, 10), speech itself "subverts intentionality," because every utterance holds the potential to "misfire" in some way, to be meaningful beyond or regardless of the explicit intentions of the speaker. Thus, discursive agency is not something finite and singular that an individual possesses. The model of discursive agency in Medina (2006, 130) positions intention in relationship to context and situation, where it is essentially unstable, "*unfinished and open*" to new contexts and interpretations (emphasis in original). "Discursive agency involves a process of constant recontextualization" (Medina 2006, xiv), and is thus distributed across interactional contexts and discourses.

Ideas about domestic violence victims commingle with ideas about truth and authority in ways that impact the legal production of an excited utterance and determine the agency of the person to whom the excited utterance is attributed. Discursive agency is, in part, an effect of "being *recognizable*" (Butler 1997, 5, emphasis in original), and is thus the product of prior discourses, social values, and expectations that are used to make sense of any utterance and speaker. As such, discursive agency is never wholly in the grasp of a speaker, because it is produced when people in interaction access prior discourses to make sense of the interaction and each other. The victim of domestic violence is recognizable within social discourses about domesticity, victimhood, intimacy, marriage, etc, and when she arrives in court, these are joined by the legal language ideology of hearsay that brings with it presuppositions about truth, trustworthiness and reliability. Discursive agency is an effect of the language ideology, or the social ideas about language *and* language users that organizes and constrains the speaker, the utterance, and its institutionally salient success and ultimate value. Discursive agency is a product of legal entextualization, but it is not located in any single or identifiable location (discourse or speaker). Indeed, the utterance entextualized as an excited utterance can itself be understood to operate with discursive agency. What emerges in this entextualization process is an utterance that acts, not a speaker; and indeed, the utterance in many ways acts on the speaker.

The legal metadiscourses that work to entextualize this discursive agency operationalize a language ideology that rationalizes and simplifies sociolinguistic and contextual complexity, in part, via the processes of iconization, erasure, and fractal recursivity (Irvine and Gal, 2000). Iconization is the process of treating "linguistic features that index social groups or activities" as though they are "iconic representations of them, as if a linguistic feature somehow depicted or displayed a social group's inherent nature or essence" (Irvine and Gal 2000, 37). The machinations that naturalize the feature for the group also tend to laminate onto the speech feature the more ideological aspects that have come to be linked historically or contextually to it. The related semiotic process of erasure "[simplifies] the sociolinguistic field" (38). Via erasure, facts seen as inconsistent with the official story are "filtered through cultural and institutional ideologies" (Ehrlich 2001, 4) and explained away, making "'victims' understandings of the events [. . .] unrecognizable or imperceptible" (2001, 1). Victims' versions of their own experience are either ignored or transformed to fit the needs of the legal process.

Erasure works in sync with fractal recursivity, which simplifies the sociolinguistic field by creating oppositions that organize and structure kinds of utterances and by extension speakers. Fractal recursivity does the work of organizing binaries, thereby "categorizing and differentiating cultural 'objects'" (Gal 2002, 80). Fractal recursions are always indexical and "relative: dependent for part of their referential meaning on the interactional context in which they are used" (80). The layers of binaries of a fractal recursion can be collapsed, making some of the more ideological aspects of the binary relationships and the events they structure indistinct or invisible. Nico Besnier (2004, 317) explains fractal recursivity as "the mimetic patterning of one opposition . . . on to another." In the context of the excited utterance exception, the legal process of determining which utterance is true also determines which utterances are not true.

Fractal Recursivity and the Excited Utterance Exception

Legal language ideologies are organized according to fractal recursivity, made all the more stable because the law is explicitly oppositional—the truth of A automatically implies falsity, if not A. The binary structure makes the objects it organizes intelligible in relationship to each other oppositionally, organizing them into binaries of <A/not A>, which works to organize utterances into hierarchies. Figure 8 illustrates the basic binary relationship between the excited utterance and other utterances.

This fractal recursion determines which of the available utterances is admissible, "by virtue of its inherent trustworthiness" (*Idaho v. Wright* 1990, 657).

As Figure 9 shows, at a basic level, the excited utterance is admissible because it is inherently trustworthy. Thus any utterance admitted as an excited utterance is inherently trustworthy, which establishes a static baseline standard for evaluating other utterances about the same event. The binary structure of the law simplifies the complexity of sociolinguistic interaction, by presupposing that some utterances are inherently trustworthy. The evaluation process either alters the indexicality of the utterance so that it can be fit into either side of the binary or renders utterances that cannot be forced into either side of the binary unrecognizable. When

A	Not A
excited utterance	other utterances
admissible hearsay	inadmissible hearsay

FIGURE 8 Basic Binary Relationship.

A	Not A
excited utterance	other utterances
inherent trustworthiness	lacking inherent trustworthiness
admissible hearsay	inadmissible hearsay

FIGURE 9 Inherent Trustworthiness.

the binary that structures this rule is operationalized in a trial, any alternative utterances will be explained away as false and/or legally inconsequential.

In the excited utterance exception, the most explicit organizing binary is <excited utterance/other (reflective, testimonial, false) utterance>. This binary is established in the definitions of the excited utterance that are used to evaluate and reestablish an excited utterance during trial and appeal. The definition in Extract 1 comes from *Haggins v. Warden, Fort Pillow State Farm* (1983), one of the central precedents used in the *US v. Hadley* (2005) appellate opinion. This definition weaves together discourses from precedent with discourses from various legal treatises. (For the sake of clarity and brevity, I have omitted the paragraphs regarding the issue of time in the evaluation of the excited utterance, as this is not the central issue here.)

Extract 1: (Haggins v. Warden, 1983, 1057)

> Three elements are necessary for the admission of an excited utterance. First, there must be an event startling enough to cause nervous excitement. Second, the statement must be made before there is time to contrive or misrepresent. And, third, the statement must be made while the person is under the stress of the excitement caused by the event.
> [. . .]
> "Testimony that the declarant still appeared "nervous" or "distraught" and that there was a reasonable basis for continuing emotional upset will often suffice" (quoting *McCormick's Handbook of the Law of Evidence* § 297 at 705-706 (2d ed. 1972).
>
> It is important to remember, however, that "the ultimate question is whether the statement was the result of reflective thought or whether it was a spontaneous reaction to the exciting event." (Id.) Thus, a court must take into account other factors that could affect spontaneity. For example, the declarant's age or physical or mental condition might indicate that a statement is not the result of reflection even if it was made some time after the exciting event.
> [. . .]
> In order to find that [Federal Rules of Evidence] 803(2) applies, *it must appear that the declarant's condition at the time was such that the statement was spontaneous, excited or impulsive, rather than the product of reflection and deliberation*. (Citing cases)" (quoting from *State v. Iron Shell*).

Definitions such as these operate according to and help to maintain the language ideology of the hearsay rule that trusts empirical, especially visually based, knowledge; understands trustworthy language to be independent from contextual and historical information; and trusts language produced spontaneously and in an excited state (Andrus 2009). In Extract 1, we see the positive and negative criteria for an excited utterance, shown as oppositions in Figure 10.

excited utterance	other utterances
references exciting event	references speaker's reflective faculties
exciting circumstances	calm or typical circumstances
spontaneous, excited, or impulsive utterance	contrived utterance
excited speaker	calm speaker
inherently trustworthy	not trustworthy

FIGURE 10 Fractal Recursion Reiterated in the Definition of the Excited Utterance.

Some version of these criteria is used in most appeals dealing with an excited utterance. In particular, the list of criteria in the first paragraph are used. Individual criteria are also used in trial arguments for or against the use of the excited utterance exception. The reasoning is founded on a seemingly natural assumption that some events are "naturally" more exciting than others, and that utterances made in response to such events will be excited and thus trustworthy. Spontaneity plays a central role in structuring this presumption about exciting events and speakers, and in fact *Haggins* (1983) expresses this oppositionally (see Figure 11).

The explicit binary construction highlights the fundamental tenet of the excited utterance: spontaneous utterances are more trustworthy than rhetorical or subjective ones.

The discourse of the excited utterance exception thus filters out alternative explanations of a purported *excited utterance*. "[Excited utterances] have long been recognized as exceptions to the general rule prohibiting hearsay because they *contain inherent guarantees of truthfulness*" (*Haggins* 1983, 18, emphasis mine). When the value of "inherent guarantees of truthfulness" is fitted into the basic binary structure of the excited utterance, we get a fractal recursion in which an excited utterance is inherently true, making all other utterances at least potentially false by contrast. See Figure 12.

Thus, the excited utterance is an unreflective utterance that bears no mark of the speaker's discursive agency. The excited utterance fractal recursion thus

"The ultimate question is

Whether the statement was the result of reflective thought	*Or*	whether it was a spontaneous reaction to the exciting event."

"It must appear that the declarant's condition at the time of the statement was such that

the statement was spontaneous, excited or impulsive	*rather than*	the product of reflection and deliberation."

FIGURE 11 Binary Structure of the Definition in *Haggins v. Warden, Fort Pillow State Farm* (1983).

excited utterance	other utterances
exciting circumstances	calm or typical circumstances
quick, spontaneous utterance	contrived utterance
excited speaker	calm speaker
spontaneous, impulsive	reflective, deliberate
truthful utterance	not truthful utterance

FIGURE 12 Development of Definitional Opposition.

presupposes another binary: <no discursive agency/discursive agency>, one that is embedded in the fractal recursion (see Figure 13) but that is not explicit.

In the precedential fabric of the excited utterance exception, then, speaking on purpose is problematically aligned with false statements, positioning discursive agency as always already unreliable. Discursive agency is the product of the legal discourses in which the *excited utterance* is debated and established; it is a product of metadiscursive language ideologies with and in which it is recontextualized. In a fractal recursion, the oppositions can be collapsed at multiple levels, potentially putting each concept in opposition with those on the other side of the opposition. If we collapse the structure of the language ideology (Figure 14), the consequences to discursive agency are highlighted when excited utterance is aligned with other utterances and untruthful speech. Further, because truthful speech is only produced when the speaker has no discursive agency the ultimate binary is <trustworthy utterance/discursive agency>.

Thus the criteria used to evaluate an utterance offered as an *excited utterance* also assume and attribute discursive agency. To put it another way, the discourse provided by Anglo-American case law limits the attribution of agency within the institutional context, by creating seemingly neutral indexical links between different but related binaries. This legal discourse sets off a chain reaction that ripples back through time to characterize the utterance said in the

excited utterance	other utterances
exciting circumstances	calm or typical circumstances
quick, spontaneous utterance	contrived utterance
excited speaker	calm speaker
truthful utterance	not truthful utterance
spontaneous, impulsive	reflective, deliberate
inherently trustworthy utterance	not trustworthy utterance
no discursive agency	discursive agency

FIGURE 13 Discursive Agency in the Fractal Recursion of the Excited Utterance.

excited utterance	other utterances
exciting circumstances	calm or typical circumstances
quick, spontaneous utterance	contrived utterance
excited speaker	calm speaker
truthful utterance	not truthful utterance
No discursive agency	discursive agency

FIGURE 14 Collapsed Fractal Recursion.

"original" speech event. That is, when the speaker of the excited utterance is recontextualized in discourses that presuppose that the impulsive speech of an excited speaker is out of her control, then the process of determining the status of the utterance will also determine the discursive agency of the speaker. The in-court speaker is authorized to speak purposefully, repeating the utterance of someone else, precisely because that "original" utterance is not (is not anymore) associated with the discursive agency of an individual.

In the *Hadley* trial (2002–2003), Prosecutor 1 successfully used the fractal recursion established in excited utterance case law to explain why the excited utterance was the true account of events:

> Of course, as an excited utterance, those words were closer in time to the event. She was still under distress by it. The officers testified about what kind of demeanor she had at the time that they arrived, that she was very upset. (June 2003: 51)

and again:

> Clearly [PH]'s statements at the scene on that night in May of 2002, before she had any further contact and influence by the defendant, to get her to lie, before she had time for reflection, which was presented in her excited utterance, those statements are certainly more credible than what she has since said then that is contrary to that—to the events of that night. (June 2003: 52)

The excited utterance established during the *Hadley* trial creates the backdrop against which alternative accounts made by the same speaker can be measured and proven untrue. The very same argument also assumes that PH is passively parroting her husband, saying what he has told her to say during phone conversations (Prosecution 1, March 2003: 73). Even when she speaks willfully, the discursive agency of the abused woman is attributed elsewhere, typically her husband. The "truth" is in no way linked to PH, who was either a victim of her husband and (1) made reflective and false utterances, or (2) was excited out of her reflective faculties and made one single, inherently trustworthy utterance. Both are the result of the violence performed by the husband. The result of this binary structure in the case at hand is the erasure of PH as an agent of discourse. As I will discuss, however, she still finds ways of disrupting the structure, albeit briefly.

"But I did have a choice. But you made sure that I didn't know that choice"

The sentencing in *US v. Hadley* (2002–2003) began about nine months after JH was found guilty of felony possession of a gun. The primary evidence against JH was the excited utterance attributed to his wife given (in somewhat different ways) by Officers 1 and 2, who responded to the 911 call. In the following exchanges Prosecution 1, attorney for the government (prosecution), questions PH, who is intent on providing a corrective for the excited utterance, which had already been admitted as evidence during the trial. In this questioning, Prosecution 1 attributes and disattributes discursive agency to PH following the structure of the fractal recursion established in the excited utterance exception. The government's case relies on the excited utterance evidence admitted during the trial. In recounting that evidence, Prosecution 1, prosecuting attorney, reiterated the excited utterance embedded in an account of the event that establishes both the speaker as excited and the event as exciting:

> . . . the officers testified that when they arrived at the scene after receiving a 911 call which had reported the defendant was beating his wife, they arrived at the scene and the wife ran out of the house screaming "He's got a gun. He's going to kill me." That was testimony heard in this matter. Also, the 911 tape was played, and we could hear yelling and screaming in the background, definitely an altercation going on. (Prosecution 1, 2002: 11–12)

Such discussion during sentencing reinforces the validity of the excited utterance, working against PH who is trying to destabilize it.[4]

PH has appeared in court for sentencing on her own and asked Defense 1 to let her give testimony. In her testimony, she has an agenda that focuses on three things: 1) she does not remember what she said to police; 2) she did not run out to the police and make a spontaneous exclamation; and 3) during cross-examination by Prosecution 1, she argues that she was not adequately informed of her rights, in particular her right not to testify to the grand jury against her husband. PH works to establish the new account of events in the first couple of minutes of direct examination done by Defense 1, attorney for the defense (March 2003: 15–17):

Extract 2:

Q (by Defense 1): Now, you're familiar with the events of May 25, correct?

A (by PH): Somewhat. I remember some of it.

[lines omitted]
Q: Did you ever tell the police that [JH] had held a gun to your head?
A: I don't remember what I told the police.
[lines omitted]
Q: So you don't remember running out to them and saying, "Oh, he's got a gun and he's held a gun to my head"?
A: I didn't run out to them.
Q: You didn't run out?
A: They came inside the house. I was inside the house. I didn't run out.
Q: Okay. So they came into the house, and is that when you told them that he held a gun to your head?
A: I don't remember what I told them. It happened so fast, I don't remember that.
[lines omitted]
Q: Okay. Did you ever see a gun?
A: Actually, no, I didn't ever see one.
Q: You didn't ever see [JH] with a gun?
A: No, I didn't ever see it.
Q: So if the police said that you said that you saw a gun and everything, then they're mistaken?
A: I didn't see him with one.

This was the first exchange between PH and an attorney in the courtroom, and in it, she altered the circumstances in which the utterance was produced, used "I don't know" and "I don't remember" evasively, and distanced herself from the excited utterance by representing the police as actively entering her house and questioning her. Using "I don't know," she also disclaimed authorship of the version of the event represented in the excited utterance. PH also argued that the police came into the house, undermining the idea that she ran out to the police and blurted the utterance. Figure 15 shows the basic binary structure being circulated in the *Hadley* trial and sentencing.

As we will see in the next section, when she was confronted with the *excited utterance* in this new and institutional context, PH also represents herself not

Excited Utterance	Other Utterances
"He has a gun. He's going to kill me"	"I never saw, only felt"
PH ran out to police	police came into the house
said during trial by police	said by PH during sentencing
utterance indexes event	utterance indexes reflective faculties
Inherently truthful	Untruthful

FIGURE 15 Fractal Recursion in *US v. Hadley*.

as the author of the *excited utterance*, which is used to measure the veracity of all other utterances, but as a person coerced to speak by those with more authority—primarily the police and Prosecution 1.

When PH is questioned by Prosecution 1, the complicated relationship between discursive agency in a private domain and discursive agency in the rigid institutional domain of the courtroom is negotiated. PH interrupts Prosecution 1, refuses to answer questions, and finally requests an attorney, which requires the Judge to adjourn for the day.

PROSECUTION 1'S ACCOUNT OF AGENCY

The exchange between PH and Prosecution 1 was a contest over discursive agency—agency that shifts depending on the topic, the speaker, the reference point (original event, grand jury testimony), and the speakers' discursive goals. The point of contention between Prosecution 1 and PH, at PH's insistence, was the spousal immunity that she claimed she would have invoked had she known it was an option.[5] In Prosecution 1's cross-examination of PH, the excited utterance provides the backdrop against which other statements can be measured; any detail that diverges from the account hypostatized in the excited utterance is considered to be untrue. Thus, any new narrative points that PH introduced, such as the contention that the she did not run out to speak with police, are understood to be false when measured against the excited utterance introduced in police testimony. As Prosecution 1 put it, "Forgetting about whatever [PH]'s problems about truthfulness or untruthfulness are, the excited utterance itself carries the weight of constitutional trustworthiness because of the circumstances in which the statements were given" (Prosecution 1, June 2003: 72). Prosecution 1 uses the established excited utterance to attribute agency to PH when she is not being truthful—PH *chooses* not to remember and not to tell the truth, "You remember, [PH], just what you want to remember" (Prosecution 1, March 2003: 20).

Prosecution 1 evaluated PH's multiple utterances using the fractal recursion of the excited utterance exception to (*dis*)attribute the discursive agency required to produce an excited utterance from PH in order to *attribute* discursive agency in all other circumstances. Figure 16 illustrates the fractal recursion that organizes the assumptions about agency articulated in Prosecution 1's response to PH's shifting account.

In her courtroom actions, Prosecution 1 operationalizes the language ideology of the excited utterance (Figure 16). As she uses it, the excited utterance is stable; it requires no testing and therefore no further binary breakdown. The "other utterance" side of the binary, however, is unstable; these utterances must be proved in cross-examination and measured against the unwavering excited utterance. The stability of the excited utterance makes it usable as the standard against which other utterances can be measured.

<table>
<tr><th></th><th>Excited Utterance</th><th colspan="2">Other Utterance</th></tr>
<tr><td rowspan="3">Utterance</td><td rowspan="3">Does not require cross-examination
• Inherently trustworthy because utterance is not the result of reflective faculties</td><td colspan="2">Require cross-examination
• Not inherently trustworthy because speaker is using her reflective faculties
• Utterance is measured against excited utterance</td></tr>
<tr><td>Trustworthy</td><td>Untrustworthy</td></tr>
<tr><td>Accounts analogous with excited utterance are true</td><td>Accounts that deviate from the excited utterance are false</td></tr>
<tr><td rowspan="2">US v. Hadley</td><td rowspan="2">In the trial: excited utterance admitted in the testimony of Officer 1 police testimony</td><td>PH's testimony given to grand jury</td><td>PH's testimony given during sentencing</td></tr>
<tr><td>PH's utterance is analogous with the excited utterance attributed to her in the testimony of Officer 1
and so
↓
Utterance is trustworthy
In this discursive situation, Prosecution 1 (attorney for government) attributes discursive agency to PH</td><td>PH's utterance is divergent from the excited utterance attributed to her in the testimony of Officer 1
and so
↓
Utterance is not trustworthy
In this discursive situation, Prosecution 1 attributes discursive agency to JH who has influenced PH
or
Prosecution 1 attributes discursive agency to PH who does not resist JH's influence (potential perjury charges)</td></tr>
<tr><td>Discursive Agency</td><td>Speaker has no discursive agency; was forced to speak by force of the exciting event</td><td>Sovereign Agency: Speaker (PH) can choose to be truthful</td><td>Sovereign Agency: Speaker (PH) can choose to be misleading
or
Ineffectual Agency: Speaker (PH) can be influenced by a more powerful agent (JH)</td></tr>
</table>

FIGURE 16 Language Ideology of the Prosecution in *US v. Hadley* (2002–2003).

Note how the nested binary affects the discursive agency of PH. Prosecution 1 used this binary, and the excited utterance that organized it, to explain and evaluate the differences between PH's discursive agency in different circumstances. Prosecution 1 ignored all alternative narratives produced by PH by using the excited utterance (attributed to PH) as the true utterance. This allows her to treat PH as an agented speaker in all other situations. She could choose to tell the truth during sentencing testimony—she has the capacity to be honest—she is just not. Prosecution 1 says, "Then how can we believe what you're saying today? You remember, [PH], just what you want to remember" (Prosecution 1, March 2003: 20). Prosecution 1 turns around PH's contention that she didn't remember what happened to assert (again) that PH is untrustworthy. PH is an agent of discourse only in relationship to potentially false utterances. Utterances that substantially match the excited utterance are understood to be true. Utterances that do not match the excited utterance are understood to be false. The standard measure, the excited utterance, was produced by a speaker with no discursive agency.

The discursive agency involved in lying is then also diverted away from PH to JH. Elsewhere, Prosecution 1 argues, "[JH] had begun talking to her at that time, as soon as he was arrested on these federal charges, to begin talking to [PH] to get her to change her statement" (Prosecution 1, March 2003: 73). Even when Prosecution 1 attributes PH the discursive agency to lie, she also disattributes agency by linking her falseness to JH. Thus, PH is only partially attributed discursive agency, and only in the most negative sense.

The discursive agency involved in making true utterances is highly constrained, because the standard of truthfulness is established outside of the speaker. The event is assumed to be what really happened, and it is perfectly indexed by an excited utterance—ignoring that the excited utterance is the product of courtroom interaction. Prosecution 1 has access to the legal discourse that can be used to align and realign the discursive agency of out-of-control speakers. This grants Prosecution 1 a sort of fundamental agency to define PH's agency: to attribute discursive agency to some of PH's utterances (different testimonial settings), while disattributing it elsewhere (the excited utterance, abusive husband). This double-bind of attribution constrains PH's discursive agency in every way. It makes it so that she cannot reclaim authority over the original narrative without looking like she is being purposefully false. The only discursive agency in which she is recognizable is associated with falseness.

PH'S ACCOUNT OF EVENTS AND AGENCY

PH is also interested in choices—in particular, her choice not to testify against her husband. She assumes (momentary) discursive agency when she argues that Prosecution 1 had kept information regarding those choices from her. PH asserts over and over that had she known about all of her choices (had she known exactly *how* her discursive agency was institutionally constrained), she would not have *chosen* to testify to the grand jury in the days following her husband's arrest. She attempts to situate events and utterances in interactional contexts—interacting with police, Prosecution 1, and other legal professionals over time. PH's rearticulation of discursive agency differs from the simple binary structure represented by Prosecution 1, revealing a complex, goal-oriented, and context-specific relationship to the narrative at stake in this legal battle. PH reframes the original event, and by refusing to stay on the topic introduced by the questioning attorneys (on both sides), she actively reframes the discursive agency attributed to her in that questioning. At the beginning of the cross-examination, while Prosecution 1 was working to establish the focus of their prior interactions and PH's grand jury testimony, the exchange in Extract 3 took place (March 2003: 19–20):

Extract 3:

Q (Prosecution 1): And you testified before the grand jury that day under oath, right?
A (PH): Yes. And you did not tell me my rights, either, with me. You withheld that from me.
Q: [PH], I'd like for you to just answer my questions.
A: Well –
Q: [PH], you testified in the grand jury –
A: – but was that fair for you to do that to me?
Q: That's not the issue here.
A: Yes, because [JH] is my husband, that is an issue.
Q: [PH], you told the grand jury that you –
A: I don't remember.
Q: – husband put a gun to your head.
A: I don't remember. I don't remember.
Q: You don't remember?
A: No.

Prosecution 1's question pattern directs PH to repeat for the court that JH had held a gun to her head. In answering, PH represented her earlier testimony to the grand jury as the product of an unfair interaction in which she had not been informed of all of her rights, and had thus been led to doing something that she didn't realize she could have avoided. She links this leading directly to her inability to remember what she said or what happened. PH consistently attempts to reinject her intimate life into the legal context, bringing up her husband—"Yes, because [JH] is my husband, that is an issue."—rather than answering the question asked. When her new topic is dismissed by Prosecution 1, she insistently repeats "I don't remember" multiple times.

We see PH's grip on her version of events each time she reintroduces her relationship and each time she comes back to the issue of her spousal immunity:

". . . you did not tell me about my rights, either." By reintroducing the issue of the spousal immunity that Prosecution 1 is avoiding, PH works to reclaim ownership over a story that is both deeply personal and has material value in her life, past and present. In altering details and coming back to the issue of being tricked, she problematizes her link to the excited utterance. She represents herself as having authority to accurately report the "original" event. When she is chastised by Prosecution 1 for not answering the question she is asked, "I'd like for you to just answer my questions," PH continues, talking right over Prosecution 1, "but was that fair for you to do that to me?" PH does not respond to the institutional authority of Prosecution 1, and in so doing, she moves to take discursive agency in a setting where it is explicitly constrained by attorney questioning and the rules of the court. She goes on to say:

> But I did have a choice. But you made sure that I didn't know that choice. Just like I'm here now, I'm here to support my husband, because I care about him and I love him, but I did not- I do not want to be here testifying against my husband. So, no, I don't know. I don't remember. I don't know. (PH, March 2003: 23)

In making this accusation, PH claimed knowledge of being denied a legal right and talked about it with authority even though she was not an authorized agent of/in the legal discourse. She explained that she had not wanted to testify and that she only had because she had not known that she had the right to refuse. She then linked her current lapse in memory directly to the fact that she never wanted to testify against her husband by using the conjunction "so": "I do not want to be here testifying against my husband. So, no, I don't know. I don't remember. I don't know." In reiterating the denial of her rights, she also established for the Court the context surrounding her grand jury testimony—she had been coerced into testifying. The legal discussions leading up to her grand jury testimony had led her to believe that she had no choice. By breaking the rules of the court with a discussion of a choice that had been hidden from her, PH forced Prosecution 1 to engage the issue of spousal rights that she had otherwise avoided.

In each of these exchanges, PH is responding to the problematic ways in which she is attributed and disattributed agency by the courtroom and the discourse of excited utterance case law. She takes agency that has not been attributed to her (control over the topic of questioning) and distances herself from agency that has been attributed to her by Prosecution 1 (agency to choose to tell the truth). Her answers during questioning belie a different, more flexible relationship to discursive agency that is deeply dependent on context and her goals.

As Figure 17 illustrates, PH resists attorney-led questioning by raising the topic of her constrained agency and her denied choice. Such a discursive action involves shifting her position within a complex web of agency attribution. By claiming that police came into her house and asked questions, she rearticulates

<table>
<tr><td rowspan="5">Sentencing Testimony
(March 2003)</td><td>Context</td><td>Legal Attribution of Agency in Cross-Examination by Prosecution</td><td>PH's Response</td></tr>
<tr><td rowspan="2">Cross-examination by prosecution regarding the sequence of events</td><td>Assumed in questioning that PH went out of her house to meet police.</td><td>PH rearticulates police interaction in order to counter agency that is attributed to her by the prosecution:</td></tr>
<tr><td>Assumed that PH will restate the facts established in the excited utterance entextualized in the testimony of Officers 1 and 2.</td><td>¤ "They came inside the house. I was inside the house. I didn't run out."
¤ "I don't remember what I told them. It happened so fast, I don't remember."
¤ "I thought it was [a gun]. But I actually don't know what I saw. I just felt…"</td></tr>
<tr><td>Cross-examination by prosecution regarding prior testimony to the Grand Jury</td><td>Assumed in the questioning that PH willingly testified before the grand jury against her husband who had been charged with aggravated assault.</td><td>PH rearticulates the Grand Jury interaction, moving away from the agency attributed to her by the prosecution during cross-examination:
¤ "The state filed charges."
¤ "For some reason you didn't tell me that I had the right not to testify against my husband. […] And you told me I had no choice but to be there."</td></tr>
<tr><td>Discussion between prosecution, defense, and Judge while PH is on the stand</td><td>She is willfully lying and in jeopardy of being charged with perjury.</td><td>PH invokes her right to an attorney, requiring the judge to adjourn court for the day.</td></tr>
<tr><td rowspan="2">Sentencing Testimony
(June 2003)</td><td colspan="3">Agency disciplined by institutional constraints:
¤ On the stand:
¤ PH does not have an attorney present;
¤ PH answers Prosecution 1's questions;</td></tr>
<tr><td colspan="3">¤ Off the stand:
¤ PH interrupts court from the audience, saying, "I did lie." "Why? Because I want to tell the truth, I have to leave?"</td></tr>
</table>

FIGURE 17 Attribution of Discursive Agency.

her interaction with police, attributing agency to the police officers. By claiming that she had not been adequately informed of her spousal immunity, she rearticulates her interaction with attorneys and attributes agency to them. In both, she situates herself as the person acted on rather than the actor.

In actively shifting her own role within the interactional web of agency stretching all the way back to the interaction with police, PH claims discursive agency within the institutional space of the courtroom. In so doing, she distances herself from an attribution of discursive agency that produces effects she does not agree with. The way the legal discourses oriented her relationship to discursive agency does not match her own view. This is not a small issue. According to the law, the central act of holding a gun to the head of PH must be associated with the only person who saw the act—PH. Thus, the court must link that act to PH by attributing statements to her and making their association seem objective rather than subjective. Such an objective relationship between the utterance and the event contradicts PH's subjective relationship to her own experience. That is, this is not an objective issue for her, but rather a subjective issue that is about her own lived experience and worldview.

The institutional roles assigned by the metadiscourse to these two interlocutors, Prosecution 1 and PH, puts them in different relationships to both the discourse in question (the excited utterance) and to discursive agency. Prosecution 1, who has discursive agency in this setting, is put on guard when PH, whose discursive agency is constructed in negative terms, claims discursive agency in the space of the courtroom. Even though it is not in front of the jury, these assertions of discursive agency require the court to spend a great deal of time considering her excited utterance and determining how it compared to the alternative accounts given in testimony. Prosecution 1 uses excited utterance legal discourse to make PH recognizable as a woman whose only true utterance is the excited utterance. Thus the fractal recursion that organizes PH's utterances also aligns her as a speaker who is fundamentally untruthful—only truthful when her reflective faculties have been stilled.

(Re)Constructing PH's Narrative in Judicial Discourse

Over the course of the trial analyzed above, we see the objectification of PH's complicated relationship to her own story. It is about a violent experience of which she was the object, and it is treated as though the version of the story circulating in the legal discourse is told in her own words. Her attempts during sentencing to reclaim and alter the trajectory of the story—to reappropriate discursive agency over her own narrative history—have limited success. As I explained above, she asserts agency in court in the very same act of displacing the discursive agency attributed to her by Prosecution 1 regarding prior utterances. Nevertheless, the discourse of PH, her alternative accounts, and her contextual reasoning, are discounted in the courtroom. In fact, they are used in the end to prove that she is fundamentally and simultaneously untruthful and a non-agent. Thus, as Goodrich as argued, the law appropriates one of PH's accounts in order to reject "alternative and competing meanings and accents, forms of utterance and discourse generally, as extrinsic, unauthorized or threatening"

(Goodrich 1986, 3). And importantly, in this case and others like it, those alternative and competing accounts are also produced by PH.

The Judge in *Hadley* (2002) wields legal power and legal and social discourses to authoritatively end the production of alternative accounts. In fact, when he brought questioning to a close at the end of sentencing in June, he said: "The Court has been very patient and has allowed counsel for both sides to put on more evidence than probably was necessary considering the simplicity of the issue" (June 2003: 74). With this, the Judge announces the end of discursive play, and as he pronounces JH's sentence, he also gives PH's.

Throughout his discussion of PH, primarily taking place on the last day of sentencing in a dialogue with Defense 1, the Judge relies heavily on popular representations of domestic violence, ideas about how the "average person" would respond to abuse, and the legal discourse of the excited utterance, in the process of making PH recognizable as an abused woman who loves her husband and thus produces utterances that cannot be trusted. In so doing, the Judge disciplines PH as he determines which of PH's utterances are true, which are false, and how she as a speaker figures into the various utterances she has produced.

Throughout his discussion of PH, primarily taking place on the last day of sentencing in a dialogue with the attorney for the defense, the Judge relies on his knowledge of abusive relationships in general, popular representations of domestic violence, and ideas about how the "average person" would respond to abuse, rather than the specific relationship between the Hadleys. In making this argument, the Judge operationalizes his social understanding of abuse and intimate relationships. This cultural knowledge is even apparent in the first of his legal findings:

> First finding: "The defendant's wife, [PH], loves her husband, and she will do anything at all that she can, within reason, to help him and to prevent him from going to jail for a long time." (Judge, June 2003: 75)

This finding is about PH, even though she is not the person on trial. This finding also reifies in legal language the domestic relationship between JH and PH as a loving one, even though he is about to sentence JH to more than twenty-two years in prison for assaulting her with a gun. This finding, informed by popular discourses about abused women and domestic love, explains PH's motives for lying while on the stand during sentencing. She "loves her husband" and wants "to help him." As evidence for this finding, the Judge cites a movie and television:

> Well, I don't know for a fact, but there are a lot of TV shows, there are a lot of stories in newspapers and magazines and things, it is common knowledge—I think there was a movie fairly recently starring a Hispanic actress—about people having domestic disputes and the police coming by

> and taking people out of the house for a short time period until they cool down. In those cases people don't say "he's got a gun." They say, "We're having a fight. I need him out of here." (Judge, June 2003: 59–60)

Here the Judge makes explicit the assumptions he is making about communication between an abused woman and a police officer, assumptions based on social knowledge that he uses to determine which of PH's stories are correct. He uses his cultural knowledge as evidence that if she said he had a gun when she ran out of the house, then he must have. Otherwise, she would have said something else—"We're having a fight. I need him out of here." His story relies on the assumption in the excited utterance that the blurted speech will accurately report the event, supported by abstract knowledge of domesticity and violence.

The Judge also openly posits hypothetical reasons why somebody in PH's situation might lie or tell the truth, requiring the attorney for the defense to quit referring to the specific details of the case and instead to think about her motivation. When Defense 1 mentions the speaker, PH, directly—"PH has claimed amnesia to a lot of it."— the Judge corrects him saying, "We're leaving her out of it right now" (June 2003: 57). He focuses on general motivations for an utterance about a gun, recognizing the existence of a gun as the only possible motivation for such an utterance. Thus, his fourth finding reinforces the placement of the gun: "When the police arrived, PH ran out of the house and made statements to the effect that 'He is trying to kill me,' or 'He's going to kill me. He has a gun.'" (Judge, June 2003: 75). This finding affirms the circumstances of utterance and the fact value of the excited utterance, but even this is couched in a generalizing framework, using the phrase "statements to the effect that" indicating that such statements are typical and nonspecific.

As he has done elsewhere in his legal findings the Judge references popular discourses of abused women and domestic love to explain PH's motives for lying on the stand during sentencing, and these findings support and are supported by the discourse of the inherently trustworthy excited utterance, which finds spontaneous utterances made under exciting circumstances to be trustworthy. These two findings work as oppositions within the fractal recursivity of the excited utterance. They also situate PH within the binary of the fractal recursion represented in Figure 18.

When he decides the sentence of JH, the Judge contends with the alternative account of the story created by PH, even including her in his legal findings. To do so, he calls on his cultural (not legal) knowledge of abused women and creates a new and final narrative that disciplines PH's. Throughout his discussion of PH, the Judge attempts to contextualize PH and her competing accounts, but he does not use her actual contexts—he does not turn to the details of her story. Instead, at the end of the sentencing procedures, he relies on popular discourses of abuse to produce a narrative based on a lay psychology of love and abuse.

Excited Utterance: PH's one trustworthy utterance	PH's other, untrustworthy utterances
Fourth finding: When police arrived, PH "made statements to the effect that 'He is trying to kill me,' or 'He's going to kill me. He has a gun.'"	First finding: PH loves her husband and will say anything to save him.
reflective faculties stilled	reflective faculties intact
quick, accidental utterance	contrived utterance
excited, spontaneous speaker	calm, purposeful speaker
no discursive agency	**discursive agency**

FIGURE 18 Discursive Agency in *Hadley*.

> The reason advanced by the defense for [PH]'s initial statements [the excited utterance] was that as a result of this dispute [PH] wanted to get the defendant out of the house. . . . So she decides to concoct a lie, a story. And she must have decided this sometime between the time that the police officers arrived and she was released from—she was released by her husband. So she comes running out of the house, and she has thought that "what I have to say is that he has a gun, because that will achieve my new goal, not my old goal." So she tells the police officers that "he has a gun," that "he is trying to kill me." When the police officers do not respond in the way that she wants, she takes them back to the house and she leads them to a gun that just happens to be in the house.
>
> [. . .]
>
> And even though she might subject herself to prosecution by admitting that she had lied in her testimony before the grand jury and she had lied to the police officers, with the love that she has for her husband, I'm not sure that she would not be willing to do that if she had in fact not been telling the truth at the beginning. (June 2003, 76–77).

Though he could have sidestepped PH's alternative accounts, by returning to the discourse of the excited utterance as Prosecution 1 does, in the above narrative he engages PH and explains her to the Court. In the process he creates a universal account in which PH is made recognizable as an abused woman who remains true to her husband even in the face of perjury and contempt charges. The Judge's narrative surreptitiously dismisses the narrative work that PH has attempted to do in her testimony, and with it any remaining narrative agency that she may have had. He renarrates PH's relationship to her husband, recasts her relationship to her narrative speech, and ultimately alters her own narration of her lived experience. We see the Judge telling us what PH is thinking in an account of the event that is even cited in the appellate opinion. As he has done elsewhere during the trial, in this account, the Judge abstracts away from the particular co(n)texts of JH and PH and toward a general narrative of domestic dispute that downplays violence and plays up both the love in the relationship, which is used as evidence that she is lying, and the truth value of the legally constructed excited utterance. The Judge creates a story to make PH "recognizable." According to Butler (1997, 5),

> One "exists" not only by virtue of being recognized, but, in a prior sense, by being *recognizable*. The terms that facilitate recognition are themselves conventional, the effects and instruments of a social ritual that decide, often through exclusion and violence, the linguistic conditions of survivable subjects. (emphasis in original)

The body is made intelligible in the act of speaking, not only by the words it speaks but also by the discourses that are brought to bear within the rhetorical situation that the utterance will become part of. The Judge works to silence PH's alternative accounts and stolen discursive agency by making her recognizable using social discourses in a situation that has legal weight. That is, the Judge uses social discourses that make PH recognizable as an abused woman in order to fully divest her of her discursive agency.

The lay psychology used to explain why she would want to lie for her husband relies on the idea that the agency of abused women has already been compromised by the abusive husband and by her love for him. In the legal discourses used to appropriate her one true utterance, itself produced by the abuse, her discursive agency is further diminished. The result is the reduction of PH's access to narrative agency—the ability to have access to authority in self-representation. PH is not allowed to be the author of her own story, but she is forced to tell the story, or linked to a story attributed to her, over and over.

The discourses brought to bear in PH's case give contour to the event about which she is speaking; they affect her narrative and inevitably her relationship to that narrative. These same discourses also limit her authoritative access to her own story in future interactions with the narrative and ultimately the ways she is recognizable in public and institutional spaces. The legal process establishes the reality of the event—what will count as a fact of the case and what will not (cf. Scheppele 1990; Amsterdam & Bruner 2000). What makes the excited utterance such a pertinent example of such hypostatization is the fact that reality is established using a narrative account attributed to a speaker, but in such a way that the narrative and the reality it represents are placed outside of the reach of discursive agency of the speaker. The words must be hers; the narrative must be hers; but the intention cannot be. The speaker is effectively stripped of the means to both personally *and* truthfully represent something that happened to her. The excited utterance is a case in which one set of utterances produced by a speaker forecloses on the possibility for another set of utterances produced by the same speaker to be understood as true accounts.

The binary structure of the American legal system creates a situation in which PH cannot account for a past event using new utterances. The phrases that the law does find intelligible are citationally attributed to the same speaker whose new utterances are found to be unintelligible (in relation to the legally established reality of the event). Caught in between her own utterances, the recognizability of the speaker herself, in relation to her own story, is constrained. At the same moment that she is limited access to discursive agency, she is made recognizable within a highly regulated set of discourses—abused woman willing to lie for an abusive husband.

Entextualizing Discursive Agency

In a case of domestic violence such as the one discussed here, where new utterances have been produced that oppose those that have been endowed with the properties of reality, PH's statements are used during trial and the appeal to establish a reality that she does not agree with, and they are used to prove that the other things she has to say are untrustworthy and ultimately to establish her as an untrustworthy speaker. Words she uttered in a prior setting (one that is completely different, includes a different set of rhetorical concerns and actors, and comes stocked with a unique set of histories and prior texts) are cited in court and attributed to her in such a way that they are understood to be inherently trustworthy. This citation preempts the setting in which they were said, and also anything that she will say about the event they report and the context in which they were said in the future. In this way, the language ideology of the excited utterance creates a situation in which the speaker's own words establish the binary inherently trustworthy utterance/not inherently trustworthy utterance that will be used to evaluate the utterances in question. The result is that the speaker's narrative agency, her agency to authoritatively represent her own experience, is cut short. Narrative agency is instead attributed to her abusive husband and to the event of abuse itself via the authoritative discourse of the Court and the law. Thus, in *US v. Hadley* (2002–2003), multiple systems of attribution confound PH's access to agency. In the context of institutional discourse and the imposed constraints on the speech of individuals within an institution, the idea that agency exists in as much as one is recognized as an agent makes intuitive sense. The powerful role of the legal institution and any assertion that it makes will outweigh any single assertion made by an individual person.

The sentencing procedures of *Hadley* (2002–2003) are an interaction in which private and public spheres collide. In each sphere, there are different discourses at work that relate the speaker to the event and the utterance, and different discourses that can be used to make sense of the interaction and the people. Such discourses are used to make PH recognizable, and they alter her access to her own narrative, directly impacting her narrative agency. When the excited utterance exception is invoked during trial and accepted by the trial judge, the statement is thereby deemed inherently trustworthy, breaking any links of agency between the utterance and the speaker that may have existed. In other words, because the language ideology of the excited utterance assumes that the speaker has no agency if the utterance is indeed an excited utterance, then if the utterance is deemed an excited utterance, the speaker is constructed as a non-agent. However, as I argued in the previous chapter, this assumption is made in a completely new context of interaction, not the context of interaction in which the original utterance was made. The excited utterance is a site in which an utterance is moved from context to context using an authoritative discourse that actively works to decontextualize the utterance—elide its history of production and reiteration. That is, the discourse of the law works to make the interactional space in which the original utterance was made seem unimportant, a process that affects the discursive agency of the speaker in the public interactional space of the institution and in the private interactional space of her social world.

Over the course of the *Hadley* trial, a narrative about a gun is produced. In that narrative, PH is established as an abused woman, speaking excitedly about a startling situation, but the role and function of domesticity and marriage are downplayed. PH's utterances to police are repeated in court as hearsay evidence. It is deemed admissible hearsay—an excited utterance—by the Court, and at the moment of this legal pronouncement, the link between PH and the utterance is broken. According to legal principle and case law, an excited utterance is made after the reflective faculties of the speaker have been stilled, making it a product of the event more than the speaker. During sentencing, PH attempts to disrupt this smooth narrative by appropriating agency where none was available to her. She counters the story, revealing her changing relationship to a story that is ultimately about her life. PH is able to appropriate this discursive agency, even if for a short time, because as the only eyewitness of the event, only she can trouble the empirical link between the event and the utterance established via the legal discourse of the excited utterance. The speaker is situated as an irremovable element of the excited utterance, the person who has visual knowledge of the event, and as such, PH is the only person who can interrupt her own account.

Yet because the excited utterance is actually a product of the courtroom, not the speaker, her interruption is short lived. The systemic attribution of agency that is embedded in the legal discourse itself is compounded by the power of the judge in the institutional hierarchy of the courtroom to arbitrate the production of the empirical link between the speaker and the excited utterance. The speaker's relationship to her own utterance is thus articulated in the discourse of the law in such a way that her attempts to claim narrative agency in her own story are cut short. The language ideology of the excited utterance metadiscursively forecloses discursive agency with the expectation that only spontaneous speech bears adequate indicia of reliability. However, in the very same discourse, one particular speaker must be linked to the excited utterance because of their visual knowledge. Thus, the excited utterance discourse constitutes an odd sort of actor—someone who must speak, but who in the moment of speaking is divided from her speech. And then, the speech is appropriated within a legal discourse that will reshape the utterance and in so doing, reshape the speaker (and her relationship to all of her utterances) by placing her within the binary structure used to measure the utterance in question. The fractal recursions used to measure the excited utterance, in which PH is attributed agency in situations in which her utterance will be proved false, results in an erasure, as Irvine and Gal (2000) define it. Erasure is not an actual eradication of a thing, but the process of making the thing seem unimportant or inconsequential. By repeating and collapsing the inherently trustworthy utterance/not inherently trustworthy utterance binary at different points, PH is shown to be a merely abused woman who is willing to lie in order to save her abusive husband. Her ability to confabulate is measured against the spontaneously produced utterance that is treated, especially in the metadiscourse of appellate law, as inherently trustworthy. But even the agency to willfully produce false discourse is curtailed in the discourse produced by the judge in which her actions are attributed to her abusive husband and some social value of love.

Only when it is forced from a speaker by an exciting event that has stilled the faculties of self-consciousness does an utterance bear adequate indicia of reliability. As I have explained in detail in an earlier chapter of this dissertation, the assumptions about agency that allow the excited utterance to function the way it does have been a component of the common law of evidence since its birth in the early Enlightenment. The idea that finds inherently reliable or inherently trustworthy a spontaneous utterance that is spoken by the body of a witness or victim but not his/her subjectivity is an idea that is dismissive of individual speaker agency. In recognizing an utterance as an excited utterance, giving it that name during trial, and ratifying the naming citationally in the appeal, the boundaries around the event, the utterance, and the speaker are set, and along with it the normative practices of the discourse itself (Butler 1993, 8). Butler argues that this citation practice of bounding is an act of erasure—the reification is enacted "through enforcing a certain criterion, a principle of selectivity" (Butler 1993, 11). The criteria that are used to establish the boundaries of the excited utterance also give contour to the body who speaks the excited utterance. The criteria used in *Hadley*—exciting event, hysterical speaker, abused woman—are used to make PH recognizable in such a way that the court is allowed to maintain authority over a narrative that it insistently links to her body.

The interactional space of the institution does not attribute agency to the speaker of the excited utterance, nor does it recognize the attribution of agency that may have occurred in prior interactions or the way agency is moved around by all of the speakers in the court in order to suit the needs of any particular argument. Defense 1's argument failed because it misunderstood the system of agency attribution when Defense 1 overattributed agency to PH as an agent of discourse. He missed the fact that a speaker like PH has discursive agency only in relationship to an objective utterance that is also attributed to her. All other utterances are considered to be false and/or the result of influence from her abusive husband. This is a troubling proposition, especially in the context of domestic violence legal precedent. The speaker of the excited utterance is constructed as a sovereign subject who is forever linked to a representation of a story in which she was the victim, and in which she has no agency. She is doubly reduced as an agent—linked to a story where she is a victim and then forced into a position of spectator rather than actor even in the process of recounting the event.

6

Conclusions: Entextualization and a Legal Accounting for Domestic Violence

> "A statement is always an event that neither the language (*langue*) nor the meaning can quite exhaust. [. . .] Like every event, [a statement] is unique, yet subject to repetition, transformation, and reactivation, [and] it is linked not only to the situations that provoke it, and to the consequences that it gives rise to, but at the same time and in accordance with a quite different modality, to the statements that precede and follow it." (Foucault 1972, 28)

As Foucault aptly puts it, utterances are events that are repeatable and that are linked to the discursive practices that make up the events, contexts, and other statements that condition the emergence of a particular utterance. Hearsay is a type of utterance with legal weight situated just this way—between events of many different types: the event it purportedly reports, the one in which it was "originally" spoken, the legal events in which it is actually spoken, the recontextualizing statements in which it is produced, and those contexts in which it will be repeated with the force of law in the future. And when the excited utterance in question is about an event of domestic violence, then it is also positioned among the multiple, effective discourses about what it means to be in an intimate relationship and what it means to be abused by one's intimate partner. Hearsay, whether deemed admissible or inadmissible, is the kind of reported speech that Matoesian (2001) describes, stocked with bits and pieces from its previous contexts that may amplify and/or interrupt the pragmatic, rhetorical, and semantic function of the utterance when it is recontextualized in the powerful discourses of the law. A particular piece of hearsay such as an excited utterance will carry with it fragments from multiple events and discourses: the domestic assault, the encounter with police, interactions with prosecuting attorneys, assumptions about who gets abused and why, expectations about how the victim will respond to the abuse, and the list goes on. As Shoshona Felman

(2002, 57) has argued, "Legal memory is constituted, in effect, not just by the 'chain of law' and by the conscious repetition of precedents but also by a forgotten chain of cultural wounds and by compulsive or unconscious legal repetitions of traumatic wounding legal cases." Similarly, this book has argued, trials and appeals are made up of myriad explicit and implicit social discourses that are deployed alongside the metadiscourses of the hearsay rule, underpinned as it is by a language ideology rooted in empiricism, and developed over a number of centuries in order to evaluate a single hearsay utterance. This conglomeration of discourses, coming from various social and legal domains, are deployed to entextualize an utterance as either admissible or inadmissible hearsay—evidence or mere hearsay. I have argued that fundamental to this process are the precedents and statutes circulating in evidentiary discourses that excuse, justify, and even laud a husband's right to use physical violence against his wife, creating a legal facticity of domestic violence that remains functional even after domestic violence has become explicitly illegal.

We find justifications of domestic violence in historical legal texts and in social discourses that expect domestic violence, excuse the actions of the abuser, and make presumptions about the victim—she has abused woman's syndrome, she lies, she provoked the abuse. Such ideas are circulated within news stories about high-profile incidents of intimate violence, for example. Domestic violence is excused, justified, or explicitly deemed inconsequential in the vast majority of case law that have occasion to comment on it, hearsay among them (cf. *Giles v. California*, 2008). When the legal trust of objectivity comes together with the legal facticity of domestic violence, we get a discourse of legal victim-blaming. Victim-blaming is legally facilitated in a number of ways, which I describe in this conclusion. The hearsay principle circulates a language ideology that links true statements to a standard of objectivity that is always located outside of the speaking subject and in the empirically experienceable world. Admitting hearsay then requires a showing that the utterance is the product of that empirical world and not the subjectivity of the speaker. The legal value of objectivity is overstated and unrealistic, misunderstanding the rhetoricity and pragmatism that are part and parcel of any linguistic interaction. As Trinch (2010, 184) argues, "A completely factual representation of the event may not be only impossible but it frankly may be quite secondary to any given narrator's more pressing concerns." The expectation of objectivity coincides with and renders invisible, inconsequential, or untrustworthy the pragmatic and rhetorical underpinnings of the statements made by victims of domestic violence.

I have argued that the rule against hearsay has proven to be legally useful in domestic violence cases because it explicitly locates truth in objectivity, in an empirical reality—outside of the speaker—which reiterates and supports the legal presumption that truth is objective, and that objectivity is functionally and structurally different from stories, which are subjective. Admissible hearsay doesn't work against the legally constructed superiority of objectivity. Indeed, discourses that admit hearsay, such as the excited utterance exception, validate the fetishization of objectivity, entextualizing an utterance that has been rendered objective—stripped of any association with the speaker's subjective goals or intentions. This process dissociates the utterance from the speaker, instrumentalizing her—turning her into a mere vehicle through which objective truth passes—which results in the production of an account that is under the control of the law not the speaker. In the context of domestic violence, and this is not incidental, she is also giving an account of a domestic assault against herself. As Trinch (2010, 188) has shown, "a written account of intimate-partner violence [is] formalized as public property." The objective account of what happened becomes a legal fact, and it is not under the control of the person said to have spoken the account originally. Not all hearsay repeats an account in which the "original" utterance was also about the person who telling the story. Often hearsay is about something that happened to somebody else that the original speaker witnessed and is reporting. In the context of domestic violence, the person who said the original utterance is also the victim of the crime she is reporting. This victim/witness gives an account that is translated into admissible and inadmissible evidence. Admissible hearsay takes the account of self as objective and thus not belonging to the speaker; inadmissible hearsay takes the account as subjective and thus untrustworthy.

The evaluation of the admissibility of hearsay in trial testimony necessitates the discussion, representation, evaluation, and animation of the speaker's emotional responses, creating and in many cases requiring a co-articulation of social discourses about womanhood, domesticity, and violence. Using reported speech in-court, whether it is admitted or not, thus risks the out-of-court speaker to whom the hearsay utterance is attributed and who is not on the stand as it evaluates her body, her speech, her relationship to her husband, and her relationship to the truth. The absence of the speaker to whom the utterance is attributed cannot be stressed enough. That is, the discussion of victimhood, truth, and linguistic agency that emerges when hearsay is elicited in in-court testimony is made possible precisely because the speaker-victim is absent. Her speech is evaluated, using a language ideology that values and trusts objectivity, which includes the behavior and emotional state of the speaker. Whether the hearsay is admitted or not, the victim/speaker is treated as a roadblock to prosecution. In order to unpack this relationship between hearsay and domestic violence, I have analyzed its roots in Anglo-American legal history, its relationship to constitutional law developed in US Supreme Court opinions, and a trial in which hearsay was admitted using the excited utterance exception. The hearsay rule is significant, has power, and is specifically consequential as a rule that identifies what can and can't be said—which stories are admissible and which are not in court. Linked as it is to speakers, it also determines who is and is not authorized to make legally intelligible statements.

Social and legal discourses combine to create a system of indexicality in which victims of domestic violence are linked to untrustworthy speech, whether or not the speech was admitted as hearsay. The social and legal discourses about domestic violence, the bulk of which justify or at least excuse domestic violence as a normal if not necessary aspect of marriage, combine with the evaluations of trustworthiness and reliability circulated in hearsay law. According to Catherine MacKinnon (1989, 237), "Law actively participates in the transformation of perspective into being," by granting "legitimacy" to some while hiding the "force that underpins the legitimacy," which itself works to run cover for force. As such, individuals who are appropriated by legal discourses are "marked by power." MacKinnon's work focuses on the relationship between gender, "the state," and legal practices, arguing that the law is not objective, but rather a particularly powerful site in which social gender inequality is reiterated and reproduced as "facts of social power in and of law." Domestic violence is such a sociolegal fact—a point where social discourses meet Anglo-American statute and case law naturalizing gendered patriarchal discourses of the home and the law. The hearsay rule participates in sociolegal patriarchal discourse—working metadiscursively to manage the relationship between speech, the body, and an event—by mobilizing a legal language ideology that values empiricism and objectivity, and which believes words have meaning independent of the factors of usage. Weissbourd and Mertz (1985) call this a legal "drive for reference." A referential or empirical language ideology is derived from a more general language ideology that locates the "real" in the material world that exists outside of and prior to language, and puts distance between the "real" and language (cf. Rumsey 1990; Trinch 2003; Ehrlich 2012). This language ideology is used to entexutalize hearsay, and in the process, it makes the speaker recognizable along a continuum of objectivity. That is, not only does the entextualization make the utterance legally intelligible, but it also entextualizes the potential for the speaker to be "recognizable," applying discourses that precede the speaker in interaction. The entextualized speaker then provides a standard of recognizability that can be used to evaluate future speakers and future speech events. This process lays the groundwork for evaluations of her speech that affect not only how her speech is taken up (and taken away) in legal settings, but also whether or not she will be identified as a legitimate speaker in a legal context.

In this conclusion, I consider the ways legal entextualization shapes that victim's narratives about domestic violence, affecting the ways they are allowed to give accounts of their life experiences in enduring ways. The language ideology that informs and forms entextualization processes also affects discursive agency and polices victim behavior at the same time as and in order to adjudicate abuser behavior. I describe how hearsay case law and structures of policing participate in this process, operationalizing discourses that blame victims for abuse in the domestic sphere, avoiding direct interaction with victims, objectifying their bodies, instrumentalizing their accounts of abuse, and hypostatizing their identities. Fundamental in this process are the use of hearsay in domestic violence and the presupposition of an untrustworthy speaker embedded in hearsay. Legal discourses about hearsay carry bits and pieces of social and legal contexts that validate and justify patriarchal power in the domestic sphere. Patriarchal structures of the home and the law support and reinforce each other (cf. Ferraro, 1995), running on an economy of victim narrative that is underpinned by a legal language ideology that presents the treatment of the victim as in the service of justice.

Intertextuality and Entextualization

One of the things I have done in the foregoing pages is give empirical substance to the critical truism that evidence is not found in events but produced in legal processes and procedures. Evidence is the product of intertextual and interdiscursive discourses that are at work in all levels of legal interaction, from statute to trial to appellate opinion. Legal texts that are already infused with social discourses are used to measure and evaluate hearsay, a process that entextualizes evidence. That is, hearsay evidence is a product of legal interactions and the statutory and precedential arguments that define the limitations of viable evidence and in the process identify a particular piece of evidence. In generally articulating the reasons hearsay can and cannot be admitted, by drawing from the many arguments and criteria available in legal texts, the viability of a particular utterance's evidentiary status is also determined.

Text and context are simultaneously produced in the same processes of recontextualization that begin when the law begins its interventions (taking statements, interviewing potential witnesses, etc.) and culminate in the trial and again in the appellate opinion. Determining the relationship between texts and contexts happens in what Blommaert (2005, 46) has called, "the *post-hoc* recontextualization of earlier bits of text" which might themselves be recontextualizations. That is, texts are formed, entextualized, when the discourses circulating in a different context identify a bit of discourse as a "text-artifact" (Silverstein and Urban 1996). The norms and values of the recontextualizing context are used to identify a bit of discourse as a text, which entextualizes it as such. Texts and contexts are not themselves discrete entities, but rather they are produced during entextualization, when a new context, stocked as it is with texts, is used to recognize some bits of discourse as texts and other bits as context. That is, in the new context some chunks of interaction are labeled texts, which makes the rest of the interaction the context (Andrus 2011). This process both makes the texts and contexts seem naturally occurring, obscuring the lines of production, and it decontextualizes the text fragments, rendering them mobile. "Texts and discourses move around, are repeatedly recontextualized in new interpretive spaces, and in the process undergo significant transformations in meaning" (Ehrlich 2012, 48). Decontextualization renders texts movable, recontextualizable in future iterations that will necessarily impact the meaning of a text and the kinds of effects it can achieve.

Because hearsay is narrative in that it reports, qualifies, and explains a series of occurances, the entextualization of hearsay evidence also determines the beginning and ending points of the events it indexes, what they mean/meant, and what is important, etc. Importantly, there is another layer of narrating, the event of telling again in which the hearsay is entextualized in court. In this trial retelling, the criminal events are recounted, along with details about the mental state of the speaker on scene. In in-court testimony, the witness gives an account of an event in which a person gave an account of something that happened, such that hearsay is a narrative in a narrative, but the context of retelling is treated as though it is ineffectual, invisible. That is, the production of hearsay assumes that the narrative reproduction of the utterance does nothing to alter, reframe, or otherwise disrupt the semantic or rhetorical—the referential or non-referential—qualities of the utterance.

The discursive resources with which hearsay is entextualized presume that an utterance is already decontextual—that the context in which the utterance was produced is not required for the utterance to remain meaningful in exactly the same way. As Bauman and Briggs (1990, 72), explain, texts are often treated "as self-contained, bounded objects separable from their social and cultural contexts of production and reception." When a text is formed, then, it is also decontextualized. This renders the text mobile while at the same time forgetting, eliding, and even obscuring the effectuality of the sociocultural and institutional contexts through which such a mobile text is moved. That is, the text is legally presumed to be always already decontextual, and so it is—it has significant power in this discursive setting, because once entextualized, it seems to have always stood on its own. To understand the full effect of entextualization and decontextualization, I want to return to the fact that hearsay is a narrative couched in a narrative. The context of retelling is fundamental to understanding the decontextualization process and all that is embedded in the resultant text-artifact. Hearsay—whether admissible or inadmissible—is decontextualized when it is entextualized in the testimony of the person who recounts the words of an absent speaker. That absent speaker is described in the narrative that is produced about any bit of hearsay evidence (itself an account of an event) when it is elicited during direct- and cross-examination. The questions and answers that precede and follow the hearsay utterance during the trial describe the speaker and the event while in the process of circumscribing her utterance referentially to a particular event. The narrative about the speaker focuses on emotional state and ability to reflect on the consequences and legal usefulness of the utterance. Thus the discursive process that results in a decontextualized text is laden with descriptions of the speaker, her rhetorical and agented potential, her emotional state, and her trustworthiness. Admissible hearsay is often entextualized against a backdrop of a highly subjective speaker who is then shown not to be in control. It is that lack of control that produces an utterance that is thought to be objective—true regardless of the speaker. However, the showing of such objectivity is founded on an absence of self-reflection, which is typically established with direct-examination and cross-examination in which the speaker is described as excited out of her senses. The process of reporting speech in this institutional setting, framed within legal discourses and question-asking parameters, pulls relevant details from the "original" and "secondary" contexts into the resultant text in order to decontextualize the resultant legal text, unlinking it from the speaker to whom the utterance is attributed.

Because of the multiple acts of narration, a hearsay utterance is both an account of something that happened and part of what happened. Recontextualization changes the semantic shape of an utterance. Moreover, not everybody is authorized to recontextualize a text in ways that maintain a text's institutional viability. "Larger patterns of social inequality" (Ehrlich 2012, 48) are always already in the contextualizing discourses that produce texts. And thus, as Ehrlich (69) puts it, "social power is inevitably implicated in the processes of decontextualization and recontextualization (Bauman and Briggs 1990) and [. . .] not all 'texts' in a given text trajectory will be accorded the same value or legitimacy." What I have argued here is that subjectivity is a co-product of entextualization. That is, the patterns of inequality with which texts are produced also produce the speakers or speaking positions associated with them. Descriptions of the speaker of hearsay are not neutral in some way, but rather they are themselves part of the discourses that circulate and reiterate patriarchal presuppositions about domesticity, marriage, wifehood, womanhood, etc. Legal processes of entextualization that are explicitly intertextual thus produce and reproduce indexical linkages between social ideas about domesticity and ideas about how language works that come together to make the domestic violence victim legally intelligible and socially recognizable. The interdiscursive network of legal language ideology manifested in hearsay law, the legal facticity of domestic violence, and social discourses about victims function indexically to reproduce social and legal discourses about domestic violence which ultimately facilitate either the appropriation or elision of the speech of domestic violence victims.

Language Ideology, Discursive Agency, and the Legal Facticity of Domestic Violence

Butler (1997, 11) argues that speech is "a bodily act." Not only is speech a physical act, but that act is complicated by the "kind of saying that the bodily 'instrument' of the utterance performs" (11). That is to say that speech requires a body—the physical body that speaks—and an utterance is made meaningful with the discursive and interactional resources with which the speaking body is made meaningful. The discourses of Anglo-American law and social discourses about domestic violence that come into play when a particular utterance is entextualized precede the individual moment of speech and specific trial. Such discourses participate in a "regulatory practice that produces the bodies it governs, that is, whose regulatory force is made clear as a kind of productive power, the power to produce—demarcate, circulate, differentiate—the bodies it controls" (Butler 1993, 1). The bodies that are evaluated via the discourse of the excited utterance are sorted using the trustworthy/not trustworthy dichotomy, and, as I have discussed in this book, the body that has been abused is most often aligned with untrustworthy speech. In moving to gain and maintain control over an utterance, the institutional practice of the excited utterance reiterates the "injuries, dominations and enslavements" that "lie behind these words" and that accompany discourse (Foucault 1972, 216).

Embedded and circulating in the discourse of the Anglo-American law of evidence, an excited utterance is assumed to be sayable by anybody in any place, without changing its semantics, pragmatics, or rhetoricity. In the same process, agency is also entextualized, becoming a part of the legal discourse of which the excited utterance is also a part. In this context, it is more useful to conceive of agency as discursive agency, distributed as it is across agents, actions, events, and objects. Once entextualized, agency is most visibly a characteristic of the excited utterance, at the same time that the utterance itself literally requires a speaker, and the law necessitates a speaker whose level of excitement can be evaluated in the tautological construction of testimonialness. That is to say, in the excited utterance, there must be a speaker but she must not have sovereign agency. Indeed, the same discursive gesture that entextualizes the excited utterance entextualizes a speaker who is essentially out of control. In the interactional space of the legal system, agency is disattributed from the speaker of the excited utterance and embedded in the discourse of the law—but her body and bodily performances remain necessary.

The attribution of discursive agency in the entextualization of hearsay instrumentalizes and subjectifies the speaker. As Butler argues, institutions and discursive practices "delineat[e] who will qualify as a subject of recognition, and [offer] available norms for the act of recognition" (2005, 22). The subjectivity of a victim of domestic violence is a product of discursive forces, productive prohibitions that define the limits of subjectivity (Butler 2005, 116). It is important to note, as Bucholtz (2010, 1) does, "Individuals do not passively inhabit identity categories to which they have been assigned; rather, they negotiate and navigate these categories in a variety of ways within social interaction." Or as Butler (2005, 19) puts it, "a subject must negotiate [norms and rules] in a living and reflective way." Subjectification isn't finite, final, or unnegotiated, but indeed it is a set of norms and prohibitions that are reperformed over and over. In that reperformance, there is room for a disruption of the norms that alter them or explicitly take them on. Take for example, PH from the case analyzed in Chapters 4 and 5. With her refusal to answer questions during cross-examination, she actively disrupts the social and legal expectations of a witness. Nor does she fit easily into expectations of an abused woman; she offers no excuses for her husband while attempting to shift the narrative attributed to her. She treats law and narrative as negotiable. Although her attempt doesn't win the day, it would not be fair to say that she loses the struggle over her narrative or subject position. The law forces a winner/loser finality, but PH's arguments show a more nuanced negotiation, in which she submits to powerful discourses at the same time that she breaks the rules of the court. Indeed, these two often happen in the same utterance. When she interjects "I did lie" from the gallery, she occupies the untrustworthy subject position carved out for her in the social and legal discourses, but she does so by breaking the rules of the court and speaking out of turn.

The discourse involved in entextualizing the hearsay utterance also characterizes the body and emotional state of the speaker. Either she is in complete control and already acting as a witness (inadmissible hearsay) or she is a hysterical, out-of-control victim (admissible hearsay). That is, the process of entextualizing an utterance presented as hearsay in the context of domestic violence makes texts, but it also has the added effect of creating subjectivities, which are used to make individual speakers recognizable. Hearsay is explicitly banned, but it has a lot of exceptions, which means that in hearsay case law there is a constant comparison between hearsay that is inadmissible and hearsay that is admissible. Depending on whether the hearsay utterance was deemed admissible or not, there is some variability in the subjectivity. The speaker subjectivity associated with inadmissible hearsay is "witness," as that concept is introduced in *Crawford v. Washington* (2004). Both *Crawford* and *Davis v. Washington/Hammon v. Indiana* (2006) argue that some utterances are inherently testimonial, because their primary purpose is to be used prosecutorially, and such utterances are always spoken by a witness. Entextualizing hearsay as inadmissible and testimonial thus has the consequence of producing a subject category called "witness" that always relates back to the concept of testimonial. This subject category has a high presumption of speaker intentionality and a very simple idea of rhetorical purpose. On the other hand, if the utterance is admitted, for example using the excited utterance exception that is commonly used in cases involving domestic violence, the speaker is assumed to be essentially out of control. The excited utterance is constituted as admissible only if the speaker is not in control of her reflective faculties. Thus, entextualizing an utterance as an excited utterance has the consequence of producing a hysterical subject. This subjectivity has a high presumption of spontaneity, equating truth-telling with a lack of intention or thoughtful reflection.

We see robust and highly effectual arguments about spontaneity and intentional speech in judicial opinions in which the US Supreme Court rules on hearsay cases by contrasting admissible and inadmissible hearsay. In the most recent iterations of this precedential structure, *Crawford v. Washington* (2004), *Davis v. Washington/Hammon v. Indiana* (2006), *Giles v. California* (2008), *and Michigan v. Bryant* (2011), the comparison hinges on the relationship between the concepts of "witness," "testimonial utterance," and "primary purpose." This constant comparison in the binary logic of the law—A/not A—has the effect of creating a series of mutual exclusions:

- hearsay (inadmissible)/admissible hearsay
- testimonial utterance/non-testimonial utterance
- witness/non-witness
- control/no control

This set of binaries is created and circulated intertextually and interdiscursively in precedent, and has the effect of managing the speaker, not just the utterance. That is, ideas about the utterance and what makes an utterance testimonial or not are based on a discussion of a speaker that results in binaries that define the actions, behavior, and motives against each other. The binary contrasting of testimonial and non-testimonial utterances results in producing two kinds of speakers, one of whom is in control (testimonial) and the other of whom is not in control (non-testimonial). This aligns further with being a victim-witness (in control and giving testimony) or a victim (out of control and speaking spontaneously). Controlled language is equated with controlled emotions, and being emotionally in control translates to speaking purposefully, which renders the hearsay untrustworthy.

The last binary set, control/no control is strongly established in *Davis/Hammon* (2006), which is explicitly binary and contrastive, defining admissible hearsay by ruling on two cases in a single opinion. The control/no control binary is a product of the primary purpose evaluation. On the one hand (*Davis*), we have a victim who is out of control, who speaks in the moment, whose only obvious primary purpose is to get help. On the other hand (*Hammon*), we have a victim who is in control, who speaks after the assault has ended, whose only obvious primary purpose is to report a crime and cause legal trouble for the abusive partner. The speech of the person who has a primary purpose that is testimonial is inadmissible, because she is acting as a witness and must be cross-examined. The speech of the person who has no testimonial intentions is admitted.

What *Davis/Hammon* (2006) teaches us is that the victim of domestic violence is caught in between the legal binaries that simplify the discursive fields in which victims live and speak. Victims are either in complete control or completely out of control; they have singular primary purposes to either want to prosecute or not. Isn't it interesting that the victim who actively calls 911 (*Davis*)—who is constructed in the legal texts as only wanting to get herself and her children safe, who is constructed as not speaking with the primary purpose of prosecuting—is the victim whose speech is treated as trustworthy enough to obviate cross-examination? The victim who doesn't call the police (*Hammon*)—who waits for police to come to her house, who is constructed as speaking testimonially with the purpose of prosecuting—is the victim whose speech is deemed rhetorical and not trustworthy, thus requiring cross-examination. In other words, the victim who is out of control must be saved by the law, and the victim who is in control is untrusted and dismissed. What we find in *Davis/Hammon* (2006) is that there is no room between distrust and distress. Either the law treats victims of domestic violence like essential liars or like women who need to be saved, often saved from their own bad decisions. It is the hysterical speech, the speech that is out of control, that is admitted as hearsay that is so trustworthy that it has fact-value that doesn't need to be tested. Of course, many victims of domestic violence are treated as both untrustworthy and distressed, as was the situation in the case analyzed in this book.

Placed within the larger framework of hearsay case law, importantly including the trial and the rehearsal of social and linguistic ideology that takes place there, these binaries put the victim in a no-win situation. Trustworthy hearsay is non-testimonial and so it is admissible; testimonial speech is untrustworthy and so it is inadmissible. That is, purposeful speech is assumed to have the singular purpose of wanting the abuser prosecuted, but in a strange turn, only spontaneous speech is actually used to prosecute. Prosecution thus hinges on a showing that the victim did not intend for the abuser to be prosecuted. In the context of hearsay, only speech that is absent of personal motivation is used/useful in prosecution. Purposeful speech is assumed to be untrustworthy, especially compounded by the presumption that victims of domestic violence lie. Social and legal discourses combine to suggest that victims of domestic violence lie to protect their abusive husbands and they lie when they falsely accuse their partners of abuse.

It may seem viable for victims to just take the stand and give their side of the story. That is, it might seem like the way out of the double bind of hearsay is to be an in-court witness. Not only is the decision to be an in-court witness not hers to make, acting as an in-court witness does not make the domestic violence victim legally intelligible, or at least not in a way that is under her control or that may even match her own view of herself and her intimate relationships, etc. PH went to court and demanded to give testimony in *US v. Hadley* (Sentencing, 2003), but it did not result in her being considered trustworthy. Indeed, one of her utterances was entextualized as an excited utterance, which was used to prove all of her other explanations of what happened to be false. The excited utterance was proved to be out of her control, and in the appellate opinion, it was deemed nontestimonial. PH was not called to give testimony during the trial. Instead, her eyewitness account was admitted in the testimony of two of the police officers who came to her house after 911 was called.

The process of entextualizing the excited utterance in the courtroom context, in the direct examination of Officer 1, decontextualized the utterance and divided it from the speaker, but only insofar as the speaker is considered to be the author of the utterance—to have a say in what the utterance means and how it will be used. The excited utterance is attributed back to the speaker who saw what happened, but she is obliged to speak it by the exciting event. She does not choose to speak it. So this utterance is decontextualized and made mobile by presuming that the speaker didn't mean to say it anyway. The accidental quality, the fact that it was not purposefully said, it what makes it admissible. The way the legal object "excited utterance" is entextualized in the legal discourse, the speaker of the utterance is compelled to speak by the event; she is not the author of the utterance and indeed she has no authority over it.

In the process of creating the legal object "excited utterance," with its presumption that the exciting event stilled the reflective faculties of the speaker and caused the production of a spontaneous account of what happened, the event itself is granted a sort of agency. However, law runs on culpability; a person must be held accountable—put on trial—for the criminal event. So the event may be put in the position of actor, but even more so, the abuser is granted a fundamental agency in relationship to his or her criminal actions. The abusive event of which he was the perpetrator is what causes the excited utterance to be spoken, and it is the utterance's spontaneous character that makes it admissible. All—event, abuser, law—works on the speaker of the excited utterance who is also a victim of domestic violence; she is situated as an essential victim—always acted on. Thus the abusive event is hypostatized in the excited utterance, in turn hypostetizing the speaker as a victim. The entextualization process, with its intersecting lines of legal reasoning, social discourses, precedents, and prior experiences, essentially links the speaker to an utterance about an event of abuse of which she was the victim, but it does so via a subjectivity that is not authorized to speak about or explain the event or the utterance further. Her reified position as the object of abuse makes it impossible for her to have access to the narrative of abuse. The displacement of discourse in the excited utterance thus results in the perpetuation of abuse by making the speaker a mere conduit for an objective account of the violence done by her husband to her person.

The objective/subjective distinction plays out in a number of ways in hearsay cases involving domestic violence, which all consistently frame the speaker and the utterance as potentially untrustworthy, with arguments about the state of the speaker's reflective faculties—her subjectivity—stilled at the time the utterance was spoken. Objectivity is operationalized in the most recent US Supreme Court opinions that use it as a measurement of the primary purpose of the utterance in question.

The disassociation between intelligible accounts about what happened and the subject position associated with being a victim of domestic violence happens in more than one way. One way has to do with the physical evidence left on the body. "Regardless of her consent or belligerence, the rhetorical situation necessitates she be examined as the potential abused object" (Shearer-Cremean 2004, 167). That is, her body gives objective (physical) evidence of abuse. The proof of the body is visible, and to observe it does not always require consent. The abused body is thus treated as objective evidence that must be gathered, rather than as subjective, a part of the person who is working with her own set of contextual constraints. This objectification is reproduced again in the construction of the excited utterance. In the production of the excited utterance, a legal fact, the subjectivity and agency of the speaker are overridden by both the legal discourse and the violent episode. The discourse of excited utterance case law also preempts any attempt that the speaker may make to regain narrative control over the violence. When PH tries to alter the story embedded in the excited utterance attributed to her—"he has a gun" and "he's going to kill me"—she is treated as a liar. Any self-aware and contextually sensitive account of the event is treated as false in comparison to the one true utterance—her excited utterance. The event that is granted agency in the production of the one true utterance is the violence done by her husband. Ostensibly for the woman's own good, the use of the excited utterance in a case involving domestic violence works to further limit her discursive agency following the lines of socially situated power structures. In this legal framework, the violence perpetrated by her husband is more powerful than anything PH can do discursively, and this power is reinforced by the legal discourse applied in the evaluation of the excited utterance.

Entextualization, Subjectivity, and Narrativity

Although this project has not specifically been about narrative, it is important to note that hearsay is not only reported speech, but as I've already briefly discussed above, it is also essentially narrative. Evaluations of hearsay are about the reliability of the story that tend to focus on the person who is said to have told the story out of court. The person giving testimony is cross-examined, but their reliability in relationship to the story is not questioned. As Trinch (2010, 182) puts it, "The person who bears witness also shoulders the burden of having done so." In the case of hearsay, that person who carries the burden of bearing witness is not in the courtroom. And when that person is narrating an event of violence at the hands of her intimate partner, that burden extends to the social, institutional, physical, and personal consequences of the story. She continues to "bear witness" institutionally; she is risked in the telling; she is the "I" of the story. But she is likely not even in the courtroom. On her front porch, she blurts something to a police officer, who then goes into the courtroom and recounts, in response to attorney-led questioning, the story s/he was told. When the event reported on the front porch is about something that happened to the speaker, as is the case of domestic violence, this story is also an account of self—an account in which the teller of the story has to relate herself to events and those with whom she has interacted. The speaker recounts an event in which she was abused.

Not all hearsay utterances give an account of self; only those that are spoken by victims bearing witness to a crime against themselves, as opposed to witnesses bearing witness to a crime against another person. Narrative accounts, such as those spoken by a domestic violence victim, are subjective—framed relative to the values and goals of the speaker. Using criteria that function as a set of presuppositions in the law about what language is and how it works, the hearsay rule works to entextualize spoken evidence that is importantly also narrative, and as such, describes what happened. Of course the law's expectations for and valuation of objectivity are unrealistic (cf. Trinch 2003; 2010). Language is interactive. According to Trinch (2010, 184), in giving accounts of domestic violence, "Narrators show an awareness of the dialectical nature of representation, because they constantly mediate between their own narrative purposes and the expectations they believe their listeners possess." That is, those telling the stories clearly indicate awareness of the expectations of their interlocutors (cf. McElhinny, 1995). Women who have been the victims of violence tell stories about what happened strategically, in order to achieve goals, to get and stay safe, and to protect their families (cf. Trinch, 2013). These goals don't always simply or easily align with each other, let alone with the law's explicit concern with policing. Moreover, accounts about what happened do more than simply point at the world, as though what happened resides stably outside of language.

Narratives give accounts of selves, which are deeply invested in and interconnected with larger social structures, personal histories, and immediate concerns. "When the 'I' seeks to give an account of itself, it can start with itself, but it will find that this self is already implicated in a social temporality that exceeds its own capacities for narration" (Butler 2005, 7). That is, any story about the self will be more than just about self, and the rhetorical and semantic work it performs are not under the control of the teller of the story. Once spoken, an utterance is open for recapitulation by those who hear it, the contexts in which it is reiterated, and future potential audiences.

According to Foucault (1986 42), self-narrative requires the speaker "to take oneself as an object of knowledge and a field of action." That is, the speaker becomes the subject of the story, and indeed, the speaker becomes the "field" on which the story plays out. Such a process is expected to "transform, correct, and purify" the self that the story is about. The account given in hearsay is a story that has legal weight and is framed as an account of self, but is actually produced across contexts and speakers who tell and retell it. The narrative captured in hearsay demonstrates the depths to which self-narrative is never fully in control of the person who tells the story about herself. Any account of self opens the self up to interrogation, so that evaluation of the account is also an evaluation of the speaker, who, in this case, was a victim of domestic violence whose discursive position is already precarious. The narrative and the speaker both find themselves preconditioned by social and legal norms—the rules of the court; and the federal rules of evidence, precedent, and the ideas about language that authorize particular utterances and particular speakers. Hearsay is attributed to a particular person, who is said to have told the story in the past but who is not speaking in the courtroom. Thus the self-narrative we find in hearsay is a product of the various contexts, speakers, audiences, and discursive networks through which it is moved. The legal discourse overlooks the differences that arise when the speaker and context change. This is particularly striking and consequential when the hearsay is attributed to a domestic violence victim who is speaking about an event of abuse of which she was the object. As I have demonstrated, cases involving domestic violence are shot through with social discourses that explain the behavior and motivations of victims of domestic violence.

The "I" of a hearsay narrative about domestic violence is risked in every interaction in which the story is told. "Narrative representations of past violence have a fundamental relation to risk, danger, and vulnerability" (Trinch 2010, 180–181). The risks of the violent situation at home are renewed as the victim's story and speech are ignored or exploited for legal purposes. The process of telling a story about oneself is always risky, and in this case, such risk is compounded when the story is about an event in which the speaker was abused and is then told to a police officer and subsequently repeated in court, entextualized as a legal fact, and then attributed to the person whose emotional demeanor proves that the utterance but not the speaker is trustworthy. The self who is entextualized in this process is a product of narrative and legal discourses. "There is no 'I' that can fully stand apart from the social conditions of its emergence" (Butler 2005, 7). That is, not only is the narrative a product of interaction but also the "I" at its center; both are produced in the social interaction that is the telling of one's story. The story is given shape—details selected and given significance—based on the interactional expectations and the auditor of the story, and if the story is about the speaker, the speaker is also a product of the social conditions in which it is told.

Victimness and untrustworthiness are attributed to the "I" of the narrative about domestic violence that is entextualized as evidence. As Butler (2005,15) puts it, "I come into being as a reflexive subject in the context of establishing a narrative account of myself when I am spoken to by someone and prompted to address myself to the one who addresses me." The self is a product of address and response, of being spoken to and being prompted to answer in a particular way. Hearsay produces an "I," but the moments of address are multiple—in the front yard, in the police station, in the district attorney's office, in the courthouse—but the self to whom the narrative is linked, who told the story one time in one way, is not always in the room. The domestic violence victim who speaks to a police officer about a very recent attack perpetrated by her intimate partner will highlight victimness pragmatically and interactionally; the police officer has arrived and has the power to stem the tide of violence, if only momentarily. Even in the same situation, a different addressee will produce a different speaker. Talking to a friend who has also been abused by her partner might produce a survivor-centric "I." Victims of domestic violence have been shown to respond differently to female and male officers (McElhinny, 1995). Address in hearsay is always in the past, and, importantly, it is recapitulated by the addressor, the person who invited the narrative in the first place. That is, the moment of address that calls for self-narration is repeated in the courtroom some time later by the person who does the addressing, not the person who was addressed, giving a significant amount of control to the addressor and the discourses circulating in the law and the courtroom. The self that is produced within the discourses of the retelling—the second set of discourses that condition the emergence of the narrator—frames her account institutionally while putting the story into her mouth.

When somebody else tells the self-narrative, recounts the story in a new context, the story will change, along with the speaker. The "I" that was the subject of her own story becomes the object of a legally recognizable story when it is recontextualized during the trial. As Shearer-Cremean (2004, 178) argues, "When an abused woman's trauma story is articulated within a discourse frame of male domination, the narrative undergoes discursive shifts and permutations that meet the requirements of the patriarchal discursive contours." The story shifts to fit the demands of the paternalistic institution that distrusts the victim of domestic violence. This process is only further hypostatized in the appellate opinion. That the "I" emerges out of the social conditions in which a narrative about the self is told, in response to the context and speaker to whom the story is told, means that the retelling of that story by another party will change the "I." The person whom the story is about is stabilized as a part of the event, in this case the object of abuse. There is no active, agented "I," even though the story is a self-narrative.

Further, and perhaps more importantly, in the retelling of the story during the trial, the "I" who emerged in the original telling is no longer the speaker. She is talked about, instead, treated as a prop in a performance in which the police articulate themselves as competent public servants. The victim of domestic violence, whose story has now been transformed into evidence or non-evidence, becomes the object of her own story. The narrative accretes meaning and stabilizes into a seemingly finite legal artifact. Once it is hypostatized in a voice that is not hers but is said to be hers, the original speaker is put on the outside of a story that is about an event that happened to her. Shifting the person who tells the story from the victim to the police officer to whom she originally spoke solidifies her legal status as a victim (whether or not the utterance is admitted as hearsay), and it makes her the spectator of her own story. This can happen in a very literal sense, as in the case of PH when her narrative is told by a different person while she is in the courtroom. And as we would expect, as the spectator, she has no authorship nor authority over the narrative. Indeed, during sentencing she is on the stand when the attorneys for both parties repeat her speech for the court, arguing successfully that her interpretation of her own story is false. PH is positioned as a passive, even untrustworthy audience to her own story. In the stripping of the context and history from the excited utterance, the event entextualized in that utterance is pulled away from the speaker. Her body gives witness to the crime, her purported excitedness makes her utterance into evidence, but the utterance in which that crime is entextualized cannot be the product of the speaker's goals, history, or context. This is the embodied double bind of the excited utterance: it must be her body, but it cannot be her subjectivity.

When a speaker like PH attempts to (re)claim an utterance and the story it tells, she is unable to—the utterance is out of her control. Adding to the injury, the discourses that make her aware of her lack of control also make the utterance (appear) permanent, entextualized into law. Determined to have been out of control when she made the "original" utterance, there is nothing that PH can do to reclaim control over the utterance. In fact, everything she does and says is used to prove the truthfulness of the excited utterance and put it further out of her control. PH learns that once spoken, the utterance is lost to the speaker, but open to appropriation, especially by more powerful discourses. The legally audible and constructed excited utterance demonstrates the extent to which an utterance can fail to belong to the speaker, as well as the implications of that lack of ownership. The rules surrounding the excited utterance circulate this paradoxical anxiety. Institutional discourses make the transient utterance seem stable, durable, *and* mobile.

When it is used in a case of domestic violence, the excited utterance reproduces the violence of the event. The combination of the excited utterance and domestic violence puts the speaker to whom the excited utterance is attributed in a double bind. The same move in the excited utterance that puts the speaker out of control of her speech requires the body of the speaker to have been present at the event. Thus the regulatory discourses of the excited utterance that require agentless speech are the very same discourses that require that the body be risked, literally and discursively. Her body witnessed and was the victim of the violent event. Adding to the injury, the account of the violent event produced by that body must not involve her subjectivity. The speaker's body is objectified as the mere vocal apparatus for an excited utterance that the event has required her to speak. Her abused body must produce the utterance, but not from a personal, historical, or contextual position.

The constraints of legal discourse obscure the production of the utterance as it is pulled into the abstracting discourse of case law. The result is that the body who speaks is also obscured. Discursive agency is linked to the event and to legal discourses, but the effects of the discourse continue to make the body intelligible, and the effects of the (discursive) event continue to mark the body.

Policing the Victim

Controlling the victim's story is a way of policing the victim of domestic violence. As Trinch (2010, 188) argues, accounts of "intimate-partner violence" that are written down for legal uses are "formalized as public property. Once the story is inscribed in the legal document, [. . .] women continue to lose control over their stories, as they can no longer tell it their way, and they can no longer decide what can be done with it. The prosecution for example, can always use a sworn affidavit against an 'uncooperative' victim who recants in a criminal investigation." Although the criminalization of domestic violence has made strides in making violence perpetrated by husbands against wives recognizable as criminal and thus open to police intervention, this book has identified some of the ways that legal interventions have failed victims of domestic violence. Legal interventions in domestic violence that increase policing and punishment have not reduced domestic violence, and I argue they have the consequence of reproducing patriarchal violence. It has been well established that our particular police state puts people in jail, but it can only do that under the auspices of fairness—legal protections of the rights of the accused, such as the presumption of innocence and the right to confrontation. Criminalizing domestic violence creates the potential to hold abusers responsible, and this requires a victim. Much of the work of punishing abusers rests on the victim status of the abused. In this way, the victim is fundamental to the crime, putting her at particular risk. The necessitation of the crime combined with the protections for the accused put legal pressure on the victim.

In Anglo-American common law, there are myriad robust precedential options that excuse and justify domestic violence and very few that do the opposite—those listed above are just the tip of the case law that maintains the legal facticity of domestic violence. Victims who enter the legal system are caught between competing expectations of how good victims will act: stay in control, lose control; come to court, don't come to court; testify, don't testify—all of these are simultaneously demanded. She should be available to testify, but should not expect to be called to the stand. If her statements were said when she was visibly out of control, then they can be admitted without her untrusted body on the stand. But when she does not take the stand, she will be accused of avoiding court in order to protect her abusive husband.

There are two quieter idealized narratives about what an abused wife should do that underpin this double bind, both of which hinge on marriage being located in civil rather than criminal law. One involves a wife who manages her husband better, quiets his violent tendencies, and doesn't need to call the police. The other is of a fully agented wife, with means of her own, and strong spirit and will, who can extricate herself and her children from a violent marriage with a simple divorce. Both of the idealized solutions to domestic violence share a common missing element: the police. They don't frame the situation as criminal. However, even though the expectations that historically made domestic violence a private civil matter still cling to it, the criminalization of domestic violence makes it a police issue. Moving a civil issue into criminal law has consequences. Criminalizing a traditionally civil issue requires old laws to be retrofitted so that they can be applied to a new crime that still carries domestic baggage with it. Anglo-American law is constructed to punish criminals, and so it is not surprising that when domestic violence was criminalized, it was fit into a system of punishment that involves police and the possibility of jailing. Policing and sentencing are two fundamental components of criminal punishment, and so domestic violence reforms have led to institutionalized ways for police officers to perceive wife abuse and arguments for longer sentences for abusers.

The focus on the criminalization of domestic violence has consequences, not only for the perpetrator but also for the victim. First, it has the effect of pretending that domestic violence is just like any publicly perpetrated crime. It is not. Despite pulling back the veil of domesticity and making domestic violence open to criminal charges, issues that are specific to a domestic relationship are ignored, treated as insignificant. Domestic violence is saturated with intimate, economic, and social concerns that, for starters, make divorce anything but simple. Social values that blame wives for the failure of marriages, that expect women to maintain intimate relationships, are compounded by age-old economic factors that may keep women financially dependent on men. We are now better able to count incidences of domestic violence, but we seem no closer to staunching wife-beating. One reason is that, in addition to ignoring sociocultural and gendered factors in which domesticity and domestic violence are imbricated, the emphasis on policing and punishing the abuser has the consequence of policing and punishing the victim.

The paternalism of the home is reproduced in the paternalism of the courtroom. Legal rules and courtroom procedures instrumentalize the victim's story, translating it into evidence that can be used regardless of the willingness of the victim, and in some cases can be used to demonstrate the depths to which the victim can't be trusted. Falseness is presented as a baseline in at least two ways. First, accusations of abuse are treated as not true. The legal mandate "innocent until proven guilty," stated positively without any hedging, implies that all accusations of guilt are incorrect until they are proven in the "crucible of cross-examination" (*Crawford v. Washington* 2004, 62). This legal precept is compounded by the broader social presumption that the accusation of abuse is not true. We saw this quite explicitly when the pop-star Rihanna was beaten by her sometime boyfriend Chris Brown. Gil Kaufman, a writer for *MTV.com,* argued that circulating the photo was necessary, because "the evidence of Rihanna's injuries settles" questions about the truth of her allegations (mtv.com, 2/20/09). That is, people initially presumed that she was lying and only believed that the assault was real after they saw photographic evidence. Of course, this makes abuse that doesn't leave marks harder to prove true, an issue I'll have to leave for another day.

The second presumption of falseness has to do with the belief that victims of domestic violence will lie to protect their husbands. Sometimes this lie is explained by attributing it to abused women's syndrome, but either way, it deepens the distrust of the victim and often leads the court to treat her as recalcitrant. We see this in *US v. Hadley*, a case in which a husband is found guilty of holding a gun to his wife's head due to the use of a hearsay utterance attributed to his wife, PH, who denied saying the utterance. Both the prosecution and the defense characterize PH's statements as essentially false. The prosecuting attorney admonishes (June 2003: 20), "Then how can we believe what you are saying today? You remember, [PH], just what you want to remember" and the defense attorney's (June 2003: 54) accusation that "[PH] is coming in and lying." We even have her husband testifying on the record, "My wife lied about that" (June 2003: 41). The legal discourse makes PH intelligible in relation to falseness, and at the end of sentencing, she stands up in the gallery and yells, "I did lie," and when she is asked to leave, she continues, "Why? Because I want to tell the truth, I have to leave?" (June 2003: 77–78). PH is consistently positioned with a true/false opposition, in which even her truth is made recognizable as a lie.

Domestic Violence in US Law

This project, though limited to a particular law developed in a language ideology specifically in the Anglo-American law of evidence, and limited by data which primarily comes from a US context, contributes to a growing transnational discussion about the systemic and troubling abuse of women that happens around the globe (cf. Alonso 1996; Hirsch 1998; Lazarus-Black 2007; Muhammad 2010). Beasley and Thomas (1994), for example, argue that domestic violence—though imbricated in different social, cultural, and legal systems—needs to be dealt with as a human rights concern subject to international law. Although the legal and marital systems are significantly different in different countries and legal systems, the patriarchal use of violence in intimate relationships is disturbingly similar in some striking ways, as is shown in the work of Lazarus-Black (2007), for example. Hirsch (1998, 2) in research on marital disputes in Muslim Swahili society is careful not to "suggest that Western women (liberated through law) are positioned to speak for Muslim women (silenced through law)." Instead she argues,

> [L]aw, as an institutional discourse that shapes approaches to social life, gives form to gendered subject positions and sets the parameters for who should speak, where, and when. Yet, from culturally and institutionally defined positions, speakers interact in ways that sometimes transform assumptions about their gendered status. (Hirsch, 1998, 3)

That is, while law shapes gender, performances of marital interactions show legal and social entailments of gendered speech are open to more nuanced negotiations.

Contrasted with this research, the international research shows that, as much as domestic violence is a pervasive, entrenched problem in multiple contexts, it is also intertwined with cultural, social, national, and racial issues that impact the specific problem and indicate different solutions. And of course, in the context of domestic violence in the United States, gender and law are complicated by discourses of race. And although this project doesn't focus on understanding the impact of race on crime rates, police response times, arrest policies, length of incarceration, and many other factors (race is not made explicit in the trial transcripts and opinions analyzed here, and I risk doing more harm than good by making assumptions about the implications of race), I would be remiss if I didn't note that issues of race and domestic violence intersect in many ways. As Beth Richie (2012) has argued, domestic violence is often thought of as a gender problem that is not impacted by race, and race as a political issue not impacted by gender. Or as Felman (2002, 6) puts it in her analysis of the O.J. Simpson trial, "the two cardinal societal traumas of race discrimination and gender discrimination" are too often pitted against each other, with one or the other treated as a more significant social issue. Such systemic competition for civil rights, Richie argues, is "strategically" used to "advance hegemonic values" (2012, 3). So for example, police surveillance is more pervasive in and more likely to result in arrests in neighborhoods with predominantly African-American or Latino/a populations, while at the same time police may take calls about domestic violence less seriously when they come from neighborhoods associated with people of color. Thus, according to Richie (2010, 6), "young women of color" may not "turn to formal systems as a remedy for their victimization because of the strong distrust of the criminal legal system" (cf. Bell & Mattis 2000). As Patricia Williams (1987, 407) has put it, "black femaleness" is often read "as unreliable, untrustworthy, hostile, angry, powerless, irrational, and probably destitute." According to Bell and Mattis (2000), such stereotypes present African American women as out-of-control, justifying their partners' uses of domestic violence. Taken together with the inattention to race from anti-violence and feminist legal reforms, there are few avenues to safety for women of color that don't also pathologize and victim-blame along color lines (cf. Williams 1987, 1991). Limited English proficiency also complicates the use of public services, such as the police. Ad hoc interpretations during police interviews produce dubious if not coerced accounts of events (cf. Berk-Seligson 2009). Trinch (2003) shows how interpretation during interviews to get a protective order adjusts the story, creating an institutional account that is no longer under the control of the narrative. Issues of race and ethnicity dovetail with those of gender, creating resource gaps and more pernicious and violent stereotypes that have widespread and damaging consequences to women of color involved in legal contexts. Race becomes an additional intertextual resource used to police victims of abuse in the process of policing abusers.

* * *

In legal and social discourses about domestic violence, it is assumed that abused women lie. Abused women are accused of lying to punish their partners when they make initial claims of abuse. Abused women are assumed to be lying to protect their partners when they recant their statements or miss court dates. They are stuck between two impossible positions. The excited utterance exception to hearsay reproduces these, adding excited, hysterical behavior as an indicator of truth, further compounding the subjectification of the victim of abuse. The victim whose case is moved into the purview of law has few sites from which she is recognizable in relationship to the truth. Indeed, she is primarily recognizable in relationship to abuse. Criminalizing domestic violence institutionalizes an intimate crime within a system that has historically rationalized and excused violence against women. Because of the historical forms and functions of criminal law, making domestic violence a punishable crime created a situation in which victims of intimate violence are recognizable as victims and as false, in opposition to perpetrators, who are innocent until proven guilty. Making domestic violence a crime allows for prosecution of abusers and better protections for victims, but such innovations are embedded in a patriarchal and institutional context that also polices victims and reinforces abuse in insidious ways.

NOTES

Introduction

1. Of course, "law" is neither singular nor omnivocalic. Peter Goodrich (1986) and others argue that legal language like any other language is dynamic according to patterns of use and the social situations in which it is used. Legal language is made up of multiple voices, applied differently by different people, and differently by the same people in different situations. Nevertheless, I use "law" for the sake of brevity, and further, following Carol Smart (1989), I use "law" to mimic the way legal discursive practices such as precedent presume singularity and omnivocality. I use the more specific term "Anglo-American" to refer to the abstract system out of which current US law developed and in which it continues to participate.

2. The US Federal Rules of Evidence (FRE) constrain and enable the fact-finding goals of the court through the presentation of evidence in testimony. The FRE control what kinds of evidence are admissible, who can give the evidence, the standards of measuring evidence, etc. There are two basic standards used to evaluate evidence: relevancy and reliability (see Philips 1992). Relevance has to do with whether the "fact" is pertinent to the case at hand and the rule of law in question (see FRE, article 4). Reliability has to do with how reliable the evidence is regardless of the person giving testimony. Some suggest that the standard of reliability developed because legal professionals mistrusted the abilities of the lay jury (See Philips 1993; Landsman 1990). Most evidence's reliability is tested via cross-examination, but the excited utterance is considered reliable enough to be admissible even though the speaker of the utterance—the person with the empirical knowledge—is not giving testimony.

3. Even though gossip has been reclaimed by feminists (cf. Spender 1982) and sociolinguistic studies (cf. Tannen 1991; Coates 1998) that show how gossip is about creating community, reproducing community values, and the like, it still maintains a negative valuation in broader culture. Indeed, whether it is positively or negatively viewed, gossip is value- and goal-laden.

4. According to Rule 801 of the Federal Rules of Evidence (FRE), a "statement" is "a person's oral assertion, written assertion, or nonverbal conduct, if the person intended it as an assertion." The "declarant" is the person who originally said the utterance, prior to the legal proceeding. The "party" is the in-court witness to whom the declarant spoke and who repeats the statement in court as part of their testimony.

5. Gilbert was a champion of Locke's ideas, thinking them important enough for law students that he abridged Locke's *Essay* for his law students (Shapiro 1991).

6. No-drop policies disallow victims of domestic violence from dropping charges against their abusers after the fact.

7. For example, in 2007, only fifty-four of 254 cases in state and Federal appellate circuits that included an excited utterance involved domestic assault or domestic violence.

8. The government had the "burden of proof" in this case. In federal courts, the accused is presumed innocent, and it is on the prosecution, the government here, to prove guilt beyond a reasonable doubt. Prosecution 1 and the Judge reestablished this fact during sentencing (*Hadley* 2003, 11). Also see United States Courts explanation of "How Courts Work" in criminal cases at http://www.uscourts.gov/FederalCourts/UnderstandingtheFederalCourts/HowCourtsWork/CriminalCases.aspx.

Chapter 01

1. I use the term "victim," rather than "survivor" or another term, following Mulla (2011), because it is the term that the law recognizes and requires in order to intervene. I heed Trinch's (2013) warning that the term not be used to essentialize but to account for the complexity of purpose, thoughtfulness, and strategic action that victims of domestic violence use to negotiate their domestic lives. To that end, I typically use the structure "victims of domestic violence" rather than "domestic violence victims."

2. Blackstone also classes wife-beating, stating that it is still only practiced by the "lower rank of people" (p. 634). The incorrect assumption that only poor or working-class people abuse their wives continues to persist.

3. For a detailed analysis of the ideology of law and domestic violence at work in *Regina v. Bedingfield* and the similarities between *Bedingfield* and *Crawford v. Washington* (2004), see Aviva Orenstein's excellent 2010 article "Sex, Threats, and Absent Victims: The Lessons of *Regina v. Bedingfield* for Modern Confrontation and Domestic Violence Cases" in Fordham Law Review 79, 2010.

4. Statutes regarding domestic violence are made at the city level. Laws have changed and been introduced at different rates across the United States and with different definitions and mandates, which means that domestic violence is responded to differently from city to city.

Chapter 02

1. Gilbert's treatise wasn't published until 1754 (I reference the 1791 edition), but after reviewing the case citations in Gilbert's unpublished manuscripts and notes, Macnair (1994) believes it was drafted in the first decade of the eighteenth century. John Pitt Taylor (1897) dates the hearsay rule back to the late seventeenth century and the reign of Charles the Second.

2. This shift has led legal scholars such as Langbein (1996) to conclude that there was no identifiable law of evidence in the first half of the eighteenth century. I'm suggesting instead that the law of evidence was developing in line with changes to the language ideology: cultural developments in how speech versus writing could be understood and trusted. Thus, I follow Wigmore's view that the nascent law of evidence was in circulation, spotty though it may have been, until it finally began coalescing toward the end of the eighteenth century and early nineteenth century.

3. Generally, the law of evidence preferred and continues to prefer objects, artifacts as evidence, which is what Starkie (1833) called "primary evidence." All forms of testimony were called "secondary evidence." "Immediate" evidence was from firsthand knowledge, whereas "mediate" evidence, such as hearsay, is secondhand.

4. To admit hearsay evidence, Taylor (1897) provides a long discussion of "original" evidence, which he distinguishes from hearsay. "There are *three classes of declarations*, which

though usually treated under the head of hearsay, are in truth *original* evidence; the *first* class consisting of cases where the fact that the declaration was made, and not its truth or falsity, is the point in question; the *second* including expressions of bodily or mental feelings, where the existence or nature of such feelings is the subject of inquiry; and the *third* embracing all other cases, where the declaration offered in evidence may be regarded as part of the *res gestae*" (1897, 497). The types of utterances listed are fairly typical of exceptions to hearsay. By not labeling them exceptions, he circumvents the potential problem of a rule that has significant exceptions. In the years that followed, other American legal scholars such as James Bradley Thayer (1898) would continue discussing and debating the validity of a rule that carried so many exceptions with it.

5. In *Language and the Law* (2006), Sanford Schane uses speech act theory to differentiate between hearsay and non-hearsay in an analysis that follows the grain of Wigmore's argument.

6. This list is certainly not exhaustive. It focuses on exceptions dealing with spoken hearsay. For those exceptions that have more than one precedent, I've only included the top one or two most cited cases (according to Shepard's Citations), and only included those with more than one thousand citations. I have not included those cases that are about textual hearsay such as DNA tests (*Williams v. Illinois*, 2012), lab reports (*Bullcoming v. New Mexico*, 2011), and business documents (*Melendez-Diaz v. Massachusetts*, 2009). I have also omitted those opinions such as *Hamdan v. Rumsfeld* (2006) because they bring up special conditions of evidence used in military prosecutions that is supplied by the federal government. Such opinions are important and have wide social impact, but they are beyond the scope of this research and would require analysis that pays close attention to their particular context(s).

Chapter 03

1. In this book, I focus on cases involving heterosexual domestic assault. There is also important work done on the problems specific to litigating homosexual domestic assault. See for example Hunter's (1992) "Homosexuals as a New Class of Domestic Violence Subjects Under the New Jersey Prevention of Domestic Violence Act of 1991."

2. I use the convention of Mrs., Mr., and Ms. with the last name, because this is the convention used in trial and appellate documents.

3. For Aviva Orenstein (1997), one of the most significant problems with the excited utterance exception to hearsay is the way the speaker's emotional state is defined. An exciting event might make some speakers silent rather than hysterical, which might also be a sign of suppressed reflective faculties.

4. In *US v. Hadley* (trial 2002; appellate opinion 2005), the case analyzed in the second half of this book, the hearsay in question is admitted and the role of the gun is played up. In fact, the charges of domestic assault are exchanged for gun possession in that case, and, in so doing, the specificities of domestic violence are suppressed.

Chapter 04

1. Of course, the trial is not the first time that evidence is discussed among the different members of the court and even between attorneys and witnesses. I am suggesting that the trial is the moment of entextualization because 1) it is the context that the other conversations about evidence anticipate, 2) it is the context that finally rules on evidence, and 3) it is the context that produces a textual account.

2. We only have a sense of what PH said that night in police testimony and in the testimony she gave during sentencing. Any use of quotation marks cites police testimony, not PH's words.

3. According to Conley and O'Barr (2005), lawyers use objections sparingly because they can potentially call the jury's attention to a fact or argument that they would rather have fall under the radar. In the case of the excited utterance, if the objection is overruled by the judge, the utterance becomes a fact of the case, something that may not suit the needs of the prosecution's case.

4. This is the key distinction between hearsay third-party statements and non-hearsay third-party statements (cf. Schane 2006).

Chapter 05

1. The concept of "discursive agency" is related to speech act theory, but importantly, discursive agency actively works against the intentionality described, especially in the speech act theories of Searle (1970) and Paul Grice (1957). For both, when someone speaks, they intend the utterance to "mean" something. In *Speech Acts*, Searle (1970, 43) reiterates Grice's theorem: "To say that a speaker *S* meant something by *X* is to say that *S* intended the utterance of *X* to produce some effect in a hearer *H* by means of the recognition of this intention." What Searle find most useful is the idea that meaning is made when the hearer recognizes intentions of speakers. Speech act theory has been criticized for this notion of intentionality by those who argue that meaning isn't under the sole province of the speaker, but rather actively negotiated in interaction. Austin (1962, 13) himself differentiated between the repetition of an utterance and a legal speech act: "[I]n the American law of evidence, a report of what someone else said is admitted as evidence if what is said is an utterance of our performative kind: because this is not so much of something *said*, as which it would be hear-say and not admissible evidence, but rather as something he *did*, an action of his." Though not referencing it by name, Austin is alluding to the *res gestae* principle. A r*es gestae* utterance coincides with a physical act in such a way as to give the act legal significance, as in staking a claim (Wigmore, vol. 6 §1732). Hearsay is not performative, in Austin's sense, because hearsay is "something said." Getting into a discussion of intentionality would certainly mean delving into the historical and linguistic relationship between *res gestae* and hearsay, which is a discussion I leave for another day.

2. The government had the "burden of proof" in this case. In federal courts, the accused is presumed innocent, and it is the job of the prosecution, the government here, to prove guilt beyond a reasonable doubt. Prosecution 1 and the Judge reestablish this fact during sentencing (2003: 11). Also see United States Courts, www.uscourts.gov, and its discussion of criminal courts for further discussion of this legal issue.

3. PH's full quote is: "When I was at the grand jury, I was afraid, scared, did not want to be there, did not want to testify. For some reason you didn't tell me that I had the right not to testify against my husband. I don't know why, but you didn't. And I did not want to be there. And you told me I had no choice but to be there. That's what you said" (2003: 22).

4. During sentencing, the government also submits the statement written by PH in front of the police on the night of the event and her grand jury testimony. Because such statements and testimony do not fit the parameters of an excited utterance—they are made in response to questions, lack spontaneity, and are made with the reflective faculties, and in the case of the grand jury testimony, they are explicitly testimonial—they had been

inadmissible during trial and the jury did not see them. It is assumed that the judge, who makes the sentencing decision, can determine the validity of a piece of evidence. "Being judicially trained, the Court can go ahead and determine for itself whether or not it believes what was stated or not" (Defense 1, June 2003: 56).

5. Prosecution 1 is not PH's attorney, so she is under no obligation to explain the nuances of the law regarding spousal immunity, for example, that PH might not know about.

APPENDIX

Cases Cited

Bacon, F. [1620] 1902. *Novum Organum*, by Lord Bacon, ed. by Joseph Devey, M.A. New York: P.F. Collier. (Accessed August 13, 2014). http://oll.libertyfund.org/titles/1432

Bourjaily v. United States, 483 U.S. 171 (1987). Supreme Court of the United States of America.

Bradley v. State of Mississippi, 1 Miss. 156 (1824).

California v. Green, 399 U.S. 149 (1970). Supreme Court of the United States of America.

Chettle v. Chettle, 161 Eng. Rep. 1399. King's Bench, Ecclesiastical, Admiralty, and Probate and Divorce Court (1821).

City of Austin v. Ritz, 72 Tex. 391 (1888). Supreme Court of Texas.

Commonwealth of Pennsylvania v. Marker, 25 Pa. D. & C.3d 119 (1982). Supreme Court of Pennsylvania.

Commonwealth of Pennsylvania v. Werntz, 161 Pa. 591 & 29 A. 272 (1894). Supreme Court of Pennsylvania.

Crawford v. Washington, 541 U.S. 36 (2004). Supreme Court of the United States of America.

Davis v. Washington/Hammon v. Indiana. 126 S. Ct. 2266. (2006). Supreme Court of the United States.

Dutton v. Evans, 400 US 74 (1970). Supreme Court of the United States of America.

Giles v. California, 128 S. Ct. 2678 (2008). Supreme Court of the United States of America.

Haggins v. Warden, Fort Pillow State Farm, 715 F. 2d (6th Cir. 1983) United States Court of Appeals.

Hamdan v. Rumsfeld, 548 U.S. 557 (2006). Supreme Court of the United States of America.

Holden v. Holden, 161 Eng. Rep. 614 (1810).

Huff v. White Motor Corp., 609 F. 2d 286 (7th Cir. 1979). United States Court of Appeals.

Idaho v. Wright, 497 U.S. 805 (1990). Supreme Court of the United States of America.

Johnson v. Southern Railway Co, 351 Mo. 1110 (1943). Supreme Court of Missouri.

Joyner v. Joyner, 59 N.C. 322 (1862). Supreme Court of North Carolina.

Keefe v. State of Arizona. 50 Ariz. 293, 297–298 (1937).

King v. Dingler, 168 Eng. Rep. 383 (1791). King's Bench Court.

King v. Woodcock, 1 Leach, at 500, 168 Eng. Rep (1789).

Lilly v. Virginia, 527 US 116, 134 (1999). Supreme Court of the United States of America.

Mattox v. United States, 156 US 237 (1895). Supreme Court of the United States of America.

Melendez-Diaz v. Massachusetts, 129 S. Ct. 2527 (2009). Supreme Court of the United States of America.

Michigan v. Bryant, 131 S. Ct. 1143 (2011). Supreme Court of the United States of America.

Mima Queen and Child, Petitioners for Freedom v. Hepburn. 11 U.S. 290; 3 L. Ed. 348. (1813).

Ohio v. Roberts, 448 U.S. 56 (1980). Supreme Court of the United States of America. Regina v.

The People v. Poland, 22 Ill. 2d 175 (1961). Supreme Court of Illinois.

The People of New York State v. Fulton Fire Insurance Co. 25 Wend. 205 (1840). Court for the Correction of Errors for New York.

The People of NY State v. Del Vermo, 192 N.Y. 470 (1908). Court of Appeals of New York.

Price v. State of Oklahoma, 1908 OK CR 32 (1908). Oklahoma Court of Criminal Appeals.

The Queen v. Brooks, 1 Denison Cr.Cas. 217 (1843).

Regina v. Bedingfield, Cox's Criminal Law Cases, Reports of Cases in Criminal Law Argued and Determined in the Courts in England and Ireland, Crown Court, 341 (1879).

Smith v. State of Tennessee, 28 Tenn. (9 Hum.) 162 (1848).

State of Louisiana v. Price, 121 La. 53 (1908).

State of North Carolina v. Black, 60 N.C. (1 Winst., 266) 262 (1864).

State of North Carolina v. Rhodes. 61 N.C. 453 (1868). Supreme Court of North Carolina, Raleigh.

State of Ohio v. Johnson. Court of Appeals. No. L-05–1001 (2006). Court of Appeals of Ohio, Sixth Appellate District.

Thompson and Wife v. Trevanian. 90 Eng. Rep. 179. King's Bench (1694).

Thurman v. City of Torrington, et al. 595 F. Supp. 1521 (C.D. 1 1984). United States District Court for the District of Connecticut.

United States of America v. Jerome Hadley (2002–2003). Trial Transcript. United States District Court Eastern District of Tennessee at Chattanooga. Trial: November 12–13, 2002; Sentencing: March 21, 2003; June 6, 2003.

United States of America v. Jerome Hadley. 431 F.3d 484 (6th Cir. 2005).

United States of America v. King. 34 F. 302 (1888). Circuit Court, E.D. New York.

United States of America v. Kelvin Newsom. 452 F.3d 593 (6th Cir. 2006). United States Court of Appeals.

United States of America vs. Michael Mitchell. No. 06–77-DLB (E.D. KY. 2007). United States District Court for the Eastern District of Kentucky, Northern Division.

United States v. Cromer. 389 F.3d 662 (6th Cir. 2004). United States Court of Appeals.

United States v. Inadi. 748 F.2d 812 (3rd Cir. 1984). United States Court of Appeals.

United States v. Schreane. 331 F.3d 548 (6th Cir. 2003). United States Court of Appeals.

White v. Illinois. 502 U.S. 346 (1992). Supreme Court of the United States.

Works Cited

Agha, A. 2005. "Introduction: Semiosis across Encounters." *Journal of Linguistic Anthropology* 15(1): 1–5.

Ahearn, L. 2001. "Language and Agency." *Annual Review of Anthropology*. 30: 109–137.

Alonso, A. M. 1996. "Rationalizing Patriarchy: Gender, Domestic Violence, and Law in Mexico." *Identities: Global Studies in Culture and Power* 2(1/2): 29–47.

Amsterdam, A. G., & J. Bruner. 2000. *Minding the Law*. Harvard University Press.

Andrus, J. 2009. "The Development of an Artefactual Language Ideology: Utterance, Event, and Agency in the Metadiscourse of the Excited Utterance Exception to Hearsay." *Language and Communication* 29(4): 312–327.

Andrus, J. 2011. "Beyond Texts in Context: Recontextualization and the Co-Production of Texts and Contexts in the Legal Discourse, Excited Utterance Exception to Hearsay." *Discourse & Society* 22(2): 115–136.

Andrus, J. 2012. "Victim Agency: Fractal Recursivity in the Language Ideology of the US Law of Evidence and Domestic Violence." *Language in Society* 41(5): 589–614.

Atkinson, J. M., and P. Drew. 1979. *Order in Court: The Organization of Verbal Interaction in Judicial Settings*. Oxford: Oxford University Press.

Austin, J. L. [1962] 2003. *How To Do Things with Words*. Oxford: Clarendon Press.

Bauman, R. 2005. "Commentary: Indirect Indexicality, Identity, Performance: Dialogic Observations." *Journal of Linguistic Anthropology* 15(1): 145–150.

Bauman, R., and C. Briggs. 1990. "Poetics and Performance as Critical Perspectives on Language and Social Life." *Annual Review of Anthropology* 19:59–88.

Bauman, R., and C. Briggs. 2000. "Language Philosophy as Language Ideology." In *Regimes of Language: Ideologies, Polities, and Identities*, edited by P. Kroskrity, 139–204. Santa Fe, NM: School of American Research Press.

Bauman, R., and C. Briggs. 2003. *Voices of Modernity: Language Ideologies and the Politics of Inequality*. Cambridge, UK: Cambridge University Press.

Beasley, M. E., and D. Q. Thomas. 1994. "Domestic Violence as a Human Rights Issue." In *The Public Nature of Private Violence: The Discovery of Domestic Abuse*, edited by M. A. Fineman and R. Mykitiuk, 323–349. New York: Routledge.

Beauvoir, S. de. [1949] 1961. *The Second Sex*. Translated by H. M. Parshley. New York: Penguin.

Bell, C. C., and J. S. Mattis. 2000. "The Importance of Cultural Competence in Ministering to African-American Victims of Domestic Violence." *Violence Against Women*, 6(5): 515–532.

Beloof, D., and J. Shapiro. 2002. "Let the Truth be Told: Proposed Hearsay Exceptions to Admit Domestic Violence Victims' Out of Court Statements as Substantive Evidence." *Columbia Journal of Gender and Law* 11(1):1–37.

Berk-Seligson, S. 2009. *Coerced Confessions: The Discourse of Bilingual Police Interrogations*. The Hague: Mouton de Gruyter.

Besnier, Niko. 2004. "The Social Production of Abjection: Desire and Silencing among Transgender Tongans." *Social Anthropology* 12(3): 301–323.

Blackstone, W. Sir. [1766] 1832. *Commentaries on the Laws of England*, Volume 1. Edited by C. Christain and L. Hovenden. New York: Collins and Hannay. [Google Books]

Blommaert, J. 2005. *Discourses*. New York: Cambridge University Press.

Blommaert, J. 2008. "Artefactual Ideologies and the Textual Production of Languages in Africa." *Language and Communication* 28(4): 291–307.

Bodine, A. 1975. "Androcentrism in Prescriptive Grammar: Singular 'They,' Sex-Indefinite 'He,' and 'He orShe.'" *Language in Society* 4(2): 129–146.

Brooks, P. 1996. "The Law as Narrative and Rhetoric." In *Law's Stories: Narrative and Rhetoric in the Law*, edited by P. Brooks and P. Gewirtz, 14–22. New Haven, CT: Yale University Press.

Bruner, J. 1991. "The Narrative Construction of Reality." *Critical Inquiry*, 1–21.

Bucholtz, M. 2001. "Reflexivity and Critique in Discourse Analysis." *Critique of Anthropology* 21(2): 165–183.

Bucholtz, M., and K. Hall. 2005. "Identity and Interaction: A Sociolinguistic Approach." *Discourse Studies* 7(4–5): 585–614.

Bucholtz, M. 2010. *White Kids: Language, Race, and Styles of Youth Identity*. Cambridge University Press.

Buller, F. 1785. *Introduction to the Law Relative to Trials at* Nisi Prius. 4th Edition. London: Strahan & Woodfall. [GoogleBooks]

Butler, J. 1990. *Gender Trouble*. New York: Routlege.

Butler, J. 1993. *Bodies that Matter: On the Discursive Limits of Sex*. New York: Routledge.

Butler, J. 1997. *Excitable Speech: A Politics of the Performative*. New York: Routledge.

Butler, J. 2005. *Giving an Account of Oneself*. New York: Fordham University Press.

Byrom, C. E. 2005."The Use of the Excited Utterance Hearsay Exception in the Prosecution of Domestic Violence Cases After *Crawford v. Washington*." *The Review of Litigation* 24(2): 409–428.

Celock, J. 2012. "Donald Pridemore, Wisconsin Legislator, Says Single Parenting Leads to Abuse." *Huffington Post*, March 12, 2012. http://www.huffingtonpost.com/2012/03/12/donald-pridemore-wisconsin-lawmaker-child-abuse-divorce-single-parents_n_1340319.html (accessed August 8, 2014).

Centers for Disease Control and Prevention. 2010. "An Overview of Intimate Partner Violence in the United States: 2010 Findings" http://www.cdc.gov/violenceprevention/pdf/ipv-nisvs-factsheet-v5-a.pdf. Accessed August 5, 2014.

Coates, J. 1998. "Gossip Revisited: Language in All-Female Groups." In *Language and Gender: A Reader,* 2nd edition, edited by J. Coates and P. Pichler. Oxford: Blackwell.

Corcoran, C. 1992. "From Victim Control to Social Change: A Feminist Perspective on Campus Rape Prevention Programmes." In *New Directions in Feminist Psychology: Practice, Theory and Research*, edited by J. C. Chrisler and D. Howard, 130–140. New York: Springer.

Coker, D. 1999. "Enhancing Autonomy for Battered Women." *UCLA Law Review* 47(1):1–112.

Cole, S., and R. Dioso-Villa 2007. "CSI and its Effects: Media, Juries, and the Burden of Proof." *New England Law Review* 41(3): 435–470.

Conley, J. M., and W. M. O'Barr. 1990. *Rules versus Relationships: The Ethnography of Legal Discourse*. Chicago: University of Chicago Press.

Conley, J. M., and W. M. O'Barr. 2005. *Just Words: Law, Language, and Power*. 2nd ed. Chicago: University of Chicago Press.

Conley, J. M., W. M. O'Barr, and E. A. Lind. 1979. "The Power of Language: Presentational Style in the Courtroom." *Duke Law Journal* 6:1375–1399.

Constable, M. 2005. *Just Silences: The Limits and Possibilities of Modern Law*. Princeton: Princeton University Press.

Cotterill, J., ed. 2004. *Language in the Legal Process*. New York: Palgrave Macmillan.

Coulthard, M. 2004. "Whose Voice Is It? Invented and Concealed Dialogue in Written Records of Verbal Evidence Produced by the Police." In *Language in the Legal Process*, edited by J. Cotterill, 19–34. New York: Palgrave Macmillan,

Doak, J., and C. McGourlay. 2012. *Evidence in Context*. 3rd edition. New York: Routledge.

Dobash, R. E., and R. P. Dobash. 1992. *Women, Violence and Social Change*. London: Routledge.

Dumas, B. K. 2004."Reasonable Doubt about Reasonable Doubt: Assessing Jury Instruction Adequacy in a Capital Case." In *Language in the Legal Process*, edited by J. Cotterill, 246–259. New York: Palgrave Macmillan,.

Duranti, A. 2004. "Agency in Language." In *A Companion to Linguistic Anthropology*, edited by A. Duranti, 451–473 2nd edition. Malden, MA: Blackwell.

Eades, D. 2008. *Courtroom Talk and Neocolonial Control*. New York: Mouton de Gruyter.

Eckert, P., and McConnell-Ginet, S. 1992. "Think Practically and Look Locally: Language and Gender as Community-Based Practice." *Annual Review of Anthropology* 21: 461–490.

Eckert, P., and S. McConnell-Ginet. 1999. "New Generalizations and Explanations in Language and Gender Research." *Language in Society* 28(2): 185–201.

Ehrlich, S. 2001. *Representing Rape: Language and Sexual Consent*. London and New York: Routledge.

Ehrlich, S. 2007. "Legal Discourse and the Cultural Intelligiblity of Gendered Meanings." *Journal of Sociolinguistics*. 11(4): 452–474.

Ehrlich, S. 2012. "Text Trajectories, Legal Discourse and Gendered Inequalities." *Applied Linguistics Review* 3(1): 47–73.

Ehrlich, S. and J. Sidnell 2006. "'I Think That's Not an Assumption You Ought to Make': Challenging Presuppositions in Inquiry Testimony." *Language in Society*. 35(1): 655–676.

Fairclough, N. 2010. *Critical Discourse Analysis: The Critical Study of Language*. 2nd ed. New York: Longman.

Felman, S. 2002. *The Juridical Unconscious: Trials and Traumas in the 20th Century*. Cambridge, MA: Harvard University Press.

Ferraro, K. J. 1995. "Cops, Courts, and Woman Battering." In *The Criminal Justice System and Women: Offenders, Victims, and Workers*, edited by B. R. Price and N. J. Sokoloff, 262–271. New York: McGraw-Hill.

Firth, H., and C. Kitzinger. 1997. "Talk about Sexual Miscommunication." *Women's Studies International Forum* 20(4): 517–528.

Foucault, M. [1970]1994. *The Order of Things*. New York: Vintage Books.

Foucault, M. 1972. *The Archaeology of Knowledge and the Discourse on Language*. New York: Pantheon Books.

Foucault, M. 1986. *The Care of the Self: The History of Sexuality*, vol. 3. New York: Pantheon.

Foucault, M. 1988. "Technologies of the Self." In *Technologies of the Self: A Seminar with Michel Foucault*, edited by L. H. Martin, H. Gutman, and P. H. Hutton, 16–49. London: Tavistock.

Foyster, E. 2005. *Marital Violence: An English Family History, 1660–1875*. New York: Cambridge University Press.

Frug, J. 1988. "Argument as Character." *Stanford Law Review* 40(4): 869–927.

Frug, M. J. 1992. "Commentary: A Postmodern Feminist Legal Manifesto (An Unfinished Draft)." *Harvard Law Review* 105(5): 1045.

Gal, S. 1995. "Language, Gender and Power: An Anthropological Review." In *Gender Articulated: Language and the Socially Constructed Self,* edited by Kira Hall and Mary Bucholtz, 169–182. New York: Routledge, 1995.

Gal, S. 2002. "A Semiotics of the Public/Private Distinction." *Differences: A Journal of Feminist Cultural Studies* 13(1): 77–95.

Gal, S. 2005. "Language Ideologies Compared: Metaphors of Public/Private." *Journal of Linguistic Anthropology* 15(1): 23–37.

Gardiner, J. K. 1995. *Provoking Agents: Gender and Agency in Theory and Practice*. Urbana: University of Illinois Press.

Gavey, N. 2005. *Just Sex? The Cultural Scaffolding of Rape*. New York: Routledge.

Gewirtz, P. 1996. "Narrative and Rhetoric in the Law." In *Law's Stories: Narrative and Rhetoric in the Law*, edited by P. Brooks and P. Gewirtz, 2–13. New Haven, CO: Yale University Press,

Gilbert, G, Sir. 1752. *An Abstract of Mr. Locke's Essay on Human Understanding*. Dublin edition. Reprinted by William Sandby. [Google Books].

Gilbert, G, Sir [1791], 1979. *The Law of Evidence*. New York: Garland Publishing. [Google Books]

Goodrich, P. 1987. *Legal Discourse: Studies in Linguistics, Rhetoric and Legal Analysis*. London: Macmillan.

Greenleaf, S. 1846. *A Treatise on the Law of Evidence.* 3rd ed. Boston: Little, Brown. [Google Books].

Greenleaf, S. 1899. *A Treatise on the Law of Evidence.* Edited by J.H. Wigmore. 16th ed. Boston: Little, Brown. [Google Books].

Grice, P. 1957. "Meaning." *Philosophical Review* 66(3): 377–388.

Han, E. 2003. "Mandatory Arrest and no-Drop Policies: Victim Empowerment in Domestic Violence Cases." *Boston College Third World Law Journal* 23: 159–191.

Hanks, S. 1996. "Exorcism and the Description of Participant Roles." In *Natural Histories of Discourse,* edited by M. Silverstein and G. Urban, 160–202. Chicago: University of Chicago Press.

Hirsch, S. F. 1998. *Pronouncing and Persevering: Gender and the Discourses of Dispute in an African Islamic Court*. Chicago: University of Chicago Press.

Horkheimer, M., and T. Adorno. 1972. *Dialectic of Enlightenment*. Translated by J. Cumming. New York: Continuum.

Hunter, M. D. (1992). "Homosexuals as a New Class of Domestic Violence Subjects Under the New Jersey Prevention of Domestic Violence Act of 1991." *University Louisville Journal of Family Law* 31, 557.

Irigaray, L. 1993. Je, tu, nous*: Toward a Culture of Difference*. New York: Routledge.

Irvine, J., and S. Gal. 2000. "Language Ideology and Linguistic Differentiation" In *Regimes of Language: Ideologies, Polities, and Identities*, edited by P. Kroskrity. Santa Fe, NM: School of American Research Press.

Irvine, J. 1989. "When Talk Isn't Cheap: Language and Political Economy." *American Ethnologist*, 16: 248–267.

Johnstone, B. 1996. *The Linguistic Individual*. New York: Oxford University Press.

Johnstone, B. 2008. *Discourse Analysis*. 2nd ed. Malden, MA: Blackwell.

Johnstone, B., J. Andrus, and A. E. Danielson. 2006. "Mobility, Indexicality, and the Enregisterment of 'Pittsburghese'." *Journal of English Linguistics*. 34(2): 77–104.

Kaufman, G. 2009. "Gossip Site Defends Posting Of Rihanna Photo: Harvey Levin says TMZ obtained the picture legally." *MTV News*. February 23, 2009. http://www.mtv.com/news/1605588/gossip-site-defends-posting-of-rihanna-photo (accessed August 8, 2014).

Kitzinger, C. 2000. "Doing Feminist Conversation Analysis." *Feminism & Psychology*. 10(2): 163–194.

Kitzinger, C., and H. Firth. 1999. "Just Say No? The Use of Conversation Analysis in Developing a Feminist Perspective on Sexual Refusal." *Discourse & Society* 10(3): 293–316.

Kroskrity, P. V., ed. 2000. *Regimes of Language: Ideologies, Polities, and Identities*. Santa Fe, NM: School of American Research Press.

Lakoff, R. 1973. "Language and Women's Place." *Language in Society* 2(1): 45–79.

Lamb, S. 1999. "Constructing the Victim: Popular Images and Lasting Labels." In *New Versions of Victims: Feminists Struggle with the Concept,* edited by S. Lamb, 108–138. New York: New York University Press.

Landsman, S. 1990. "The Rise of the Contentious Spirit: Adversary Procedure in Eighteenth Century England." *Cornell Law Review* 75(3): 497–608.

Langbein, J. H. 1996. "Historical Foundations of the Law of Evidence: A View from the Ryder Sources." *Columbia Law Review* 96(5): 1168–1202.

Latour, B. 1993. *We Have Never Been Modern.* Translated by Catherine Porter. Cambridge, MA: Harvard University Press.

Laws Resolutions of Womens Rights, Or, the Lawes Provision for Woemen: A Methodicall Collection of Such Statutes and Customes, with the Cases, Opinions, Arguments, and Points of Learning in the Law, as Doe Properly Concerne Women. [1632] 2005. Clark, NJ: The Lawbook Exchange. [Google Books].

Lazarus-Black, M. 2007. *Everyday Harm: Domestic Violence, Court Rites, and Cultures of Reconciliation*. Urbana: University of Illinois Press.

Lerner, G. 1986. *The Creation of Patriarchy*. New York: Oxford University Press.

Lewis, D. 1993. "The Urban Criminal Justice System and the Juror's Perception." *Fordham Urban Law Journal* 20: 561–569.

Linell, P. 1998. "Discourse Across Boundaries: On Recontextualizations and the Blending of Voices in Professional Discourse." *Text* 18(2): 143–157.

Locke, J. 1690. *An Essay Concerning Human Understanding*, Vol. 2, Books 3 and 4. Based on the 2nd Edition. Produced by Steve Harris and David Widger. [Project Gutenberg]. http://www.gutenberg.org/files/10616/10616.txt. Accessed July 21, 2014.

MacKinnon, C. A. 1989. *Toward a Feminist Theory of the State*. Cambridge, MA: Harvard University Press.

Macnair, M. 1994. "Sir Jeffrey Gilbert and His Treatises." *Journal of Legal History* 15(3): 252–268.

Mardorossian, C. M. 2002. "Toward a New Feminist Theory of Rape." *Signs* 27(3): 743–775.

Martin, S. E. 1999. Police Force or Police Service? Gender and Emotional Labor." *The Annals of the American Academy of Political and Social Science*, 561(1): 111–126.

Matoesian, G. 1993. *Reproducing Rape: Domination Through Talk in the Courtroom*. Chicago: University of Chicago Press.

Matoesian, G. 2000. "Intertextual Authority in Reported Speech: Production Media in the Kennedy Smith Rape Trial." *Journal of Pragmatics* 32(7): 879–914.

Matoesian, G. 2001. *Law and the Language of Identity: Discourse in the William Kennedy Smith Rape Trial*. New York: Oxford University Press.

McConnell-Ginet, S. 1998. "The Sexual (Re)Production of Meaning: A Discourse-Based Approach." In *The Feminist Critique of Language: A Reader*, edited by D. Cameron, 198–210. 2nd edition. New York: Routledge.

McCormick, C. T., K. S. Brown, and G.E. Dix. 1999. *McCormick on Evidence*. 5th ed. St. Paul, MN:Thomson/West.

McElhinny, B. 1995. "Challenging Hegemonic Masculinities: Female and Male Police Officers Handling Domestic Violence." In *Gender Articulated: Language and the Socially Constructed Self*, edited by Kira Hall and Mary Bucholtz, 217–243. New York: Routledge.

McElhinny, B. 2003. "Theorizing Gender in Sociolinguistics and Linguistic Anthropology." In *The Handbook of Language and Gender*, edited by J. Holmes and M. Meyerhoff, 21–42. Malden, MA: Blackwell.

Medina, J. 2006. *Speaking from Elsewhere: A New Contextualist Perspective on Meaning, Identity, and Discursive Agency*. Albany: State University of New York Press, 2006.

Mellinkoff, D. 1963. *The Language of the Law*. Boston: Little Brown.

Mertz, E. 1996. "Recontextualization as Socialization: Text and Pragmatics in the Law School Classroom." In *Natural Histories of Discourse*, edited by M. Silverstein and G. Urban, 229–249. Chicago: University of Chicago Press,

Mertz, E. 1998. "Linguistic Ideology and Praxis in U.S. Law School Classrooms." In *Language Ideologies: Practice and Theory*, edited by B. B. Schieffelin, K. A. Woolard, and P. V. Kroskrity, 149–162. New York: Oxford University Press.

Minow, M. 2000. "Between Intimates and between Nations: Can Law Stop the Violence." *Case Western Law Review* 50 (4): 851–868.

MTV News Staff. 2009. "Rihanna's Father Speaks: 'I Hope She Will Stand Up For Women All Over The World.'" *MTV News* February 14, 2009. http://www.mtv.com/news/1605139/rihannas-father-speaks-i-hope-she-will-stand-up-for-women-all-over-the-world/ (Accessed August 8, 2014).

Mueller, C. B., and L. C. Kirkpatrick. 1996. *Evidence under the Rules: Text, Cases, and Problems*. Law School Casebook Series. 3rd ed. Boston: Little Brown.

Muhammad, K. G. 2010. *The Condemnation of Blackness: Race, Crime, and the Making of Modern Urban America*. Cambridge, MA: Harvard University Press.

Mulla, S. 2008. "There Is No Place Like Home: The Body as the Scene of the Crime on Sexual Assault Intervention." *Home Cultures* 5(3): 301–326.

Mulla, S. 2011. "Facing Victims: Forensics, Visual Technologies, and Sexual Assault Examination." *Medical Anthropology: Cross-Cultural Studies in Health and Illness* 30(3): 271–294.

Murphy, J. 1993. "Lawyering for Social Change: The Power of the Narrative in Domestic Violence Law Reform." *Hofstra Law Review* 21(4): 1243–1293.

O'Barr, W. M. & J. M. Conley (1996). "Ideological Dissonance in the American Legal System." In *Disorderly Discourse: Narrative Conflict and Inequality*, edited by C. Briggs, 114–134. Oxford: Oxford University Press.

Ochs, E. 1992. "Indexing Gender." In *Rethinking Context: Language as an Interactive Phenomenon*, edited by A. Duranti and C. Goodwin, 335–358. Cambridge, MA: Cambridge University Press.

Olsen, F. E. 1983. "The Family and the Market: A Study of Ideology and Legal Reform." *Harvard Law Review*. 96(7): 1497–1578.

Orenstein, A. 1997. "'My God!' A Feminist Critique of the Excited Utterance Exception to the Hearsay Rule." *California Law Review* 85(1): 159–224.

Orenstein, A. 2010. "Sex, Threats, and Absent Victims: The Lessons of *Revina v. Bedingfield* for Modern Confrontation and Domestic Violence Cases." *Fordham Law Review* 79; Indiana Legal Studies Research Paper No. 156. http://ssrn.com/abstract=1561852 or http://dx.doi.org/10.2139/ssrn.1561852. Accessed September 10, 2011

Park, R. 1987. "A Subject Matter Approach to Hearsay Reform." *Michigan Law Review* 86: 51–122.

Peters, C. J. 1996. "Foolish Consistency: On Equality, Integrity, and Justice in Stare Decisis." *The Yale Law Journal* 105(8): 2031–2115.

Philips, S. U. 1992. "Evidentiary Standards for American Trials: Just the Facts." In *Responsibility and Evidence in Oral Discourse*, edited by J. Hill and J. T. Irvine, 248–259. New York: Cambridge University Press.

Philips, S. U. 1998. *Ideology in the Language of Judges*. New York: Oxford University Press.

Phillips, S. M. 1820. *Treatise on the Law of Evidence* (2nd American ed. from the 3rd London ed.). New York: Gould & Banks. [Google Books].

Richie, B. E. 2012. *Arrested Justice: Black Women, Violence, and America's Prison Nation*. New York: NYU Press.

Ritivoi, A. D. 2006. *Paul Ricoeur: Tradition and innovation in rhetorical theory*. Southern Illinois University Press.

Ross, J. 2006. "After Crawford Double-Speak: "Testimony" Does Not Mean Testimony and "Witness" Does Not Mean Witness." *The Journal of Criminal Law and Criminology* 97(1): 147–217.

Rumsey, A. 1990. "Wording, Meaning, and Linguistic Ideology." *American Anthropologist* 92(2): 346–361.

Sarat, A., and T. R. Kearns. 1996. "Editorial Introduction." In *The Rhetoric of Law*, edited by A. Sarat and T. R. Kearns, 1–28. Ann Arbor: University of Michigan Press.

Schane, Sanford A. 2006. *Language and the Law*. London: Continuum.

Scheppele, K. L. 1990. "Facing Facts in Legal Interpretation." *Representations* 30(1): 42–77.

Schneider, E. 2000. *Battered Women and Feminist Lawmaking*. New Haven, CT: Yale University Press.

Searle, J. R. 1970. *Speech Acts: An Essay in the Philosophy of Language*. Cambridge, UK: Cambridge University Press.

Shapiro, B. 1991 *Beyond Reasonable Doubt and Probable Cause*. Berkeley: University of California Press.

Shearer-Cremean, C. 2004. "The Epistemology of Police Science and the Silencing of Battered Women." In *Survivor Rhetoric: Negotiations and Narrativity in Abused Women's Language*, edited by C. L. Winkelmann and C. Shearer-Cremean, 166–197. Toronto: University of Toronto Press.

Shuy, R. 1998. *The Language of Confession, Interrogation, and Deception*. Thousand Oaks, CA: Sage.

Shuy, R. 2010. *The Language of Defamation Cases*. New York: Oxford University Press.

Shuy, R. 2011. *The Language of Perjury Cases*. New York: Oxford University Press.

Silverstein, M. 1979. "Language Structure and Linguistic Ideology." In *The Elements: A Parasession on Linguistic Units and Levels*, edited by P. R. Clyne, W. F. Hanks and C. L. Hofbauer, 193–247. Chicago: Chicago Linguistic Society.

Silverstein, M. [1981] 2001. "The Limits of Awareness." In *Linguistic Anthropology: A Reader*, edited by A. Duranti, 382–401. Malden, MA: Blackwell.

Silverstein, M. 1992. "The Uses and Utility of Ideology: Some Reflections." *Pragmatics* 2(3): 311–323.

Silverstein, M. 1993. "Metapragmatic Discourse and Metapragmatic Function." In *Reflexive Language*, edited by J. A. Lucy, 33–58. Cambridge, UK: Cambridge University Press.

Silverstein, M., and G. Urban. 1996. "The Natural History of Discourse." In *Natural Histories of Discourse*, edited by M. Silverstein and G. Urban,1–17. Chicago: University of Chicago Press.

Smart, C. 1989. *Feminism and the Power of Law*. London: Routledge.

Spender, D. 1980. *Man Made Language*. London: Routledge.

Stanko, E. 1981. "The Impact of Victim Assessment on Prosecutorial Screening Decisions: The Case of the New York County District Attorney's Office." *Law & Society* 16(2): 225–239.

Stanko, E. 1982. "Would You Believe this Woman? Prosecutorial Screening for 'Credible' Witnesses and a Problem of Justice." In *Judge, Lawyer, Victim, Thief: Women, Gender Roles, and Criminal Justice*, edited by N. H. Rafter and E. A. Stanko, 63–82. Boston: Northeastern University Press.

Stanton, E. C. 1848. *Declaration of Sentiments and Resolutions*. Seneca Falls: Women's Rights Convention. http://ecssba.rutgers.edu/docs/seneca.html. Accessed on November 17, 2013.

Starkie, T. 1833. *A Practical Treatise on the Law of Evidence and Digest of Proofs in Civil and Criminal Proceedings.* 2nd ed. London: J. & W. T. Clarke. [Google Books].

Steinem, G. 1983. *Outrageous Acts and Everyday Rebellions*. New York: Holt, Rinehart, and Winston.

Stokoe, E. 2010. "'I'm Not Gonna Hit a Lady': Conversation Analysis, Membership Categorization and Men's Denials of Violence Towards Women." *Discourse & Society* 21(1): 59–82.

Stygall, G. 2004. "Textual Barriers to United States Immigration." In *Language in the Legal Process*, edited by J. Cotterill, 35–53. New York: Palgrave Macmillan.

Suk, J. 2006. "Criminal Law Comes Home." *The Yale Law Journal* 116(1): 2–70.

Tannen, D. 1991. *You Just Don't Understand: Women and Men in Conversation*. London: Virago.

Taylor, J. P. 1897. *A Treatise on the Law of Evidence Administered in England and Ireland; with Illustrations from Scotch, Indian, American, and other Legal Systems.* 9th ed. London: Maxwell.

Thayer, J. B. 1898. *A Preliminary Treatise on Evidence at the Common Law*. Boston: Little, Brown. [Google Books].

Tiersma, P. M. 1999. *Legal Language*. Chicago: University of Chicago Press.

Tjaden, P., and N. Thoennes. 2000. "Extent, Nature, and Consequences of Intimate Partner Violence" U.S. Department of Justice and the Centers for Disease Control and Prevention. http://stacks.cdc.gov/view/cdc/21858. Accessed August 5, 2014

Tracy, K., and R. R. Agne. 2004. "'I Just Need to Ask Somebody Some Questions': Sensitivities in Domestic Dispute Calls." In *Language in the Legal Process*, edited by J. Cotterill, 75–90. New York: Palgrave Macmillan.

Trinch, S. 2003. *Latinas Narratives of Domestic Abuse: Discrepant Versions of Violence*. Amsterdam: John Benjamins.

Trinch, S. 2010. "Risky Subjects: Narrative, Literary Testimonio and Legal Testimony." *Dialectical Anthropology* 34 (2): 179–204.

Trinch, S. 2013. "Recalling Rape: Moving Beyond What We Know." In *Legal-Lay Communication: Textual Travels in the Law*, edited by C. Heffer, F. Rock, and J. Conley, 288–306. New York: Oxford University Press.

Trinch, S., and S. Berk-Seligson. 2002. "Narrating in Protective Order Interviews: A Source of Interactional Trouble." *Language in Society* 31(3): 383–418.

Tyler, T. R. 2006. "Is the CSI Effect Good Science?" 115 *Yale LJ Pocket Part* 73.

United States of America. [1973] 2013 "Federal Rules of Evidence." 1 December 2013. http://www.uscourts.gov/uscourts/rules/rules-evidence.pdf

United States of America. *Amendments to the Constitution of the United States of America*. 12 August 2008. http://supreme.lp.findlaw.com/constitution/amendments.html. Accessed November 17, 2013.

Urban, G. 1996. "Entextualization, Replication, and Power." In *Natural Histories of Discourse*, edited by M. Silverstein and G.Urban, 21–44. Chicago: University of Chicago Press.

Velez-Mitchell, V. 2009. "Commentary: Brown-Rihanna case's dangerous message." *CNN News* March 10, 2009. http://www.cnn.com/2009/SHOWBIZ/03/10/velez.mitchell.rihanna/ index.html?iref=allsearch (Accessed August 8, 2014).

Vena, J. 2009. "Rihanna's Family Opens Up About Chris Brown Arrest." *MTV News* February 19, 2009. http://www.mtv.com/news/1605395/rihannas-family-opens-up-about-chris-brown-arrest/ (Accessed August 8, 2014).

Weissbourd, B., & Mertz, E. 1985. "Rule-Centrism Versus Legal Creativity: The Skewing of Legal Ideology through Language. *Law and Society Review* 19(4): 623–659.

West, C., and D. Zimmerman. 1987. "Doing Gender." *Gender & Society* 1(2): 125–151.

Wigmore, J. H. [1904]1940. *Evidence in Trials at Common Law*. 3rd ed. Boston: Little, Brown. [Google Books]

Williams, P. J. 1987. "Alchemical Notes: Reconstructing Ideals from Deconstructed Rights." *Harvard. CR-CL Law Review* 22: 401.

Williams, P. J. 1991. *The Alchemy of Race and Rights*. Cambridge, MA: Harvard University Press.

Woolard, K. 1998. "Introduction: Language Ideology as a Field of Inquiry." In *Language Ideologies: Practice and Theory*, edited by B. B. Schieffelin, K. A. Woolard, and P. V. Kroskrity, 3–47. New York: Oxford University Press.

Woolard, K. A., and B.B. Schieffelin. 1994. "Language Ideology." *Annual Review of Anthropology* 23:55–82.

INDEX